The
CIVIL WAR
Treasury

The
CIVIL WAR
Treasury

VOLUME I

1860-1862

Albert A. Nofi

MALLARD PRESS
An imprint of BDD Promotional Book Company
666 Fifth Avenue
New York, NY 10103

To M.S.N.
For putting up with it all.

Acknowledgements

A great many people were of considerable assistance in the preparation of this volume, and, though I selfishly reserve for myself credit for any errors, I should like very much to thank them.

Dr. David G. Martin, of Longstreet House, was an invaluable source of advice, ideas and information, which he culled from his extensive collection. Helena Rubenstein, Daniel Scott Palter, Jeff Briggs and the other fine folks at West End Games were generous in providing access to their fine company library. Prof. John Boardman, of Brooklyn College, was very helpful in certain matters linguistic, mathematic and heraldic and also for Renfrew. Kelly Richter made several useful contributions and is, moreover, a devoted student of the war, dioramist and friend of the Harbor Defense Museum at Fort Hamilton, New York. I owe Anthony Staunton, from "Down Under," thanks and a cold one for use of his Medal of Honor materials. Richard L. DiNardo, Dennis Casey, Jay Stone, James Dingeman and several other stalwarts of the New York Military Affairs Symposium provided a number of interesting items. The people at the Hunter College Library and the Brooklyn College Library were of great help, while those at The New York Public Library, were enormously cooperative, and particular thanks must go to the folks in the Rare Book Collection, the Newspaper Division and to Margaret Moore, for her ever-cheerful welcome. Matilda Virgilio Clark graciously provided access to certain family records. John Hardacrem must be thanked for his letter in the June-July 1987 issue of *Blue & Gray*, which suggested some comment on the present state of historic Civil War sites. Among other people whom I should like to thank are Eric Smith, James R. Furqueron, Dave Wesley, Robert Capriotti, Daniel David of Sky Books International, Linda Grant DePauw, Editor of *Minerva*, a unique journal dedicated to the study of women and the military, Mike and Danny Kilbert of the New York Complete Strategist, who helped determine war game popularity, Thomas Brooks, John Southard, William Koop, the editor of *The Volunteer* and Valerie Eads, the editor of *Fighting Woman News*, for their advice and assistance. Nor should I neglect to mention James F. Dunnigan, who, while editor of *Strategy & Tactics*, helped shape my approach to military history, nor Daniel and Diana Alejandro, who want to write books someday. I owe a particular debt of gratitude to the officers and men of the recreated *15th New York Engineers, Co. A, 124th New York Volunteers, Clark's Battery (B, 1st New Jersey Artillery)* and the *1st New Jersey Cavalry*, who greatly assisted in the preparation of this volume by means of their demonstrations of Civil War kit, equipment and tactics, their cheerful responses to questions and their interest in and devotion to the study of the Civil War.

Bob Pigeon, of Combined Books, deserves special mention for coming up with the idea for this volume.

Finally and particularly I should like to thank my wife and daughter, Mary S. Nofi and Marilyn J. Spencer, for their support, cooperation and understanding.

—A.A.N.

Copyright © 1990 by Combined Books, Inc.

All rights reserved.

Editorial development and design by Robert L. Pigeon, Jr., John Cannan, and Lizbeth Nauta of Combined Books, Inc., 26 Summit Grove Avenue, Suite 207, Bryn Mawr, PA 19010.

Produced by Wieser & Wieser, Inc., 118 East 25th Street, New York, NY 10010.

First published in the United States of America in 1990 by the Mallard Press.

Mallard Press and its accompanying design and logo are trademarks of BDD Promotional Book Company, Inc.

ISBN 0-792-45212-7

Printed in Hong Kong

Contents

Preface

This, the first of two volumes entitled *The Civil War Treasury*, does not pretend to be a sweeping historical account of the greatest crisis in the life of the Republic. Rather, it looks at that monumental struggle in terms of bits and pieces of reality. Herein are anecdotes of encampments and battles, of soldiers and citizens. There are extracts from memoirs and letters, profiles of people and regiments and ships, songs and poems, newspaper clippings and notices and not a few serious treatments of particular aspects of the war, such as musketry and artillery. No attempt has been made to attain completeness or balance, for much must be left out so that much may be included. The object is to give the reader a deeper understanding of the human side of the struggle and a look at something of its more technical aspects as well, both topics alike frequently neglected in more traditional treatments. Thus, there is no continuous narrative nor is there much logical continuity. The materials are, however, arranged in a roughly chronological fashion and there is a brief introduction to each chapter which outlines the principal political and military developments of the year in question. In addition, several major themes link the longer pieces together, so that, for example, a camp recipe appears under "Army Life," while the adventures of a lady spy fall under "Incidents of War," and a discussion of railroads under "The Ways of War." Then there are short items, at times but a single line, which tell something about the war and the people and times, whether humorous, pointed, or merely informative. In the interests of economy, references have been kept to a minimum, although they have been maintained in the original.

Some of the items in *The Civil War Treasury* have been taken exactly as found in letters, newspapers and early books on the war. A few will be familiar, others obscure. Many are well documented, others but poorly so. At times a tale likely to be apocryphal has been included if it seems to show the spirit of the times, or just because it's too good to omit, though care has been taken to note the dubious provenance of such items. It should be remembered that many Civil War stories are genuine folk tales and exist in several versions, often involving different people at different times and in different places. As the Civil War was an era of particularly formal and florid speech, a number of original items have been rewritten to make them both shorter and more readily understandable to our simpler tastes, where the flavor will not suffer from the operation. At times language which would today be considered offensive has been permitted to stand: in such cases the reader is reminded that the age was one of particularly open bigotry, directed in various degrees against blacks and other non-whites, as well as most immigrants and non-Protestants.

Unless materials are being quoted directly, a number of a historical conventions have been adopted in accord with modern practice. Spelling conforms with current usage, so that, for example, "reconnaissance" and "center" have been used rather than the more authentic "reconoissance" and "centre." Similarly, military terminology has usually been modernized, so that, for example, army corps have been given roman numerals, which was not the case during the Civil War. To facilitate distinguishing Union formations from Confederate ones, the designations of the former have been given in *italics*.

I.

1860

The American Union: it must and shall be preserved.
—Andrew Jackson

How can the Union be preserved?
—John C. Calhoun

The irrepressible conflict.
—William H. Seward

Government cannot endure permanently half slave, half free.
—Abraham Lincoln

The crimes of this guilty land will be judged away but with blood.
—John Brown

The American Civil War was long in coming. The question at issue was a simple one, secession, the separation of a state from the Union of States, a subject on which the Constitution was silent.

Secession became a divisive issue in American society because there developed significant social, cultural and economic differences between the Southern states and the rest of the nation. The South, rural, agricultural and aristocratic, saw its interests threatened as the rest of the nation became increasingly urban, industrial and democratic. This divergence of interests between the South and the rest of the country existed even before the Revolution, and the differences increased into the early nineteenth century. There were disputes over tariffs, over government sponsored internal improvements and over the distribution of public land, all of which the Northerners and Westerners favored, and the Southerners opposed, since they were of little benefit to its primarily agricultural economy.

Complicating the issue, was the fact that the population of the North and the West grew at a rate faster than did that of the South, a development itself largely as a result of the divergent character of the regions. This trend led to a decline in Southern influence in the Congress, as the House of Representatives took on an increasingly Northern character. Then Southern influence in the Senate began to be threatened, as new states tended towards a Northern or Western socio-economic pattern. Even without further complicating factors, the differences between the sections would have been sufficient to raise tensions, though it is hardly likely that these tensions would have led to an open break. Throughout history the "right of rebellion" has been morally justifiable and, given the differences between North and South, an argument could be made in favor of secession on this basis. But exercise of the "right of rebellion" is contingent upon several important moral questions: ultimately it boils down to a question of whether or not the majority of the people involved are suffering some form of oppression which cannot be resolved by any other fashion than a resort to arms. In the case of the Civil War there was no such justification. Indeed, there was more justification for rebellion against the South. For there was one complicating factor which simultaneously was at the root of and more important than all the other issues taken together. It was a factor of overwhelming importance: slavery.

Slavery was the cause of the differences between the South and the rest of the Union. Slavery had created the planter aristocracy of the South. Slavery, which had made the South the preeminent agricultural region of the world, had hampered its industrialization. Slavery retarded the growth of the Southern population by discouraging the immigration which swelled the ranks of Northerners and Westerners.

Moved by practical and moral considerations, many perceptive Southerners had raised objections to slavery in the period after the Revolution, not least among them Thomas Jefferson and George Washington. And, indeed, the institution seemed in decline into the early years of the nineteenth century, but began to revive with the introduction of the cotton gin. In addition, the character of the society created by slaveholding, the enormous profits, the gentility, the elegance, blinded most, both North and South, to the pernicious effects of the institution on the nation.

By the middle of the nineteenth century—when the rest of the Western world had abandoned the institution—most of the white people of the South, relatively few of whom actually owned slaves, had come to view slavery as vital to the survival of Southern society. There had developed in the South an almost spiritual belief in the righteousness of slavery. The slaveholders represented wealth and status, something to which the non-slaveholders could aspire. The fact that slavery had a racial dimension enhanced the status of the impoverished white: whatever else he was, he was "free, white and twenty-one," a matter which was of considerably greater importance to the average Southerner than states rights. This development was in direct contrast to the growing belief in Western Civilization that slavery was inherently wrong. By 1840 the United States was the only major Western country in which slavery was still legal. Nor was there an absence of opposition to slavery.

Active resistance to slavery was remarkably widespread, among both blacks and whites. The Underground Railroad operated everywhere, involving people from every level of society, in both the North and South. Though initially resisted even in the North, the Abolitionist movement grew steadily. Slavery came under fire in books and plays and songs, in sermons and editorials and lectures. Southerners continuously tried to defend the institution, but slavery was indefensible, regardless of the arguments advanced. In the end, the advocates of slavery converted only themselves, while its opponents gradually converted most Northerners and not a few Southerners. The impact of the debate over slavery was tremendous, totally distorting legitimate concerns over states' rights, concerns which even Northern states possessed, but concerns which would never have become so inflammatory save for slavery.

Slavery was the overriding issue of the age. Families were broken up, friendships dissolved. Every major Protestant sect in the nation split in two, one branch opposing slavery and one favoring it. While Northerners snapped up 300,000 copies of

The first African slaves landed on the shores of what would become the United States in Virginia in 1619.

Between 1619 and 1865 an estimated 500,000 kidnapped Africans were sold into slavery in the United States.

FAR LEFT:
The barbarity of antebellum America—a slave auction in Charleston, South Carolina.

Of the approximately one million white families in the South, over a third, some 385,000, owned at least one of the 3,953,760 slaves in the region in 1860, for an average of 10.26 slaves per family, though in fact most slaveholding families had only one or two slaves: about 100,000 families had 10 or more slaves, 46,279 had at least 20 slaves, about 10,000 had at least 50 and 2,292 had at least 100.

Caricature of the rambunctious U.S. House of Representatives. During the trying times preceding the Civil War, many public servants came armed with weapons and windy rhetoric.

Harriet Beecher Stowe's *Uncle Tom's Cabin* within a year of its publication in 1851, Southerners avidly read detailed rebuttals by pro-slavery authors. While former slaves—such as Frederick Douglas, Sojourner Truth and Harriet Tubman—and Abolitionists —such as William Lloyd Garrison and Charles Sumner—stumped the North pointing out the evils of slavery, pro-slavery advocates toured the South, lecturing on its importance to "civilized living." Some extremists even advocated reopening the trans-Atlantic slave trade.

Violence grew commonplace. It became impossible to publicly express anti-slavery views in the South and an incipient Southern Abolitionist movement was destroyed in a series of lynchings and riots. Though a few Southerners, such as Robert E. Lee, were committed to the notion that slavery was a moral outrage, they largely kept their opinions to themselves thereafter. The situation of pro-slavery advocates in the North was little better, and there were sometimes riots when slaveholders attempted to reclaim their "property" under the Fugitive Slave Act. Compromise was several times attempted, but each time came to nought. The fundamental issue was individual freedom, and despite Constitutional sanction, slavery was inherently incompatible with the promise of America.

Despite the acrimony, the generation before the Civil War was one of expansion, as the increasingly divided United States grew and prospered on an unprecedented scale, finding time to expand into the sparsely inhabited West and to wage a successful war on Mexico which added greatly to the national territory. But even these achievements were tainted with the quarrel over slavery. The question of permitting slavery in newly acquired territories became a burning issue. Fanatical slavocrats sought national expansion specifically for the purpose of securing new slave states, and American filibusters were active in Mexico, Nicaragua and Cuba. By the mid-1850s the issue had become one without reasonable solution or compromise. The lines were drawn, the tinder was ready. And the tinder began to take fire.

In 1854 Congress passed the Kansas-Nebraska Act, in effect, a final effort at compromise. The idea seemed reasonable: let the citizens of each territory decide whether they wished to become a free state or a slave state through election. But a number of factors were at play. Both territories were relatively unsuited to slaveholding on a significant scale. In addition, with Northerners far more numerous than Southerners, it was not difficult to predict the probable outcome of any exercise in "popular sovereignty." So war came to Kansas, as pro-slavery thugs invaded the state to keep free soilers out, while anti-slavery fanatics retaliated in kind. The disorders continued into 1859, with the anti-slavery faction gradually gaining the upper hand. By then, the Supreme Court had dealt the final blow to any possibility of compromise. In 1857 the Dred Scott decision was handed down, which effectively ruled that no state could bar slavery from within its borders and went on to declare that even free blacks could not be citizens, both provisions alike being viewed as gross violations of states' rights and civil liberties throughout the North and West.

Tensions rose still higher. In late 1859 John Brown, a veteran of "Bleeding Kansas" attempted to spark a slave insurrection, sending thrills of horror throughout the South. And in 1860, the Democratic Party fell to pieces, so that Abraham Lincoln, a mildly successful Republican lawyer from Illinois, was elected president by 39.9 percent of the voters.

Lincoln's views on slavery could hardly be called radical. Nevertheless, he was a opponent of the institution, believing it morally wrong, though he was not inclined to abolition. But he was opposed to the further extension of slavery. And that alone was too radical a position for the slaveholding fanatics. On 20 December 1861, as the results of the election became clear, South Carolina, in which slaves actually outnumbered freemen, passed an "Ordinance of Secession." With that, civil war was a virtual certainty.

Incidents of War

Zachary Taylor's Uniform

Zachary Taylor, whose success in the field against Mexico in 1846-1848 led him to the White House in 1849, was never much of a dresser. As U.S. Grant—no clothes horse himself—put it, "In dress he was possibly too plain, rarely wearing anything in the field to indicate his rank, or even that he was an officer." Indeed, Grant could recall only two instances on which the general wore his full rig. The first occasion was at a formal review of his little army held at Corpus Christi on the eve of the Mexican War. The second was during a visit to Taylor's headquarters by the Flag Officer commanding the U.S. squadron off the mouth of the Rio Grande.

Since Taylor was aware that naval officers were punctilious in matters sartorial and ceremonial, he decided to go all out so that the army would not be outshone by the navy. His uniform was searched out and made ready and on the appointed day the general donned full kit, sword, feathers, sash, epaulets, aguilettes and whatnot. When the naval gentleman arrived it turned out that, knowing of Taylor's reputation as a careless dresser, he had put aside his personal preferences and worn civies, as a compliment to his host.

During the Mexican War Capt. Robert E. Lee was almost killed by an over-zealous sentry, escaping with but a singed uniform.

The proving ground for many Civil War Generals, a contest in the Mexican American War. (Courtesy of the West Point Museum Collections, United States Military Academy, West Point, New York)

The first American to gain the ramparts of Chapultepec Castle on 13 September 1847, against the heroic resistance of the cadets of the Mexican military academy, was Lt. George E. Pickett, who, almost 16 years later, would fail in an attempt to storm Cemetery Ridge at Gettysburg.

The Orphan Commission

As the coming of war causes armies to expand, it is not unusual for the number of high ranking officers to expand as well. Nor is it unusual for fierce competition to develop as to who should get to fill the newly created slots. And so it was in the Mexican War. Up to a point. On 3 March 1847 Congress authorized an increase in the number of generals in the army to serve for the duration of the war. President James K. Polk found little difficulty in filling most of the slots available, as there was considerable competition to secure the coveted promotions. But one major generalcy seems to have been cursed.

The president first offered the commission to Sam Houston of Texas, a wise choice given the man's military and political reputation. But Houston had just been elected senator from Texas and declined. So the president turned to Texas' other senator, Thomas J. Rusk, a man of considerable military experience—he had been surgeon general of the Army of the Republic of Texas and a regimental commander at San Jacinto—who, however, also preferred to remain in the Senate. And so, the president tried again, offering the commission to Senator Thomas Hart Benton of Missouri. Benton was politically a wise choice. A moderate on slavery, he had opposed the annexation of Texas, but had become a strong supporter of the war. And Benton was willing to accept the job. But he attached a condition, supreme command. This the president wisely rejected, considering that Winfield Scott was the obvious man for that task. That made three times that the commission had been spurned.

At this point Polk decided to offer the post to a man whom he had already appointed a brigadier general of volunteers,

Gideon J. Pillow. Pillow gladly accepted. Totally without military experience, Pillow was otherwise well qualified for the job: he was a power in the Democratic Party, had been the principal architect of Polk's nomination for the presidency, and was Polk's law partner.

Pillow commanded a division during Winfield Scott's Mexican Campaign with little skill, though some courage, acquiring two wounds. He engaged in continuous quarrels with his superior, and was constantly in communication with the president. Polk, claiming that Pillow was being persecuted, sustained him in his quarrels with Scott, a Whig and potential presidential candidate. As a result, Pillow continued to be a thorn in the latter's side throughout the war.

With the coming of peace, Pillow returned to politics in Tennessee, failing in two bids to become vice-president. In 1860, Pillow became a Douglas Democrat. On the secession of Tennessee his political clout and alleged military reputation secured for him command of the state's troops. He shortly afterwards transferred to Confederate service as a brigadier general, expressing considerable annoyance that he was not appointed to a higher post, such as supreme commander. Pillow's career in the Civil War was even less distinguished than it had been in the Mexican War: his principal feat of arms being at Ft. Donelson, where he accepted command from the fainthearted John B. Floyd, only to pass it on to the honorable Simon Bolivar Buckner, so that the latter could surrender the place whilst Pillow and Floyd escaped. So perhaps Houston and Rusk and Benton were prescient in turning down the commission which Pillow so eagerly accepted.

Possibly one of the worst Confederate generals of the war, Gideon D. Pillow.

In the Matter of Bragg vs. Bragg

Braxton Bragg, who would eventually rise to the highest levels of the Confederate Army, was not an easy man to get along with. Indeed, he seems to have quarrelled with everyone in the service from the time he graduated from West Point. U.S. Grant once recounted a tale which, whether true or not, gives some notion of Bragg's temperament.

It seems that Braxton Bragg was once the Quartermaster on a small frontier post. As the second ranking officer, he naturally

assumed command when the senior officer had to absent himself for a time. Bragg performed his duties as acting post commander with great diligence, and, of course, had to tend to the quartermaster's duties as well. It chanced that, in the course of his duties as post commander, Bragg made a request of the post quartermaster. Due to some technicality, the post quartermaster found it necessary to reject the request.

The rejection caused an inquiry from the acting post commander, to which the post quartermaster replied. Several such communications passed back and forth, and the matter remained unresolved. Finally the real post commander returned. Reviewing the actions which the acting post commander had taken in his absence, the post commander came upon the correspondence between the latter and the quartermaster, that is, between Mr. Bragg and Mr. Bragg, with the result that he cried out, "My God, Mr. Bragg, you have quarrelled with every officer in the Army, and now you are quarrelling with yourself!"

Bales of cotton are loaded into a Mississippi River steamer.

Nicaragua, William Walker and the International Slavocrat Conspiracy

In the spring of 1848 several American officers toured various natural wonders in central Mexico, including a vast cavern in which they almost managed to get lost—possibly forever—which would surely have had a significant effect on the Civil War, for the party included the future Union generals U.S. Grant, Andrew Porter, Charles P. Stone and Zealous B. Tower, and the future Confederate generals Richard Anderson, Henry H. Sibley, George Crittenden, Simon B. Buckner and Mansfield Lovell.

In 1836 Cadet Lewis A. Armistead, who would die leading a brigade in Pickett's Charge at Gettysburg, was expelled from West Point for breaking a dinner plate over the head of Jubal A. Early, who rose to command a corps in the Confederate Army.

While it hardly seems likely, Nicaragua was a factor in the coming of the American Civil War. As with most Latin American countries, Nicaraguan domestic politics have always been rather acrimonious. Despite this, independence from Spain was attained in 1821 without bloodshed. This surprising development occurred because a liberal government had taken power in Spain and the landholding oligarchy which had long dominated Nicaragua preferred to go it alone rather than risk the dangers of continued ties to the Mother Country. Briefly associated with Mexico, and for a time a part of the Central American Confederation, Nicaragua became completely independent in 1838.

The next two decades were exciting ones. There were continuous problems with the Anglophile Miskito Indians on the east coast, several abortive attempts to reunite the Central American nations, a couple of border wars and an ongoing struggle between the Conservatives and the Liberals. Now, although the Conservatives tended to favor a more paternalistic, quasi-feudal socio-economic system and the Liberals preferred a more unbridled capitalism, both groups were essentially factions of the same landholding oligarchy: it was more a question of "ins" and "outs" than of genuine ideological commitment. In any case, in the mid-1850s the Liberals were out and the Conservatives were in and there was a desultory civil war in progress. Feeling that they needed help, the Liberal leadership decided to call in the *norteamericanos*.

By happenstance, at the time Nicaragua had acquired some importance as a result of the California gold rush. People and goods bound for the gold fields could transit Nicaragua at a great savings in time and with considerably less risk than a voyage around the Horn or a trip through the pestilenced jungles of Panama. Several groups were competing for control of this route. One such was the Accessory Transit Company, which counted among its stockholders Cornelius Vanderbilt. The Liberals made Vanderbilt a proposition: help us get back into power and we will do right by Accessory Transit. It was an offer Vanderbilt found himself unable to refuse. And he knew just the man to get the job done, William Walker.

William Walker (1824-1860), a native of Tennessee who stood only about five feet tall, had an interesting and exciting life. Extremely well educated for a man of his day (B.A., Nashville, '38; M.D., Pennsylvania, '43; advanced medical degree, Paris, '44; Grand Tour, '45), Walker had a varied career as a physician and journalist before discovering his true vocation as a filibuster. Filibusters, private enterprise soldiers of fortune, were very active in the Caribbean and Central America in the nineteenth century, and Walker was among the most remarkable and most colorful of the lot. His first essay in freelance imperialism was in 1853, when, with a small band of freebooters, he attempted to set himself up as president of Lower California, following it up with an attempt to take over Sonora in early 1854. That spring Mexican forces threw Walker out of the country and he fled to the safety of the United States, where he was arrested when he turned up in San Diego in May. Although tried for violations of the neutrality laws, a sympathetic jury let him off. As a result, when approached by Vanderbilt and the Nicaraguan Liberals, Walker was more than willing to lend a hand.

With a band of 58 men whom he grandiloquently named "The American Phalanx," Walker landed in Nicaragua in June of 1855. In a short time he managed to organize an army sufficiently strong as to oust the incumbent Conservative regimen after some serious fighting and installed a Liberal president. That ought to have been the end of it, but Walker had other ideas in mind. After some careful preparations, he ousted the new Liberal president and took the job for himself in July of 1856.

El presidente Exmo. Sr. Don William Walker had great plans. He intended to use Nicaragua as the base on which to build a military empire in Central America. Among his first acts was the legalization of slavery, a measure designed to secure the support of slaveholding interests in the American South. He was moderately successful in this, his efforts being endorsed by many prominent Southerners, who pressured the United States into recognizing his regime, and he attracted a number of American recruits as well. But his ambitions were too obvious and he stirred up resistance among the normally fractious Central American republics, while arousing the hostility of Britain and France. Worse yet, he quarreled with "Commodore" Vanderbilt. Not one to take things lying down, Vanderbilt promoted a coalition against Walker and the "gray-eyed man of destiny" was thrown out of office in 1857 by Nicaraguan patriots aided by expeditionary forces from El Salvador, Costa Rica and Guatemala. With about 150 followers, Walker

retreated to Greytown, on the Caribbean coast, where he was taken into custody by some American warships and returned to the United States.

Walker tried a comeback later that same year, only to be captured and deported. Walker spent the next couple of years trying to raise funds for another go at establishing a private empire. In August of 1860 he landed with a small band of adventurers on the east coast of Honduras, intending to march overland into Nicaragua. Everything went wrong. The expedition blundered into British controlled territory on the Miskito Coast. Arrested by the British authorities, Walker and his men were turned over to Honduran justice. On 12 September 1860

Walker was made the object of the attentions of a firing squad.

Although they received no government support, the activities of such freebooters as William Walker helped permanently pollute relations between the United States and Latin America. In addition, they exacerbated sectional tensions in the United States. There was no well-financed, cohesive slavocratic conspiracy behind the filibusters. However, the enthusiastic support which they often received from prominent slaveholders and secessionists such as Joseph Brown, Alexander H. Stephens, Thomas L. Clingman and Robert Toombs—later a governor, vice-president and a pair of brigadiers in the Confederacy—convinced many anti-slavery men that such did in fact

In 1854, America's endeavors in the Pacific led to Commodore Perry's landing in Japan which opened that country to Western commerce. This lithograph displays the uniforms in use by the American military at the time. (Courtesy Civil War Library and Museum).

At a "Commercial Convention" in 1859, representatives of most of the Southern states resolved that the African slave trade should be reopened, a measure which was enthusiastically endorsed by a delegate from Mississippi named Jefferson Davis.

In 1482 Pope Pius II roundly condemned the slave trade, a measure which had to be repeated by Pope Paul III in 1557, Urban VIII in 1639, Benedict XIV in 1741 and Gregory XVI in 1839.

exist: in similar fashion the slaveholders were convinced that there was an Abolitionist conspiracy to rob them of their property, murder them in their beds and outrage their daughters.

There is yet another way in which William Walker and the other filibusters influenced the Civil War. A number of men who served on such expeditions later rose to some prominence in the Civil War. Confederate Brig. Gen. Allison Nelson held the same rank in Narcisco Lopez' expedition to Cuba in 1849-1851, and among his comrades was future Union Brig. Gen. Isaac H. Duval. John T. Pickett also took part in a filibustering expedition to Cuba, making him a less than ideal choice for the job which Jefferson Davis gave him during the war, commissioner to Mexico. Robert C. Tyler and Thomas A. Smith, later

a Rebel and a Yankee brigadier general, served as officers during William Walker's first Nicaraguan expedition. Chatham R. Wheat, who later led the Confederacy's famed "Louisiana Tigers," had a remarkable career as a filibuster, serving in Cuba with Narcisco Lopez, in Mexico as a mercenary under Juan Alvarez—who, upon attaining the Presidency in 1855, made Wheat an officer in the Mexican Army—and under Walker in Nicaragua, before going off to fight under Garibaldi in Italy. Even Pierre G.T. Beauregard, depressed over the slow pace of promotion in the peace time Regular Army, is said to have contemplated joining Walker: how different might the course of the Civil War have been had Beauregard been standing next to Walker on that fatal Wednesday morning in 1860?

"King Cotton"—the basis of the Southern economy.

16

The Men

Winfield Scott

The most distinguished American soldier between Washington and the Civil War, Winfield Scott (1786-1866) was born near Petersburg, Virginia. As a young man he briefly attended William and Mary College, but left in 1805 because he disapproved of the irreligious sentiments of most of his fellow students. Scott read law and was admitted to the Virginia bar in 1806. In 1807, caught up in the war-fever sparked by the Chesapeake-Leopard affair, Scott enlisted as a private in a local militia cavalry troop. Finding the military persuasion to his liking, he secured a commission in the Regular Army in May of 1808, being posted to New Orleans.

Scott's early career was marred by a court martial for having called his commanding officer, Brig. Gen. James Wilkinson—who never won a battle nor lost a court martial—as big a traitor as Aaron Burr, with the result that he was suspended from active duty for a year, 1809-1810. Returning to service, Scott was made a lieutenant colonel upon the expansion of the army at the outbreak of the War of 1812.

Scott had a notable career in the second war with Britain. By the end of 1813 he had served with distinction at Queenston, Ft. George and in the abortive Montreal Campaign, this last under the command of his nemesis Wilkinson. In March of 1814 Scott was promoted brigadier general and given a brigade under Maj. Gen. Jacob Brown, one of the nation's finest—and least remembered—field commanders. Scott's brigade fought well at Chippewa (5 July) and with particular distinction at Lundy's Lane (25 July), during which Scott was severely wounded. For his performance at Lundy's Lane Scott became a national hero and was brevetted a major general. With the coming of peace, Scott proved to be as able an administrative soldier as he was a combat soldier.

In the immediate aftermath of the war, Scott was placed in charge of the selection board which oversaw the reduction of the Regular Army, revised the standard drill manual and had the pleasure of heading the board of inquiry investigating James Wilkinson's disgraceful performance during the late war: true to his reputation, and through no fault of Scott's, Wilkinson got off on a technicality. Over the following decade Scott made two trips to Europe to keep abreast of military develop-

ments, headed various boards and commissions and prepared or revised a number of manuals. Passed over when Jacob

A highly dubious tradition credits Abner Doubleday, who rose to become a Union major general, with the invention of baseball in 1839, when he was just 19 and a cadet at West Point.

George B. McClellan had to secure special permission of the secretary of war to be admitted to West Point in 1842, since he was only 15 years old.

So effective was the military government of Winfield Scott during the American occupation of Mexico in 1848 that, upon conclusion of the peace treaty, some residents urged the gringo general to stay behind and become president of Mexico.

One of the unheralded military geniuses in all of American history, Winfield Scott.

In his four years at West Point, Cadet U.S. Grant is said to have never attended a single dance.

In 1836 Lt. Robert Anderson's star pupil in artillery tactics at West Point was Cadet Pierre G.T. Beauregard, who considered Anderson his favorite instructor and who, 25 years later, would direct the bombardment of Ft. Sumter, which Anderson would command.

Brown retired as general-in-chief in 1828, Scott attempted to resign, but was refused. The next few years were busy ones for the energetic Scott. He was peripherally involved in the Black Hawk War, negotiated treaties with several Indian nations and, in late 1832, was sent by President Andrew Jackson to deal with the Nullification Crisis.

Nullification, a theory advanced by John C. Calhoun, held that the laws of the United States did not necessarily apply to the individual states: a state could, if it desired, enact legislation to "nullify" a particular law with regard to itself. In the early 1830s this notion became popular in South Carolina, highly resentful of protective tariffs, which it perceived as harmful to its agricultural trade with Europe. As a result, in 1832 South Carolina, confident in the support of the other Southern states, nullified the tariffs of 1828 and 1832. Jackson, although himself a southerner and slaveholder, was determined to assert the primacy of the Federal government. Securing from Congress the "Force Bill," which authorized the use of the army if necessary to suppress defiance of Federal law, Jackson sent Scott to Charleston to secure compliance with the tariff. Scott performed his task perfectly. A judicious show of force and considerable tact, plus a broad lack of support from the other Southern states and some modification of the tariff, caused South Carolina to back down, though still asserting the verity of nullification: indeed, the state legislature nullified the Force Bill! The Nullification Crisis further enhanced Scott's already high prestige.

Scott's career over the next decade reads like a catalog of American military activities. He commanded in the early part of the Second Seminole War (1835-1837), in which War Department mismanagement, disloyal subordinates and Seminole tenacity combined to cause his only failure. He helped resolve the "Aroostook War"—a potentially dangerous border dispute which had already involved the militias of Maine and New Brunswick—with Canada (1837-1842) and he directed the removal of over 16,000 Indians from the Southeast to the Indian Territory (1838). Finally, in 1841 he was promoted major general and named general-in-chief.

Scott's principal activity as general-in-chief was the conduct of the War with Mexico (1846-1848). Initially a supporter of Zachary Taylor's invasion of Northern Mexico, Scott became convinced that the only way to "conquer a peace" was to seize Mexico City, and he bent all his efforts towards that objective. The invasion of Mexico was effected with tremendous daring—the Duke of Wellington said "Scott is lost."—and extraordinary success, at remarkably little cost, despite a number of disloyal subordinates and a hostile president. The Mexican War confirmed Scott's reputation as a talented soldier and brought him considerable fame abroad. But while Zachary Taylor's bloody though indecisive victories secured for him the White House, Scott's political ambitions were frustrated when he was decisively defeated by Franklin Pierce in 1852, though by way of consolation he was made a lieutenant general by brevet in 1855, the only man in American history to hold that rank. In the years between the Mexican War and the Civil War, Scott continued to command the army, most often from New York City, about as far from the War Department bureaucracy as he could conveniently get. During this period he continued to write, helped settle the Northwest Boundary dispute with Britain and supervised the resolution of the "Mormon War" and the Kansas-Nebraska troubles. A stickler for military propriety—which earned him the nickname "Old Fuss and Feathers"—and increasingly infirm, Scott nevertheless continued to be an able administrator with a alert mind.

Although Scott, himself a Southerner, disapproved of secession, he did not believe that the Federal government had the constitutional authority to use force to prevent it. Nevertheless, when called upon, he was ready to serve. Despite his age and extreme infirmity, Scott probably had the clearest understanding of what was coming. However, when he asserted that the war would be long, he was regarded by most people—though apparently not by Lincoln—as a senile old fool. Even before the fighting began, Scott outlined what his enemies contemptuously called the "Anaconda Plan." This called for the imposition of a naval blockade on the South, the concentration of enormous armies in Virginia and the Mississippi Valley and a long war. Scott also realized that there was no one who had experience commanding such enormous forces—his own largest command in Mexico had been fewer than 20,000 men—but believed that Robert E. Lee might have the makings of a good general. When Lee turned him down, he selected Irvin McDowell, who was replaced after Bull Run by George B. McClellan.

Scott and McClellan ought to have made a good team. But the latter's flaws of character—and lack of intestinal fortitude—created tensions between the two. As a result, Scott retired from the army on 1 November 1861, concluding a military career of over 53 years. Even after he was gone, Lincoln would say of him "I cannot but think we are still his debtors." Scott died at West Point a little more than a year after the war had ended, largely on the basis of his "Anaconda Plan."

Although always counted among the nation's greatest soldiers, Winfield Scott's reputation is overshadowed by the overwhelming drama of the Civil War. As a result, Civil War commanders of far less skill are much better known. Nevertheless, his Mexican Campaign was among the most remarkable in history, with little, if anything in the Civil War surpassing it for daring, economy and decisiveness. It is difficult to escape the conclusion that, few, if any, American commanders since Washington were Scott's equal.

At the time of the Civil War an estimated 25 percent of Southern whites had at least one black ancestor.

The first state to abolish slavery was Rhode Island, which did so in 1774, two years before the Declaration of Independence.

Josiah Henson

Josiah Henson (1789-1881) was born a slave in Maryland. After passing through a series of owners, he ended up on a plantation near Rockville. As a boy Henson developed a desire to learn to read. By selling apples he raised the eleven cents necessary to buy a copy of Webster's speller and proceeded to teach himself. The first words he wrote, tracing them in charcoal, were "Isaac Riley," his master's name. The latter, however, took a dim view of slaves reading and administered a savage beating, with the result that Henson gave up the attempt. As he grew older, "Sie" Henson became a trusted retainer of the Riley family and was often taken on business trips by his master. On one such trip to Kentucky, Henson became a Methodist preacher. On his return to Rockville Henson continued his duties, while tending to the spiritual needs of the Riley slaves and was once credited with calming a potentially disastrous outbreak by some 400 slaves. Meanwhile, Henson worked towards his freedom and in 1828 bought himself and his family out of servitude, removing to Kentucky.

After a short time in Kentucky, Henson's former master began to dun him for additional money. Henson began to suspect that his former master was about to double-cross him, claiming that he was not, in fact free, and sell him "down the river" to New Orleans, a not uncommon swindle. His suspicions being confirmed—any white person could lay claim to any free black with relative impunity under the "Fugitive Slave Law"—, Henson took his family off to Canada in 1830, to the great disappointment of his former master, who put a price on his head.

In Canada, Henson found the freedom which he desired, prospered and finally learned to read. Becoming involved in the problems of fugitive slaves, some hundreds of whom trickled into Canada each year, he joined with several other successful former slaves to found the British-American Institute, a school for the "coloured inhabitants of Canada." Between times he became involved in the Underground Railroad and over the years is credited with helping 118 slaves escape bondage, often undertaking risky journeys into the South in the course of his work. Meanwhile he found time to write, and in 1849 published *The Life of Josiah Henson, formerly a Slave, Now an Inhabitant of Canada*.

Henson's memoirs came to the attention of a Brooklyn woman, who was of a literary inclination. Combining this with her anti-slavery activities, the woman, Harriet Beecher Stowe, sister of the prominent Abolitionist the Rev. Henry Ward Beecher, used Henson's memoirs to provide the background for a 40-part serial which she wrote for *The National Era*, an anti-slavery newspaper. So popular was this venture that Stowe turned the serial into a novel, calling it *Uncle Tom's Cabin, or Life Among the Lowly*, one of the greatest "best sellers" in history, a work which sparked much controversy in its day and ever since as well. Stowe, when challenged as to the veracity of anything in her book, would ever afterwards refer to Henson's memoirs.

A slave dealer inspects his "commodity" during an auction.

Human beings on sale in the city of New Orleans.

Henson himself grew quite wealthy, richer, he observed, than his former master. After the Civil War he toured England, lecturing and meeting the greats of the land, including Queen Victoria and the Archbishop of Canterbury, to whom when asked where he had been educated, he replied "I graduated, Your Grace, from the University of Adversity."

In 1877 Henson toured the United States, visiting President Rutherford B. Hayes at the White House and paying a call at the old Riley Plantation. When his former master's invalid widow, upon recognizing him, said "Why, Sie, you are a gentleman," he replied, "I always was, madam."

Henson was proud to have been the model for Uncle Tom in Harriet Beecher Stowe's novel, commenting that "If my humble words have in any way inspired that gifted lady to write such a plaintive story that the whole community has been touched with pity for the sufferings of the poor slave, then I have not lived in vain."

RIGHT:

The protective ramparts of Fort Washington overlook the golden Potomac River. This construction was part of the extensive defensive network protecting the U.S. from naval attack.

Since a free black was at risk of being stolen by slave catchers, relatively prominent and prosperous freedmen in the South often preferred to own their wives and offspring and even parents, rather than liberate them.

Sylvanus Thayer

A native of Massachusetts, Sylvanus Thayer (1785-1872) graduated from Dartmouth in 1807, and then entered West Point, graduating in 1808 and being commissioned in the engineers. Save for a brief tour as an instructor at the academy, he spent the next four years working on coast defenses in New York and New England. On the outbreak of the War of 1812 he served as engineer on the staffs of Henry Dearborn and Wade Hampton on the Canadian border. Although he saw no action in the war, he emerged as a captain and brevet major. He spent 1815-1817 touring European military academies and in July of 1817 was appointed Superintendent of West Point, which was then virtually a dying institution.

Thayer spent 16 years at West Point and is the founder of the academy as a genuine institution of higher learning and military art. Effecting a thorough reform of the academy, he instituted a formal, four year academic curriculum, created the post of Commandant of Cadets, prescribed regular military exercises, established stringent entrance and academic requirements and recruited capable instructors such as Dennis Hart Mahan. Not all of Thayer's reforms were welcome, and there were student riots in 1818 and 1826, which he put down firmly. In 1833 Thayer clashed with President Andrew Jackson when the latter reinstated some cadets who had been expelled. As a result, Thayer requested that he be relieved.

Thayer spent the next 25 years engaged in harbor improvements and coast defense work in New England, while serving on various army boards. In 1858 ill-health forced him to go on leave of absence. He was promoted colonel of engineers and brevet brigadier general upon his retirement in 1863. After the war he endowed a school of engineering at Dartmouth and lived quietly in his native Massachusetts. One of the most important soldiers in American history, Thayer had an enormous influence on the development of engineering, education and technology in the United States, and was the true founder of West Point.

As a young man, William T. Sherman disliked his red hair so much he once attempted to dye it, only to make matters worse, for it turned "an odd shade of green."

William Tecumseh Sherman was considered the best chef in his class at West Point, cooking an excellent hash over the fireplace in his room, an activity which was strictly against the rules.

John C. Fremont

On the eve of the Civil War no American soldier was better known that John C. Fremont (1813-1890). A native of Georgia, Fremont had a varied and adventurous life. Expelled from Charleston College at 18, the influence of South Carolina's Joel R. Poinsett secured for him an appointment as teacher of mathematics aboard the sloop-of-war *Natchez*—midshipmen in those days learned their trade at sea. In 1838, Poinsett—after whom the plant is named—managed to get Fremont made a second lieutenant in the prestigious Corps of Topographical Engineers. Over the next seven years Fremont was engaged in surveying and exploring the West. In 1841 he wed Jessie Benton over the objections of her father, the powerful Senator Thomas Hart Benton of Missouri, who later did well by his son-in-law, promoting various expeditions which the latter led.

Fremont's trips into the Rockies had already made him something of a national hero when, acting on secret orders, he led a column into California on the eve of the Mexican War, sparking the so-called "Bear Flag Rebellion" and being instrumental in securing the territory for the United States. Fremont was shortly appointed governor by Commodore Robert F. Stockton, but soon ran into difficulties with Brig. Gen. Stephen W. Kearny, who had arrived with orders to set up a civil government. Placed under arrest, Fremont was subject to a court martial. Though cleared of mutiny charges, he was found guilty of disobedience and conduct prejudicial to military order. Although President James K. Polk intervened to suspend sentence, Fremont resigned in early 1848.

Settling in California, Fremont soon acquired vast lands, grew rich from the gold rush, and was elected to the Senate. Meanwhile, various railroad interests employed him to explore possible routes over the Rockies. An early supporter of the infant Republican Party, Fremont was its first candidate for president, going down to defeat in 1856 at the hands of James Buchanan: had he won he would have been the youngest man ever elected.

The outbreak of the Civil War found him in California. In a move designed to cement various elements to the Republican

A military and political gad-fly to President Lincoln, John C. Fremont.

In 1859 Barton Key, son of Francis Scott "The Star Spangled Banner" Key, was killed by outraged husband, Tammany politician, and future Union general, Daniel Sickles, who was acquitted by reason of temporary insanity, the first time such a plea had ever been made.

Cadet Philip Sheridan was supposed to graduate from West Point in 1852, but was suspended for a year for a "quarrel of a belligerent character" with Cadet William R. Terrill, who later died at Perryville as a Union brigadier general.

Future Maj. Gen. Daniel Sickles guns down Philip B. Key, son of Francis Scott Key, who maintained a liaison with his wife. The resulting murder trial was one of the most sensational scandals of the 1850s.

Party—the Blair family, the Abolitionists and the German-Americans, among all of whom Fremont was immensely popular—Lincoln made Fremont a major general of volunteers on 14 May 1861 and sent him to command in Missouri.

Fremont's war service was acrimonious, but important to the Union cause, despite the fact the he was uniformly unsuccessful in the field and occasionally embarrassing to the president. He helped in holding Missouri for the Union, but issued a premature order freeing the slaves which Lincoln was forced to retract. Combined with a lack of success in the field, this prompted Lincoln to remove him in November of 1861, despite the hysterical pleadings of Jessie Fremont and an absolutely dishonest and dishonorable attempt by Fremont to avoid receipt of the appropriate orders. As a political sop, Fremont was placed in command of West Virginia in March of 1862, and he promptly involved his forces in a series of reverses at the hands of Thomas "Stonewall" Jackson, culminating in his defeat at Cross Keys on 8 June. When his command became the *I Corps* of John Pope's *Army of Virginia* shortly thereafter, Fremont asked to be relieved rather than serve under an officer who was his junior in rank. He did not return to active duty.

In 1864 Fremont was briefly involved in an attempt by some Radical Republicans to prevent the renomination of Lincoln. For the balance of his life he devoted himself to his business affairs, suffering a series of devastating failures, including an *in absentia* conviction for fraud by a French court, and was only kept solvent by the literary efforts of his wife. From 1878 to 1887 he was governor of the Arizona Territory and at his death was receiving a pension as a major general on the retired list. As with most "political" generals, whether North or South, there were sound reasons for Fremont's appointment. Unlike most, his prewar achievements to some extent justified the confidence initially placed in him. His failure as a commander was due to his ambition, his indecisiveness and his penchant for the dramatic.

Samuel P. Houston

One of the giants of American history, Sam Houston (1793-1863) was a native of Virginia. His father dying when he was 14, Houston's mother took her nine children to Tennessee. Houston, who was largely self-educated—he nevertheless managed to secure a reading knowledge of classical Greek—ran off to join the Indians about 1808, living with the Cherokee for three years, among whom he acquired the name "The Raven." In 1812 he ran a school for a time, but the following year volunteered for the war with Britain. Houston's war service was entirely in the then southwest, against the Creek Indians. During his five years of military service he was severely wounded, became a close friend of Andrew Jackson and rose to first lieutenant.

In 1818 Houston resigned his commission rather than take part in Indian removal. He became an Indian agent among the Cherokee, while he read law. Admitted to the bar in Tennessee, Houston acquired a considerable reputation, became a major general of militia and was elected to Congress in 1823 and again in 1825. In 1827 Houston was elected governor of Tennessee. By the age of 34 Houston's career had been remarkable, and great things might well have been expected of him. But in January of 1829 he made a disastrous marriage which lasted less than three months and about which he never afterwards spoke. He resigned his governorship and headed west for Arkansas, where the Cherokee had been "removed."

Houston lived among the Cherokee for three years. Despondent, he took to drink for a time, earning the name "Big Drunk," but then married Tiana Rogers, a Cherokee woman—a collateral ancestor of Will Rogers—who helped reform him. Meanwhile, the pressures for Indian "removal" were again at work and in 1832 Houston went to Washington to see what his old friend Andrew Jackson, now president, could do to protect the Cherokee. In Washington he got nowhere, for Jackson was a strong backer of Indian removal. Worse, he had a violent encounter with an anti-Indian member of the House and was sentenced to a public condemnation for contempt of Congress: however, since the Speaker was a Jackson man, Houston's formal condemnation sounded more like a commendation. While Jackson could not—or would not—do anything for the Cherokee, he suggested that Houston go to Texas—at that time a part of Mexico which had been heavily settled by Americans—to negotiate with various Indians who were raiding into the United States. Houston took up the assignment and headed west. For the rest of his life he was closely identified with Texas.

Troubles between the Texans, both American and Mexican, and the Mexican government of Antonio Lopez de Santa Ana had been brewing for a long time, and reached a boiling point in late 1835. The Texans resorted to arms and Houston was named a major general and commander of the revolutionary army. Shortly after Texas declared its independence from Mexico—on 2 March 1836, his birthday—Houston led the revolutionary army to victory at San Jacinto (21 April 1836). Three months later he was elected President of the Republic of Texas. Houston served two terms as President of Texas (1836-1838 and 1842-1844). When Texas was admitted to the Union—a matter which was long delayed because of its slave-holding status—Houston was elected to the United States Senate, serving until 1859, when he was elected governor of Texas, becoming the only man in American history to have been the governor of two states. But Texas had changed, and Houston had not. Over the years the original small population had been swamped by outsiders, mostly from the South. The political status of the Mexican-Texans had deteriorated tremendously, while the Old America-Texans had lost power to

In 1855 the North Carolina legislature declared that the Melungeon Indians were descendants of the "Lost Colony of Roanoke" and therefore eligible to marry whites, while the Tennessee legislature declared that they were "persons of color" and prohibited from marrying whites.

One of the mythic figures of the growing United States, a messenger of the Pony Express during a harrowing ride.

A number of men who became prominent in the Civil War had soldiered for the Republic of Texas. The most distinguished of these was Confederate Gen. Albert Sidney Johnston, who went to Texas after the Revolution and served for a time as commanding officer of the Texas Army. Other notable veterans of Texas, Confederates all, were Maj. Gen. George B. Crittenden and brigadier generals Thomas Green, Joseph L. Hogg, Jerome Bonaparte Robertson, Ben McCulloch and Thomas Green.

James J. Pettigrew, who would die a Confederate brigadier general during the Gettysburg Campaign, graduated from the University of North Carolina in 1847 with such high distinction in mathematics that he was immediately appointed a professor of the subject at the United States Naval Observatory.

the newcomers. A strong Union man, Houston found that Texas was heavily secessionist.

Houston's years in office were difficult ones. He openly opposed secession, believing it would be a disaster for the South, and remained staunchly Unionist to the end. When, in March of 1861, he refused to endorse the Ordinance of Secession and would not take the oath of allegiance to the Confederacy, he was removed from office in an illegal proceeding. Houston died a broken man in 1863, with "Texas" on his lips, one of the forgotten heroes of the Civil War.

A relic of a bygone age; the U.S.S. Saratoga which served in the War of 1812 and was one of the "black ships" which Commodore Perry took with him to Japan. By the Civil War, ironclads made such wooden vessels obsolete.

Dennis Hart Mahan

Some years before the war Pierre G.T. Beauregard was briefly under arrest for participating in a duel with shotguns.

Although raised in Virginia, Dennis Hart Mahan (1802-1871) was born in New York. He entered West Point in 1820 and was intimately connected with it for the rest of his life. Mahan's intellectual brilliance soon attracted the attention of the Superintendent, Sylvanus Thayer, who appointed him an acting instructor in mathematics while still a cadet. Graduating first in the class of 1824, Mahan was commissioned in the engineers and assigned at Thayer's request as a faculty member at West Point. He spent 1826-1830 in France, studying the military educational system there and completing the prescribed course at the School of Application of Engineering and Artillery at Metz. Upon his return to West Point he began a notable academic career, holding several professorships and becoming dean of the faculty in 1838.

Mahan's work affected virtually every aspect of the academy's curriculum. He wrote at least six textbooks which remained standard for many decades, introduced the study of the Napoleonic Wars as interpreted by Baron Henri Jomini, and furthered the work, begun by Thayer, of turning the academy into one of the foremost military and engineering institutions in the world, while educating virtually all of the men who would rise to the highest levels of military leadership during the Civil War. Mahan's most important work, *Elementary Treatise of Advance-Guard, Out-Post, and Detachment Service of Troops* (1847), popularly known as *Out-Post*, became the standard hand book of military training for the regular army and militia.

In 1871 Mahan stepped off the side of a river steamer in the Hudson, apparently a suicide, as he was despondent over a recommendation that he retire. His son, Alfred Thayer Mahan, had a distinguished naval career and was the author of the popular *The Influence of Sea Power Upon History*.

An artery of American commerce, the frozen New York harbor during a harsh winter.

The Women

Harriet Tubman

Nicknamed "Moses", Harriet Tubman (c. 1821-1913), who became the most famous "conductor" on the Underground Railroad, was named Araminta when born as a slave on a plantation in Dorchester County, on Maryland's Eastern Shore. At the age of 22 the young field hand was forced to marry John Tubman, a fellow slave. In 1849 she left him, and slavery forever, fleeing northwards and adopting the name Harriet.

Tubman, a small, uneducated woman who never lost her slave accent, became involved with various Quaker anti-slavery groups and was soon active in the Underground Railroad. Over the next decade she conducted 20 hazardous missions into the South, bringing more than 300 people to freedom. A hard, tough, fearless and at times ruthless woman, she was almost caught several times, but always managed to elude her pursuers. In a remarkable coup, she brought both her parents out of bondage in 1857 and settled them at a house which she had acquired in Auburn, New York. Ms. Tubman, who was a legend among the slaves and well known in the Abolitionist community—John Brown counted her among his friends—, never held a formal position with any organization, supporting herself by working as a cook, lecturer and contributor to various Abolitionist journals, dictating what she wished to say, since she never learned to read.

On the outbreak of the Civil War, Ms. Tubman went to the Carolina Sea Islands, where her fame had not reached, to serve the black community there, helping to finance a school and working as a nurse. She became involved in a number of military operations, as spy, scout and, in one instance, leader of a raiding party. After the war she continued to work for the rights of black Americans and founded a home for indigent freemen.

Slaves, captured while trying to escape the tribulations of life in the South, are returned to their masters to face harsh punishments.

Lincoln

Young Abe at War

In 1830 Congress passed the Indian Removal Act, which called for the relocation of all Eastern Indians to lands west of the Mississippi, for which the munificent sum of $500,000 was appropriated to pay "compensation." Removal brought great suffering upon tens of thousands of Indians. There was also a great deal of bloodshed in Illinois and Wisconsin.

Dissatisfied with the lands allocated to them by the Federal government, lands which they had to dispute with their blood enemies the Sioux, Omaha and Menominee and longing for

their ancestral Illinois—guarantied to them in perpetuity by a treaty dating from 1804—500 Sauk and Fox warriors crossed the Mississippi into Northern Illinois in April of 1832. Under the leadership of Black Hawk (c. 1767-1838), a Sauk, and accompanied by some 1,500 women and children, the movement was more of a migration than a raid. Nevertheless, panic spread rapidly among the white settlers. As nearly 5,500 militiamen and volunteers turned out, the Federal government began moving over 1,300 regular troops from Jefferson Barracks in Missouri and various coast defense posts in the East.

The Indians won a skirmish with the militia at Stillman's Run, but, concluding that the odds against them were too great, decided to retire into Wisconsin. A few days later the militia caught them as they were attempting to cross a river. Although the Indians came off with the worst of it in the ensuing Battle of Wisconsin Heights, they did succeed in escaping. By this time some 400 regulars had turned up. Not being a stupid man, Black Hawk endeavored to surrender, only to have his offer rejected twice. Aided by about 900 militia, the Regulars, under Brig. Gen. Henry Atkinson, began driving the Indians westward. On 2 August Col. Zachary Taylor—who later went on to greater things—led a column of troops through swampland to corner Black Hawk's band against the Bad Axe River, just south of La Crosse, Wisconsin. The next day there occurred the so-called Battle of the Bad Axe, a massacre which left only 150 survivors. American casualties in the war were 26 killed and 38 wounded. Many of the Indians were driven into the river at bayonet point and shot down in the water or drowned. Thus was Illinois made safe for civilization. Black Hawk himself was soon captured and imprisoned for about a year in Fortress Monroe. Upon his release, he settled in Iowa, where he helped drive out the Sioux, Omaha and Menominee to establish a Sauk reservation. However, his influence over his people soon passed to the younger Keokuk, who became a great favorite with the Americans.

Among the many men who served in the militia during the Black Hawk War was Abraham Lincoln, then aged 23. Lincoln volunteered on 21 April and was immediately elected captain of his company—his first success at the polls. He appears to

Aside from Lincoln, a number of other men who later rose to some importance in the Civil War took part in the Black Hawk War. The Confederacy's Gen. Albert Sidney Johnston and Maj. Gen. George B. Crittenden were infantry officers. Robert Anderson, the defender of Fort Sumter, who rose to become a Union major general, served as a colonel of Illinois volunteers. In addition, John A. McClernand, who became a Union major general, served as a militiaman, while Edwin Vose Sumner, later an able Union major general, and Philip St. George Cook, later a Union brigadier general, served as officers in the Regular Army.

Lincoln as he appeared during the 1860 presidential election. Though only pulling roughly 40 percent of the popular vote, Lincoln managed to defeat three other candidates to win the highest office in the land. (Courtesy Civil War Library and Museum)

Abraham Lincoln was born on 12 February 1809, near Hogdenville, Kentucky, less than a 100 miles from where Jefferson Davis had been born in Christian County, Kentucky, nine months earlier, on 3 June 1808.

During the election of 1860, Northern voters cast a quarter of a million more votes against Lincoln than did the entire South.

have been popular with the men, not least for his willingness to help with the chores. On one occasion, Lincoln wrestled another captain to see whose company would get a more desireable campsite: he lost, but history has failed to note the name of the man who beat him. Although the story is probably as old as close-order drill, Lincoln is alleged to have been the green officer who forgot the proper sequence of commands which would get the troops through a defile and so ordered them to "break ranks and reform immediately on the other side of that gate."

Lincoln's company was mustered out on 27 May. Military life appears to have agreed with young Abe sufficiently to prompt him to reenlist on 29 May. This time, however, he served as a private, being mustered out on 16 June. Lincoln saw no action during his 53 days of military service. Much of his time was spent slogging through swamps in search of Black Hawk and his men. He did, however, endure some physical hardship and helped to bury five men who had been killed and scalped by the Indians. During his brief military career Lincoln was twice under arrest for minor infractions of military law.

In later life, Lincoln rarely referred to his military service, and then only with some self-denigrating bit of humor. Nevertheless, he seems to have been mildly proud of having served. How well his brief brush with the military life served him when he was commander in chief of the greatest armies and navies the Republic had ever put in the field cannot be determined. But Lincoln's military experience—or lack of it—seems to have stood him in better stead than Jefferson Davis'.

Commercial traffic on the Ohio River before the war. Before 1861, America's rivers served as vital avenues of commerce. After the out break of the Civil War, they became highways of invasion patrolled by monstrous ironclads.

The "Railsplitter" Maiden Speech

Lincoln first stood for public office in 1834, running for the Illinois legislature as a Whig. He had a number of strikes against him. He was young, awkward and unknown. Moreover, the flowery "speechifying" of his opponents and their supporters and of his supporters as well, had gone on for some time, with much tooting of personal horns and praises about individual virtues, so that they had "rolled the sun nearly down." In short, the crowd was getting bored. And then it was Lincoln's turn.

Gentlemen, fellow-citizens: I presume you all know who I am. I am humble Abraham Lincoln. I have been solicited by many friends to become a candidate for the legislature. My politics are short and sweet, like an old woman's dance. I am in favor of a National Bank. I am in favor of the internal improvement system and a high protective tariff. These are my sentiments and political principles. If elected, I shall be thankful; if not, it will be all the same.

Though no masterpiece of rhetoric, Lincoln's little speech must have done the trick. He won the election, served several terms in the legislature and later went on to the House of Representatives, where his opposition to the War with Mexico later cost him his seat.

On the basis of photographs some medical experts have concluded that Abraham Lincoln suffered from Marfan's Syndrome, a collagen disorder which, among other things, causes long, thin bones and a shortened lifespan.

Lincoln began to grow his famous beard shortly after the Election of 1860, primarily at the urging of eleven year old Grace Bedell of Westfield, N.Y., who, on 18 October had written ". . . you would look a great deal better for your face is so thin."

Violently anti-Northern and racist cartoon of supposed Yankee arrogance. Drawn by Adalbert John Volck, it depicts a crowd of militant abolitionists, including Henry W. Beecher, Horace Greeley, Benjamin Butler, Edwin Stanton and even Winfield Scott, executing a caucasian on the altar of "Negro worship."

The Units

The Old Army

The United States Army on the eve of the Civil War was remarkably small given the population, wealth, and extent of the nation. Yet it was sufficient unto the need. Under no immediate threat from any power, the United States required an army primarily for police duties on the frontier and as a national cadre which would provide the leavening to turn the militia into a combat-ready force in the event of mobilization. This system had worked rather poorly during the War of 1812 (1812-1814), due largely to sectional disunity, political ineptitude and poor leadership. But the Mexican War (1846-1848) had turned out quite well, due to a considerable measure of national unity, reasonably sound political direction and excellent leadership, not least because of the presence of a goodly number of West Point graduates in both the Regular and Volunteer establishments.

At the end of 1860 the Regular Army had an authorized strength of 16,367 officers and men, of whom 14,663 were actually present with the colors. The combat strength of the Army comprised ten regiments of infantry, four of artillery and five of mounted troops. These totalled 198 companies, of which 183 were normally stationed west of the Mississippi. Although every four years several thousand men were brought to Washington for presidential inaugurations, it was unusual for so many troops to be in one place at the same time. As a result, when it became necessary to concentrate a considerable force, as during the Mexican War or the Utah Expedition, a great administrative muddle often ensued.

The ten infantry regiments each comprised twelve companies in three battalions on paper, but in practice had only ten companies active. Although the oldest regiment dated back to 1784, their enumeration had suffered considerably from a series of consolidations at the end of the War of 1812, when, among other peculiarities, the senior regiment acquired the designation *3rd Infantry*, which it still bears. The *1st Infantry* was formed in 1791, the *2nd* and *5th* date to 1808, the *4th*, *6th* and *7th* to 1812, the *8th* to 1838 and the *9th* and *10th* to the expansion of the Regular Army in 1855. Although on occasion all ten companies of a regiment might serve together, this was a rare occurrence in peace time, when many army posts had but one or two companies. The principal peace-time role of the infantry was to assist the mounted troops in policing the frontier.

Prior to 1821 the artillery had constituted a corps on the model of the Royal Artillery. In that year the existing autonomous batteries—several of which dated back into the eighteenth century and one to 1776—were grouped into four regiments. This was a purely administrative measure, however, designed to provide jobs for colonels of artillery, and the batteries continued to be deployed individually until the twentieth century. Each artillery regiment comprised ten foot companies and two light companies. A number of the foot companies were assigned to coast defense duties: the garrison of the Charleston harbor forts in December of 1860 comprised two companies totalling 65 officers and men, plus eight bandsmen. The balance of the artillery was scattered in the West, where most served as infantry, since artillery was of little use against Indians.

There were three types of horse soldiers in the army, dragoons, mounted rifles and cavalry. Despite the different designations, all three types had the same organization: initially ten companies divided into five squadrons, an additional squadron was added shortly before the Civil War, permitting the formation of three battalions at need. The *1st Dragoons*—which served as cavalry, not dragoons, a form of mounted infantry—had been organized in 1833, as the frontier began to move onto the prairies, and the *2nd Dragoons* was added in 1836. The *Regiment of Mounted Rifles* was raised in 1846 for service in the Mexican War, and rendered excellent service, being dubbed "Brave Rifles" by Winfield Scott. In 1855 two cavalry regiments were added, the *1st* and *2nd*, to provide additional mounted troops to help police the vast territories recently annexed from Mexico.

In addition to the combat arms, the Regular Army included the Corps of Engineers and the Corps of Topographical Engineers. The Engineers performed numerous civil and military services, designing coast defenses, supervising harbor development, clearing obstacles to navigation on the Western rivers, and the like. The "Topos" were generally considered the intellectual elite of the Army, and were responsible for surveying the Western territories, no minor task. Although the Corps of Engineers included a small contingent of enlisted personnel, the Topos were composed entirely of officers.

The administrative needs of the Regular Army were tended to by a number of staff departments which were often mired in bureaucratic detail. These included the Adjutant General's Department, the Inspector General's Department, the Judge Advocate General's Department, the Quartermaster General's Department, the Subsistence Department, the Medical Department, the Pay Department, and the Ordnance Department. There was, in addition, a Chief Signal Officer, but he had neither staff nor department.

If the Old Army was small, it was well officered. Very few of the officers lacked serious military training or experience. Of the 1,080 officers on active duty at the end of 1860, 821 (76 percent) were graduates of West Point. A number of the others had graduated from one of the dozen or so private or state military high schools and academies which existed at the time. In addition, a small percentage had risen from the ranks. All of the senior officers were combat veterans, some, like general-in-chief Winfield Scott, having distinguished themselves in several wars. Nor were the men they led unworthy of them. Although the troops were by no means the best representatives of American manhood, being prone to desertion, brawling and drunkenness and frequently not American at all but Irish or

German immigrants, they were good material. Well trained, they proved intensely loyal, only 26 deserting to join the Confederacy.

On 3 May 1861, shortly after the Civil War broke out, the Regular Army was expanded. Nine new infantry regiments were authorized, numbered *11th* through *19th*, each to comprise three battalions of eight companies. In addition the *3rd Cavalry* was raised and the *5th Artillery*, comprised of a dozen light batteries. But this may well have been an error. Had Regular Army personnel been dispersed among the Volunteers, the latter would have been brought up to a relatively high degree of military skill rather rapidly. Certainly those Volunteer Army regiments and brigades which had former Regulars officers and enlisted men in their ranks became militarily proficient far sooner than those which lacked such experienced personnel. Although some individuals recommended such a course, the political and military leadership of the nation decided against it. So the Regular Army, which enrolled about 75,000 men during the war, but peaked at about 50,000, served in separate regiments and brigades and divisions, discharging its duty with great courage and skill wherever it served, and providing a mark against which the officers and men of the Volunteer Army could measure themselves. It was not, perhaps, the best way for the Old Army to have served, but it served honorably and well.

The Richmond Howitzers, a Virginia militia company which would prove a tough outfit in the coming war, once buried a pet crow in an elaborate military ceremony which included two eulogies in English plus an oration in Latin and an ode in Greek.

Not long before the Civil War broke out the heavily Irish 69th New York refused to parade in honor of Mr. Charles Renfrew —the Prince of Wales travelling incognito—leading the State Adjutant General to charge the entire regiment with mutiny, charges which were still pending in April of 1861, when they were dropped so that the regiment could march off to war.

Men of the 8th New York *in the uniforms worn by soldiers of the Mexican American War. That great conflict served as the training ground for many Civil War commanders.*

War and Society

The Militia in Pre-War America

Only 3 percent of all firearms made in the United States in 1860 were produced in the South.

Invited to drill his hometown militia company while on graduation leave from West Point in the summer of 1846, the newly minted 2nd Lt. Thomas J. Jackson bungled the job so badly that he marched the men off the parade ground and right out of town.

It has been customary to deride the military policy of the United States in the period before the Civil War. Indeed, it occasionally has been said that the United States had no military policy in that period. Citing the experience of the Civil War, some authors have suggested that the nation was woefully unprepared for war. This is unreasonable. In fact, quite the reverse was true, for the nation had a realistic and intelligent military policy, given the war which was expected, as demonstrated by the experience of 1812-1814, 1846-1848, 1898, 1917-1918 and even 1941-1945.

The expected war was a conflict with an overseas power, and most specifically with Britain, which was, after all, the only country in the world having the wherewithal to seriously threaten the United States. The principal underpinning of American military policy for most of the nation's history was the triad of the navy, the coast defense system and the militia. A British invasion of the United States would require a prodigious effort, one which would take months or even years to mount. During this grace period the navy would harass British merchant shipping while the militia would have time to turn

A garrison at New York.

32

out and, leavened by the Regular Army, be brought to a reasonable degree of efficiency. By the time the British were in a position to assault American shores or drive southwards from Canada, considerable forces would be available for service either in the field or behind the most elaborate coastal fortifications in history.

Given the war which was expected, this was a reasonable strategy. But the war which was expected was not that which occurred. Nor was there very much which could have been done to prepare for the war which happened. As a result, the nation was indeed unprepared, unprepared for an internal conflict. So the militia had to go to war with little or no serious preparation.

The history of the militia in the United States has been long and varied, and its popularity and effectiveness have risen and fallen over the years. In the period immediately after the War with Mexico the militia of most states was relatively good. In 1852, for example, New York State had over 45,000 active militiamen in eight divisions, plus a regiment each of riflemen and cavalry and a small corps of artillery, all relatively well-armed and well-drilled. But through the 1850s the popularity, and, more importantly, the effectiveness of the militia declined. The institution virtually ceased to exist in several states: Jacob D. Cox, a lawyer who became one of the best amateur soldiers of the war, did not even own a uniform in 1861 despite being a brigadier general in the Ohio militia. In many states the militia became little more than an excuse for the local menfolk to get together occasionally and have a few.

Although by and large the militia in the Southern states seems to have been marginally better than that in the North, if only because of the potential danger of slave insurrections—a danger more apparent than real since the last serious outbreaks occurred in the 1830s—, no state was really prepared for war in 1860, not even for a limited war. New York, noted for maintaining an effective militia—Canada was right next door, and it was also useful in suppressing urban riots—had less than 20,000 active militiamen on the eve of the Civil War.

The militia began to become popular again late in the 1850s, as much for its social, political and entertainment value as for its military. Famed drill masters, such as the young Ephraim Elmer Ellsworth of the *Chicago Zouaves*, toured the country with their regiments, holding drill competitions and exhibitions in many cities, providing a showy, romantic notion of the military life which would eventually be shattered on the battlefield: Ellsworth himself was among the first to fall, shot by James T. Jackson on 24 May 1861, as he pulled down the Confederate flag which had flown over Jackson's hotel in Alexandria, Virginia.

In 1860 there were about 4,200,000 men liable for service under the terms of the Militia Act of 1792. On paper several states had substantial contingents. Maine, for example, had 60,000 men enrolled in the state militia, while Tennessee had over 150,000. But the important figure was that of active militia, men who were organized, uniformed, equipped and drilled in some fashion, and on that score Maine had only 1,200 militia and Tennessee about twice as many. Nevertheless, despite its very uneven military quality, it was the militia which provided the backbone of both armies in the early months of the war, many militia outfits enlisting together for war service. The accompanying table gives an approximate estimate of the strength and effectiveness of the militia of the several states in 1860.

State or Territory	Men Quality (1,000s)
Alabama	2.5 Fair
Arkansas	1.5 Poor
California	1.0 Fair
Colorado Territory	0.0
Connecticut	1.0 Fair
Dakota Territory	0.0

Showcase militia—Elmer Ellsworth's Chicago Zouaves in their natty uniforms modeled after a similar French military costume.

For some years before the Civil War Ambrose P. Hill courted one Ellen Marcy, who jilted him and in 1860 married his erstwhile West Point roommate, George B. McClellan, a fact to which the troops later attributed Hill's singular aggressiveness against his successful rival, so that during one attack a Union veteran was heard to cry "My God, Nellie, why didn't you marry him?"

When Louis M. Goldsborough entered the United States Navy in 1817 at the age of eleven, as was then the custom, family connections—his father was Chief Clerk of the Navy Department—managed to get his warrant as midshipman predated to 1812, so that he gained five years seniority, which meant he was a naval officer from the age of six.

Delaware	0.2 Poor	Missouri	1.5 Fair
District of Columbia	0.5 Poor	Nebraska Territory	0.5 Fair
Florida	0.5 Poor	New Hampshire	1.0 Poor
Georgia	2.0 Fair	New Jersey	1.0 Satisfactory
Illinois	1.0 Poor	New Mexico Territory	0.5 Fair
Indiana	0.5 Poor	New York	19.0 Good
Indian Territory	0.0	North Carolina	1.5 Satisfactory
Iowa	1.5 Poor	Oregon	0.5 Poor
Kansas Territory	1.0 Fair	Ohio	5.5 Poor
Kentucky	4.0 Fair	Pennsylvania	19.0 Fair
Louisiana	3.0 Good	Rhode Island	2.0 Fair
Maine	1.2 Poor	South Carolina	7.0 Good
Maryland	1.0 Poor	Tennessee	2.5 Fair
Massachusetts	5.6 Good	Texas	1.5 Fair
Michigan	1.2 Fair	Utah Territory	2.0 Fair
Minnesota	1.5 Fair	Vermont	0.9 Fair
Mississippi	2.5 Fair	Virginia	13.7 Good

Members of a New Jersey Militia unit.

Washington Territory	0.0
Wisconsin	2.0 Fair

As can be seen, there were perhaps 115,000 active militiamen in the United States on the eve of the Civil War, mostly of indifferent quality. By no stretch of the imagination was any state actually ready for war in 1860, at least not that which came in the following year. Although South Carolina, where secession had become something of a secular religion, had made some efforts to build a state arsenal and accumulate arms, its preparations were trivial compared with the demands of even a small war.

The secessionist states—Virginia, the Carolinas, Georgia, Florida, Alabama, Mississippi, Louisiana, Texas, Arkansas and Tennessee—had about 38,000 active militiamen in 1860, while the three Border States—Maryland, Kentucky and Missouri—had some 6,500 more, most of whom would "go South" in the secession crisis. Deducting those portions of the Virginia and Maryland militia which adhered to the Union, the Confederacy started off with over 40,000 relatively trained and equipped men, while perhaps 75,000 militia remained in the loyal areas, along with about 16,000 men of the Regular Army. Of course, the Confederacy began mobilizing before the Union. By 1 April 1861 the seceded states—South Carolina, Georgia, Florida, Alabama, Mississippi, Louisiana and Texas—had at least 45,000 men under arms in Confederate service, of whom about 5,000 were at Charleston and some 2,000 at Pensacola, when the Union had yet to call a single man. The secession of the "Upper Tier" slave states and disloyalty in the Border States over the next few weeks would immediately add over 25,000 more. Of course, by then Northern manpower began to muster.

*John Brown
while facing his arraignment.*

John Brown lies wounded on the floor of the Federal arsenal of Harper's Ferry after Federal troops put down his attempt at slave insurrection.

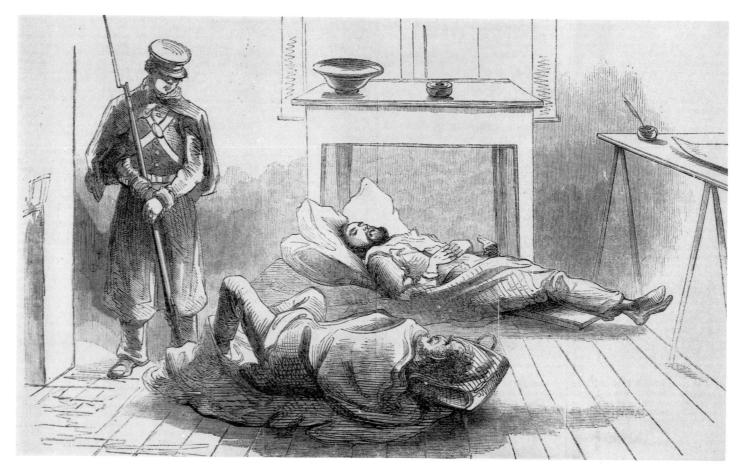

Federals advance on John Brown.

The Mormon War

The Mormons had a long and difficult struggle to establish a niche in American society. Founded by Joseph Smith in Fayette, New York, in 1830, the "Church of Jesus Christ of Latter Day Saints" was dogged by religious intolerance from the start. As a result, its adherents were driven several times to relocate, often under severe pressure and even armed force: the Missouri militia destroyed a Mormon settlement in 1838 as did the Illinois militia in the mid-1840s. Finally, after the murder of Smith at Navuoo, Illinois, in 1846, Mormon leadership decided to seek safety in an unsettled region in the west. Since the United States was then at war with Mexico, President Polk, who, like most Americans lacked sympathy for the Mormons, decided it would be in the national interest to be nice to them, lest "they turn up in California at some delicate moment in the progress of the conquest." As a result, the government granted the Mormons permission to settle in Utah. To further secure the adherence of the Mormons to the national cause, Polk authorized the recruitment of a Mormon battalion for war service.

The Mormons responded well to the appeal for troops, almost 550 men were mustered into service at Ft. Leavenworth in June of 1846, representing about a fifth of military aged Mormons. The Mormon battalion served for a year. Initially under the command of Lt. Andrew Jackson Smith of the *2nd Dragoons*, a "gentile" who would later become a Union major general, the battalion was shortly taken over by Capt. Philip St. George Cooke of the *1st Dragoons*, later a Union brigadier, who commanded as acting lieutenant colonel: among Cooke's officers was George Stoneman, who would later command the cavalry of the *Army of the Potomac* for a time. Cooke whipped the battalion into shape, discharged unfit personnel and took off for California, blazing a new trail from Santa Fe, New Mexico, along the Gila River and thence westwards to San Diego, along a route which was later followed by many of the "'49-ers" and eventually by the Southern Pacific Railroad. The Mormon battalion, which saw no combat but lost about 30 percent of its strength to disease, mustered out in California in June of 1847. About 50 of the men reenlisted, and a few settled in California, but most went to Utah, where in the interim Brigham Young had settled the first Mormon families.

In 1848, of course, Utah officially became part of the United States, along with most of the rest of the Southwest. The rapidly growing Mormon community in Utah petitioned for statehood in 1849. This was rejected, and Utah was established as a territory, though as a concession to the Mormons, Brigham Young was made governor. Over the next few years relations between the Mormons and the United States deteriorated steadily. Things came to a head in the mid-1850s. California-bound wagon trains passing through Utah began to be harassed by Mormon extremists. A number of clashes occurred, and several massacres took place. Meanwhile, the impression grew that the Mormons were contemplating separating themselves from the United States. This impression was fueled partially by the Mormon extremists' arrogant attitude towards non-Mormons, partially by Mormon practices such as polygamy, which were in violation of American law, and partially by Young's dictatorial style of leadership. Further "proof" of disloyalty was to be found in the "Danites," a 2,000-strong militia which the Mormons had organized for self-defense against Indians and other marauders. Convinced that treason was afoot, President James Buchanan removed Brigham Young from office and appointed Alfred Cumming of Georgia. Young refused to step down, whereupon a military expedition was authorized to "quell the rebellion."

Early in the summer of 1857 some 2,500 troops were despatched from Ft. Leavenworth to reestablish Federal authority in Utah. The expedition, commanded by Col. William A. Harney, comprised the *5th* and *10th Infantry Regiments*, two batteries of light artillery and Col. Albert Sidney Johnston's *2nd Cavalry*, which included Robert E. Lee, George H. Thomas and William Hardee among its field officers. Harney, a fair cavalryman, was nevertheless a poor administrator and the expedition got off to a bad start. The Danites proved able irregulars, and harassed the advancing column in a variety of ways, attacking supply trains, stampeding horses and cattle, and setting grass fires. Poorly led and ill-supplied, the troops proved unable to effect an advance on Salt Lake City, falling back on Ft. Bridger. That November Johnston was breveted a brigadier general and assigned to command, by which time the campaigning season had passed. The expedition wintered at Ft. Bridger amid considerable privation, until Johnston was able to sort out the administrative mess. Meanwhile, among the Mormons, the extremists appeared to have gained the upper hand. Additional attacks on wagon trains occurred, efforts were made to stir up the Indians, and preparations were taken in hand for the defense of Salt Lake City. A major clash appeared inevitable.

In the spring Johnston was ready to advance, reinforced

The room in which Robert E. Lee was born seems to have also been the birthplace of two signers of the Declaration of Independence, his uncles Richard Henry Lee and Francis Lightfoot Lee.

On the eve of the Civil War the United States Army had 183 of its 198 companies (92.4 percent) west of the Mississippi, or, to put it another way, one soldier for every 120 square miles west of the "Father of the Waters" and one for every 1,300 square miles east of it.

American troops campaigning in the Valley of Mexico during the Mexican American War. (Courtesy of the West Point Museum Collections, United States Military Academy, West Point, New York)

with both regulars and volunteers to about 5,500 men. With the renewal of the advance, however, came efforts at mediation. As a result, Brigham Young decided to rein in his more extreme followers, disowned any suggestion of disloyalty and agreed to step down in favor of the new governor. In June of 1858 the Utah expedition entered Salt Lake City. Direct occupation of the Mormon capitol was brief, however, for the troops were shortly relocated to Ft. Floyd, a newly constructed post about 60 miles to the southwest. This effectively ended the " ebellio ", though Federal troops remained in the territory for several years.

A great many of the officers who would later distinguish themselves in the Civil War took part in the Utah expedition. In addition to Johnston, Lee, Hardee and Thomas, Barnard E. Bee—who fell at Bull Run after bestowing upon Thomas J. Jackson the nickname "Stonewall"—commanded a battalion of volunteers, and Winfield Scott Hancock, later a Union major general and hero of the Battle of Gettysburg, also took part. Altogether it appears that at least 50 future Union generals and 30 future Confederate generals served on the expedition to suppress the alleged Mormon attempt to secede from the Union.

Salt Lake City

A port outside Washington D.C. The half finished Washington Monument can be seen over the tree line.

A peaceful Richmond, Virginia before war reached its gates.

The U.S.M.A. Ring Knockers Fraternal Association

Between 1802 and 1860, 1,875 men graduated from West Point, of whom about 85 percent were still alive at the outbreak of the Civil War, of whom about 1,100 (58.7 percent) saw service during the war.

At West Point in the decades before the war, it was customary for cadets who were indulging in a little illicit alcohol to turn their backs when imbibing, so that their classmates could honestly testify that they had not witnessed a fellow-cadet drinking.

Robert E. Lee in 1850.

West Point was the alma mater of most of the senior military commanders on both sides during the Civil War. Indeed, not a few battles were almost reunions of old Academy classmates: Pointers commanded on both sides in 55 of the 60 largest battles, and on one side in the other five. What follows is a list of the graduates who attained some measure of distinction, arranged with their classmates, so one can more readily see who went to school with whom, and what was their relative class standing. Most of the men listed became generals, but some others were distinguished soldiers of lesser rank. A few graduates of note in other fields of endeavor have been included and are designated by an asterisk. Men who failed to graduate for whatever reason have been included with what would have been their graduating class, the year in which they left the academy being indicated by a letter: a = "freshman" ("fourth class"), b = "sophomore" ("third class") and so forth.

To really understand who went to school with whom, it is important to realize that after 1818, when a four year curriculum was introduced, a cadet's tour at West Point spanned seven classes, his own plus the three which graduated immediately prior to it and immediately after it. However in 1854 the Academy course was lengthened to five years by a decision of Secretary of War Jefferson Davis. Cadets entering in that year were divided into two groups: those over 18 were given a four year course, graduating in 1858, while those under 18 were subject to the new five year program, and graduated in 1859. The curriculum was changed back to four years on the outbreak of the Civil War, and, in consequence, there were two graduations in 1861: the May class having entered the Academy in 1856, and the June class in 1857. As a result, the men subject to the five year program—the 1859, 1860 and May 1861 graduates—would have known cadets in a total of eight classes, as would be the case for a small a number of cadets who took more than the normal four years to graduate, such as Joseph K.F. Mansfield, Philip Sheridan, James W. Forsyth, Israel B. Richardson and John B.S. Todd. Note that the figure in parentheses after each year indicates the number of men in the graduating class, while the figure after each man's name shows his rank in the class. However, before 1818 there was no class standing, and the number merely indicates the order in which the cadets were commissioned.

Class (#) Union (Rank)	Confederate (Rank)
1805 (3)	
Joseph G. Totten (3)	
1808 (15)	
Sylvanus Thayer (3)	
1814 (30)	
James Wolfe Ripley (12)	
Charles M. Thurston (15)	
1815 (40)	
Benjamin Bonneville* (35)	Samuel Cooper (36)
1817 (19)	
Ethan Allen Hitchcock (?)	
1818 (23)	
Richard Delafield (1)	
1819 (29)	
Daniel Tyler (14)	
1820 (30)	
George D. Ramsey (26)	John H. Winder (11)
1822 (40)	
John J. Abercrombie (37)	Isaac R. Trimble (17)
David Hunter (25)	
George A. McCall (26)	
Joseph K. F. Mansfield (2)	
George Wright (24)	
1823 (35)	
George S. Greene (2)	
Lorenzo Thomas (17)	
1824 (31)	
Dennis Hart Mahan (1)	
Robert P. Parrott* (3)	
1825 (37)	
Robert Anderson (15)	Daniel S. Donelson (5)
William R. Montgomery (28)	Benjamin Huger (8)
Charles F. Smith (19)	

1 8 6 0

1826 (41)
Silas Casey (39)
Amos B. Eaton (36)
Samuel P. Heintzelman (17)

1827 (38)
Napoleon B. Buford (6)
Philip St. George Cooke (23)

1828 (33)

1829 (46)
James Barnes (5)
Catharinus P. Buckingham (6)
Thomas A. Davies (25)
Ormsby McK. Mitchel (15)

1830 (42)
Robert C. Buchanan (31)
Edgar Allan Poe* (b)

1831 (33)
Jacob Ammen (12)
Samuel R. Curtis (27)
William H. Emory (14)
Andrew A. Humphreys (13)
Thomas J. McKean (19)
Horatio P. Van Cleve (24)

1832 (45)
Erasmus Darwin Keyes (10)
Randolph B. Marcy (29)

1833 (43)
Benjamin Alvord (22)
John G. Barnard (2)
George W. Cullum (3)
Rufus King (4)
Henry W. Wessells (2)

1834 (36)
William S. Ketchum (32)
Thomas A. Morris (4)
Gabriel R. Paul (18)

John B. Grayson (22)
Albert S. Johnston (8)

Leonidas Polk (8)
Gabriel James Rains (13)

Jefferson Davis* (23)
Thomas F. Drayton (28)
Hugh W. Mercer (3)

Albert G. Blanchard (26)
Benjamin G. Humphreys (b)
Joseph E. Johnston (13)
Robert E. Lee (2)

John B. Magruder (15)
William N. Pendleton (5)

Lucius N. Northrop (22)

Philip S. G.Cocke (6)
George B. Crittenden (26)
Richard G. Gatlin (35)
Humphrey Marshall (42)

Daniel Ruggles (34)
Henry C. Wayne (14)

Goode Bryan (25)

1835 (56)
Montgomery Blair* (18)
Herman Haupt (31)
John H. Martindale (3)
George G. Meade (19)
George W. Morell (1)
Henry M. Naglee (23)
Marsena E. Patrick (48)
Henry Prince (30)
Benjamin S. Roberts (53)
James H. Stokes (17)

1836 (49)
Robert Allen (33)
Henry H. Lockwood (22)
Montgomery C. Meigs (5)
John W. Phelps (24)
Thomas W. Sherman (18)
Daniel P. Woodbury (6)

1837 (50)
Lewis G. Arnold (10)
Henry W. Benham (1)
Alexander B. Dyer (6)
William H. French (22)
Joseph Hooker (29)
Eliakim Parker Scammon (9)
John Sedgewick (24)
John B. S. Todd (?)
Israel Vogdes (11)
Thomas Williams (12)

1838 (45)
William F. Barry (17)
Robert S. Granger (29)
Irvin McDowell (23)
Justus McKinstry (40)
Andrew Jackson Smith (36)

1839 (31)
Edward R.S. Canby (30)
Gustavus A. DeRussy (c)
Henry Halleck (3)
Joseph A. Haskin (10)
Henry J. Hunt (19)
Edward O. C. Ord (17)
Eleazer A. Paine (24)
Andrew Porter (a)
James B. Ricketts (16)
John C. Robinson (c)
Isaac I. Stevens (1)

Jones M. Withers (44)

Joseph R. Anderson* (4)
Danville Leadbetter (3)
Lloyd Tilghman (46)

Lewis A. Armistead (c)
Braxton Bragg (5)
Robert H. Chilton (48)
Jubal A. Early (18)
Arnold Elzey [Jones] (33)
St. John R. Liddell (a)
William W. Mackall (8)
John Pemberton (27)
William H.T. Walker (46)

P.G.T. Beauregard (2)
William J. Hardee (26)
Edward Johnson (32)
A. W. Reynolds (35)
Henry Hopkins Sibley (31)
Carter L. Stevenson (42)
James H. Trapier (3)

Jeremy F. Gilmer (4)
Alexander R. Lawton (13)

According to a tradition of dubious provenance, whilst a cadet at West Point, Pierre G.T. Beauregard had a romance with Virginia Scott, daughter of Winfield Scott, the most distinguished officer in the army, who, when her family broke off the affair, entered a convent, where she died in 1845.

Thomas W. Sherman, who eventually rose to a brigadier generalcy in the Union Army, secured an appointment to West Point in 1832 by asking President Andrew Jackson for it after having walked to Washington from his native Rhode Island.

When Ulysses S. Grant married Julia Dent on 22 August 1848, the best man was James Longstreet.

During the 1850s both Charles K. Graham and George S. Greene, who led Union brigades at Gettysburg and on other fields, were employed as engineers in the design and construction of New York's Central Park.

The first astronomical observatory in the United States, the Cincinnati Observatory, was established in 1845, largely through the efforts of Ormsby MacKnight Mitchel, a West Point classmate of Robert E. Lee and Joseph E. Johnston, who became a Union major general during the war and died of yellow fever in 1862.

First Lieutenant Thomas J. Jackson while he served in the ranks of the United States military.

1840 (42)
George W. Getty (15)
William Hays (18)
William Tecumseh Sherman (6)
George H. Thomas (12)
Stewart Van Vliet (9)

Richard S. Ewell (13)
Paul O. Herbert (1)
Bushrod R. Johnson (23)
Thomas Jordan (41)
James G. Martin (14)
John P. McCown (10)
William Steele (31)

1841 (52)
John M. Brannan (23)
William T.H. Brooks (46)
Don Carlos Buell (32)
Schuyler Hamilton (24)
Albion P. Howe (8)
Nathaniel Lyon (11)
Joseph B. Plummer (22)
John F. Reynolds (26)
Israel B. Richardson (38)
Isaac P. Rodman* (7)
Alfred Sully (34)
Zealous B. Tower (1)
Amiel W. Whipple (5)
Horatio G. Wright (2)

Abrahama Buford (51)
Richard B. Garnett (29)
Robert S. Garnett (27)
John Marshall Jones (39)
Samuel Jones (19)
Claudius W. Sears (41)

1842 (56)
Napoleon J. T. Dana (29)
Abner Doubleday (24)
Henry L. Eustis (1)
John Newton (2)
John Pope (17)
William S. Rosecrans (5)
George Sykes (39)
Seth Williams (23)

Richard H. Anderson (40)
James Monroe Goggin (c)
Daniel H. Hill (28)
James Longstreet (54)
Mansfield Lovell (9)
Lafayette McLaws (48)
Gustavus W. Smith (8)
Martin Luther Smith (16)
Earl Van Dorn (52)

1843 (39)
Christopher C. Augur (16)
Frederick T. Dent (33)
Wiliam B. Franklin (1)
Ulysses S. Grant (21)
Charles S. Hamilton (26)
James A. Hardie (11)
Rufus Ingalls (32)
Henry Moses Judah (35)
John J. Peck (8)
Joseph H. Potter (22)
Isaac F. Quinby (6)
Joseph J. Reynolds (10)
Frederick Steele (30)
Nelson G. Williams (a)

Samuel G. French (14)
Franklin Gardner (17)
Roswell S. Ripley (7)

1844 (25)
Winfield Scott Hancock (18)
Alexander Hays (20)
Alfred Pleasanton (7)

Simon B. Buckner (11)
Daniel M. Frost (4)

1845 (41)
John W. Davidson (27)
Washington L. Elliott (c)
Gordon Granger (35)
George W. Morgan (c)
John P. Hatch (17)
Thomas G. Pitcher (40)
Fitz John Porter (8)
David A. Russell (38)
William F. Smith (4)
Charles P. Stone (7)

Barnard E. Bee (33)
Louis Hebert (3)
Edmund Kirby Smith (25)
William H.C. Whiting (1)

1846 (59)
Darius N. Couch (13)
John G. Foster (4)
Alfred Gibbs (45)
Charles C. Gilbert (21)
George H. Gordon (43)
George B. McClellan (2)
Innis N. Palmer (38)
Jesse L. Reno (8)
Truman Seymour (19)
George Stoneman (33)
Samuel D. Sturgis (32)

Birkett D. Fry (c)
William M. Gardner(55)
Thomas J. Jackson (17)
David R. Jones (41)
Dabney H. Maury (37)
Samuel Bell Maxey (58)
George E. Pickett (59)
William D. Smith (35)
Cadmus M. Wilcox (54)

1847 (38)
Romeyn B. Ayres (22)
William W. Burns (28)
Ambrose E. Burnside (18)
James B. Fry (14)
John Gibbon (20)
Charles Griffin (23)
Lewis C. Hunt (33)
John S. Mason (9)
Thomas H. Neill (27)
Ebgert L. Viele (30)
Orlando B. Willcox (8)

Henry Heth (38)
Ambrose P. Hill (15)
George H. Steuart (37)

1848 (38)
John Buford (16)
Hugh B. Ewing (d)

William N. R. Beall(30)
Nathan G. Evans (36)
William E. Jones (10)
Walter H. Stevens (4)

1849 (43)
Absalom Baird (9)
Quincy A. Gillmore (1)
Richard W. Johnson (30)
John G. Parke (2)
Rufus Saxton (18)

Seth Maxwell Barton (28)
Johnson K. Duncan (5)
Charles W. Field (27)
John W. Frazer (34)
James McQ. McIntosh (43)
John C. Moore (17)
Beverly H. Robertson (25)

1850 (44)

Richard Arnold (13)
William P. Carlin (20)
Eugene A. Carr (19)
Cuvier Grover (4)
Elisha G. Marshall (25)
Adam J. Slemmer (12)
Gouverneur K. Warren (2)

William L. Cabell (33)
Armistead L. Long (17)
Jean J. A. A. Mouton (38)
Robert Ransom, Jr. (18)
Lucius M. Walker (15)
Charles S. Winder (22)

1851 (42)

George L Andrews (1)
Marcellus M. Crocker (c)
Kenner Garrad (8)
Alvan C. Gillem (11)
William H. Morris (27)
James St. Clair Morton (2)
William D. Whipple (13)

Lawrence S. Baker (42)
Junius Daniel (33)
Benjamin H. Helm (9)

1852 (43)

George Crook (38)
Milo S. Hascall (14)
John P. Hawkins (40)
August V. Kautz (35)
Alexander McD. McCook (30)
Henry W. Slocum (7)
David S. Stanley (9)
Charles R. Woods (20)

George B. Anderson (10)
George B. Cosby (17)
John H. Forney (22)

1853 (52)

Alexander Chambers (43)
William Dwight (d)
James B. McPherson (1)
John McA. Schofield (7)
Philip H. Sheridan (34)
Joshua W. Sill (3)
William Sooy Smith (6)
William R. Terrill (16)
Davis Tillson (b)
Robert O. Tyler (22)

William R. Boggs (4)
John S. Bowen (13)
John R. Chambliss (31)
Henry B. Davidson (33)
John Bell Hood (44)
James A. Smith (45)
Henry H. Walker (41)

1854 (46)

Oliver O. Howard (4)
Thomas H. Ruger (3)
Stephen H. Weed (27)

James Deshler (7)
Archibald Gracie, Jr. (14)
George W. C. Lee (1)
Stephen D. Lee (117)
John Pegram (10)
William D. Pender (19)
J. E. B. Stuart (13)
John B. Villepigue (22)

1855 (34)

William W. Averell (26)
David McM. Gregg (6)
William B. Hazen (28)
Alfred T.A. Torbert (21)
John W. Turner (14)
Alexander S. Webb (13)
Godfrey Weitzel (2)
James A. Whistler* (c)

Francis R.T. Nicholls (12)

1856 (49)

George D. Bayard (11)
Samuel S. Carroll (44)
James W. Forsyth (28)
Orlando M. Poe (6)
William P. Sanders (41)
Francis L. Vinton (10)

William H. Jackson (38)
William W. Kirkland (c)
Fitzhugh Lee (45)
Lunsford L. Lomax (21)
Hylan B. Lyon (19)
James P. Major (23)

1857 (38)

John M. Corse (b)
Charles H. Morgan (12)
George C. Strong (5)

Edward P. Alexander (3)
Robert H. Anderson (35)
Samuel W. Ferguson (19)
John S. Marmaduke (30)

1858 (27)

Charles G. Harker (16)

Bryan M. Thomas (22)

1859 (22)

Martin D. Hardin (11)
Edwin H. Stoughton (17)

Joseph Wheeler (19)

1860 (41)

Weslery Merritt (22)
James M. Warner (40)
James H. Wilson (6)

Stephen D. Ramseur (14)

1861 (45)

Adalbert·Ames (5)
May
Judson Kilpatrick (17)
Edmund Kirby (10)
Emory Upton (8)

John Pelham (d)

Thomas L. Rosser (d)
Pierce M. B. Young (d)

1861 (34)

Alonzo Cushing (12)
June
George A. Custer (34)

John H. Kelly (d)

Felix H. Robertson (d)

1862 (28)

Randall S. Mackenzie (1)

James Dearing (c)

Even a cursory examination of the listings reveals that there was no particular pattern to the way in which each class yielded higher ranking officers. Thus, some years (1822, 1835, 1843) produced a numerous "crop" of Union generals, while some others (1828, 1849, 1854) yielded a good crop of Rebels, and still others (1837, 1838, 1842) produced generals in about equal proportions.

On 27 June 1860 Maj. Albert J. Myer, who was by training a surgeon, was appointed Chief Signal Officer of the United States Army, and thus head of the first independent Signal Corps in history, which consisted of precisely one man, himself.

The Sibley tent, an elaborate teepee-like affair for up to 20 men designed before the war by Maj. Henry Hopkins Sibley, later a Confederate general, had one drawback: the stove issued for it had a chimney too short to reach the opening from whence it was supposed to emerge, so that the tent rapidly filled with smoke, which may help explain why it saw little use during the war.

As a result of an accidental wound to the knee in 1839, Lt. Lucius B. Northrop went on "indefinite" sick leave from the army until January of 1861, whereupon his health recovered sufficiently for his friend Jefferson Davis to name him Commissary General of the Confederacy, a post in which he was highly incompetent.

In 1842 future Union Brig. Gen. Joseph Andrew Jackson Lightburn attempted to secure an appointment to West Point, only to be passed over in favor of future Confederate Lt. Gen. Thomas J. Jackson, the "Gallant Stonewall."

Whilst conducting a survey of Barataria Bay, Louisiana, in 1840, Lt. Pierre G.T. Beauregard supervised an estimated 10,000 soundings.

West Point graduates from the class of 1860 serving in the Federal army in the field as desperately needed drill instructors and commanders.

Grant upon his graduation from West Point.
(Courtesy Civil War Library and Museum)

LEFT:
U.S. Grant with an artillery battery engaged at Chapultepec during the Mexican American War.
(Courtesy Civil War Library and Museum)

The Seminole Wars

The first ironclad warship in the United States Navy was the so-called *Stevens Ram*, which, though authorized in 1842 and actually begun in 1854, was never completed and was scrapped on the stocks in 1874.

The Indian Wars are an inherent part of the folklore and history of the United States. Yet the most difficult of these, the three Seminole Wars, are among the least well known, perhaps because, in the end, it was the Indians who won.

The Seminoles are by origin natives of Georgia, a branch of the Creek nation who migrated into Florida in the mid-eighteenth century, primarily to get away from Britain's American colonists. As a result of the American Revolution, Florida passed to Spain. The Seminoles were not inclined to cross the border into the United States looking for trouble. Indeed, the trouble went in the other direction. Knowing that the racially tolerant Seminoles would give them refuge, blacks fleeing bondage would often head south. This presented a problem for slaveholders in Georgia, concerned about the security of their "property." As a result, slave catchers would sometimes cross into Florida, where they would often be given a warm welcome by the Seminoles. In complete violation of international law, some of these slave catching expeditions were accompanied by American troops, who received much the same treatment at the hands of the Seminoles. Things came to a head in 1817.

On the assumption that the Seminoles were being subsidized by a foreign power, about a thousand regulars and nearly 7,000 militiamen and volunteers under Maj. Gen. Andrew Jackson deliberately invaded Florida and seized several Spanish posts. A number of Seminole chiefs and two British merchants were executed out of hand, a matter which caused a furor in Congress and in Parliament, though Jackson weathered the storm. Thus ended the so-called "First Seminole War." As Spain was incapable of defending its interests in Florida, it sold the place for $5,000,000 and the United States took possession in 1821, with Jackson as governor. Seeing the way the wind was blowing, the Seminoles retreated into the swamps and jungles. An uneasy peace prevailed for a decade. Then, in 1830, with Andrew Jackson in the White House, the Indian Removal Act was passed, a massive swindle designed to grab the remaining Indian holdings east of the Mississippi through so-called "compensated" relocation to the Indian Territory, in what is now Oklahoma. By 1835 it was the turn of the Seminoles.

The Seminoles were not interested in relocating, having grown attached to the local swamps. A bloody war ensued.

Led by several able war chiefs, including Osceola (c. 1800-1839), some 3,000 to 5,000 poorly equipped Seminole warriors led over 11,000 regulars—virtually the entire Regular Army and the Marine Corps—and 30,000 militiamen and volunteers on a merry chase through the bogs and marshes and jungles for seven years. The struggle degenerated into the most brutal guerrilla warfare. Osceola himself was captured in 1838 through the treacherous violation of a safe conduct; imprisoned in Charleston, he died there the following year. But there were other chiefs to take his place, notably Alligator, Jumper and Micanopy and they carried on the struggle. By 1842 perhaps $40,000,000 had been spent. The death toll was enormous, at least 2,000 whites and an unknown number of Seminoles and blacks had died. Some Seminoles, perhaps 3,500, had been relocated, but the outcome seemed hardly worth the effort. As a result, Congress decided to drop the matter. Thus ended the Second Seminole War.

Three years later Florida entered the Union as a slave state. Things remained calm for another decade. Then, with increasing settlement, concern arose anew about the remaining Seminoles. A new effort was mounted to convince the Seminoles to go west. They refused. And so there was a Third Seminole War. The new war was a desultory affair, involving less than 3,000 troops, all militiamen save for some regular officers and staffs. The Seminoles stayed in their swamps and the army pretty much stayed out of them. There was little fighting. In 1858 a negotiated settlement was reached in which most of the Seminoles agreed to move to Oklahoma for a substantially better financial deal that any other Indians had ever received. Nevertheless, not all the Seminoles left Florida. Some retired deep into the Everglades. Not until 1934 was a treaty of peace concluded with the descendants of these holdouts.

The Seminole Wars brought no honor to the nation and little luster to American arms. But they did provide a remarkable number of Old Army officers with a lot of hard experience. Among the veterans of the Seminole Wars who would rise to prominence in the Civil War were Robert Anderson, George H. Thomas, Nathaniel Lyon and John Gibbon, as well as Braxton Bragg. Although exact figures are difficult to determine, at least 100 future Union and Confederate generals fought in the Seminole Wars.

In a period of 31 months from 1842 to 1845, the Corps of Engineers removed from the Lower Ohio, the Mississippi, the Missouri and the Arkansas Rivers 133,331 obstacles to navigation, including 21,681 snags, 36,840 roots, logs and stumps, and 74,810 trees.

Overlooking the Potomac is the birthplace of George Washington, Mount Vernon, at the time of the Civil War.

River traffic on the placid waters of the Potomac. After the Federals lost First Manassas, the Confederates provided further embarrassment by placing batteries on the shore of the river to shut down Federal use of the waterway.

The New Jersey Slaves

The appearance of 18 people held in bondage in New Jersey in 1860 seems a contradiction of the notion that New Jersey was a "free" state. The apparent anomaly was the result of something called "gradual emancipation." In the late eighteenth and early nineteenth centuries, several states, including New York, Pennsylvania and New Jersey, adopted this policy. It was designed to put an end to slavery with a minimum of social and financial dislocation. These states halted all trading in human beings and enacted legislation freeing all slaves upon attainment of a particular age, such as 25. Several states added provisions which permitted a slave to refuse freedom under certain circumstances: advanced age was one. As a result, there were still small numbers of slaves in several northern states, including New York, Pennsylvania and New Jersey, into the 1850s. By 1860 only New Jersey remained, with 18 people held as slaves, all quite elderly. As a result, New Jersey was technically a slave state until the Thirteenth Amendment was ratified on 18 December 1865. Gradual emancipation was a way to get rid of slavery without dealing a potentially fatal financial blow to slaveholders—no one seems to have wondered about the rights, financial or otherwise, of the slaves— and without throwing elderly slaves out into the street.

Gradual emancipation was stoutly resisted in the heavily slaveholding regions, and, as time went on, by the increasingly radical Abolitionists as well, who had at first seen it as a practical and reasonable solution to the problem. Gradual emancipation seems to have been a notion uppermost in Lincoln's mind during the political crisis between his election and the firing on Ft. Sumter. However, things had gone much too far long before then for such a policy to have worked.

Wade Hampton, who later became one of the South's finest cavalrymen, was probably the largest slaveholder in the country, with some 3,500 human beings numbered among his chattels.

Army Life

Water and Molasses

When, from time to time higher powers decreed that the troops deserved a party, careful preparations were made to insure that a good time would be had by all without discipline suffering in the bargain.

Typically on such occasions a whole beeve was provided for each company, to be split and roasted over open fires. Regimental bands supplied the music and the troops themselves would often sing or dance for the entertainment of their comrades, while the officers might kick in for an extra special treat, such as something sweet. The most delicate aspect of such regimental parties was the matter of drink.

Feelings about drink ran deep in mid-nineteenth century America. It was a hard drinking time, though the temperance movement was strong. To provide alcoholic refreshments to the troops might engender serious political problems for an ambitious officer. Moreover, the real stuff loosened the bonds of discipline. Yet how could one have a party without a little

taste of something interesting? As a result, an Old Army expedient was often resorted to, "water and molasses."

Water and molasses was easy to make. For each company one mixed together:

1	barrel water
3	gallons molasses
1	quart undiluted vinegar
0.5	pounds ginger

The resulting concoction was actually quite good as a substitute for the harder stuff. The ginger provided flavor and the vinegar a certain bite, while the molasses gave color and enough sugar to hike up one's metabolism a mite. Given the circumstances water and molasses was just the thing to provide a little extra to insure a convivial atmosphere at a regimental blow-out. As one observer noted, it would "cheer but not inebriate."

The site of John Brown's raid, Harper's Ferry. The town would later become the object of both Federal and Confederate attentions.

War and the Muses

Dixie

Perhaps the most popular of Civil War songs, and certainly the most enduring, the sprightly "Dixie" was written in April of 1859 by a Northerner, Daniel D. Emmett of Ohio. A well-known tunesmith of the era, Emmett—composer of the popular "Old Dan Tucker" and "The Blue-Tail Fly" (better known as "Jimmy Crack Corn")—wrote it to fill a hole in a so-called "Negro minstrel show" in New York. In 1861 Herman Arnold, a German who had immigrated in 1852, added a few notes and rescored it somewhat, apparently in the belief that he was adapting an old folk-song. On 18 February 1861 Arnold's band played his version for the first time, during the parade marking the inauguration of Jefferson Davis as Provisional President of the Confederacy: the escorting 1st Alabama had the distinction of being the first regiment to march to the tune. The new version proved immensely popular and soon became the unofficial anthem of the South, a status which it enjoys to this day, despite the fact that Emmett is said to have written an anti-Southern version, which included lines like ". . . the land of treason." Impressively, the tune was only a little less popular among Northerners, and on 8 April 1865 Lincoln requested an army band play it for a visiting foreign dignitary, "It has always been a favorite of mine, and since we've captured it we have a perfect right to enjoy it."

In a demonstration of the gallantry, honor, courage, nobility and gentility of Southern manhood, on 22 May 1856 Sen. Charles Sumner of Massachusetts was beaten into unconsciousness whilst sitting at his desk in the Senate by Rep. Preston Smith Brooks of South Carolina, who objected to a speech in which Sumner had denounced Brooks' uncle, Andrew P. Butler, as a servant of "the harlot Slavery."

In 1860 the South produced only 4 percent of all locomotives made in the United States.

Dixie

I wish I was in de land ob cotton,
Old times dar am not forgotten,
   Look away, look away, look away, Dixie Land!
In Dixie Land whar I was born in,
Early on one frosty mornin',
Look away, look away, look away, Dixie Land!

   Den I wish I was in Dixie
      Hooray, hooray!
   In Dixie land I'll take my stan'!
   To lib an' die in Dixie
      Away, away,
      Away down south in Dixie
      Away, away,
      Away down south in Dixie

Ole Missus marry "Will-de-Weaber,"
William was a gay deceber
   Look away, look away, look away, Dixie Land!
But when he put his arm around 'er
He smiled as fierce as a fourty-pounder
   Look away, look away, look away, Dixie Land!

His face was sharp as a butcher's cleaber,
But dat did not seem to grieb 'er,
   Look away, look away, look away, Dixie Land!
Ole Missus acted de foolish part,
An' died for a man that broke her heart,
   Look away, look away, look away, Dixie Land!

Now, here's a health to de next ole Missus,
An' all de gals dat want to kiss us,
   Look away, look away, look away, Dixie Land!
But if you want to drive 'way sorrow,
Come 'an hear dis song to-morrow,
   Look away, look away, look away, Dixie Land!

Dar's buckwheat cakes an' Injun batter,
Makes you fat, or a little fatter,
   Look away, look away, look away, Dixie Land!
Den hoe it down and scratch your grabble,
To Dixie's Land I'm bound to trabble,
   Look away, look away, look away, Dixie Land!

The Portent

The two most vehemently secessionist states, South Carolina and Mississippi, were also the only states in which black slaves constituted a majority of the population, 57.2 percent in the former and 55.2 percent in the latter.

The total "value" of slaves in the United States in 1860 was approximately $2,000,000,000, or an average of about $500.00 for each man, woman and child held in bondage.

RIGHT:
A railroad in central Georgia.

In a Richmond barbershop, Southerners read and discuss the recent tumultuous events gripping the nation.

Though noted principally as the author of Moby Dick, Typee and other great novels of men and the sea, Herman Melville was also a poet of considerable ability. His *Battle-Pieces* and *Aspects of the War* (1866) includes a number of important works, among them this short poem.

The Portent

Hanging from the beam
  Slowly swaying (such the law),
Gaunt the shadow on your green,
  Shenandoah!
The cut is on the crown
  (Lo, John Brown),
And the stabs shall heal no more.

Hidden in the cap,
  Is the anguish none can drown;
So your future veils its face,
  Shenandoah!
But the streaming beard is shown,
  (Weird John Brown),
The meteor of the war.

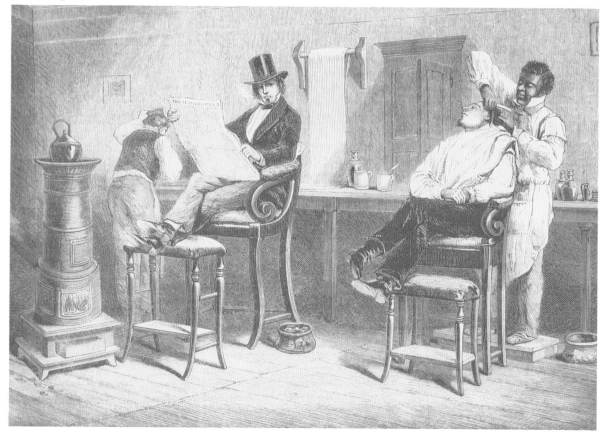

In order to get a closer look at the execution of John Brown, secessionist fanatic Edmund Ruffin donned a Virginia Military Institute uniform and marched two miles, shouldering a musket in the ranks of boys young enough to be his grandsons.

When still a teenager Jesse Grant, father of Ulysses, lived for a time with the family of John Brown.

When John Brown was hanged at Charlestown, Virginia, on 2 December 1859, one of the Virginia militiamen present was Pvt. John Wilkes Booth.

Fragments of the gallows on which John Brown was hanged were sold for $1.00 apiece, a good day's wage for a common laborer in 1859.

The trial of John Brown and his accomplices. Brown was found guilty and hung only to become a martyr for militant abolitionists.

The man who some say set the spark for the conflagration of the Civil War.

Confederate gunners bombarding Ft. Sumter are reported to have cheered each time the defenders got off a shot in reply.

Although some 4,000 shells were fired at or by Ft. Sumter over a period of 34 hours, not a single man was killed nor even wounded in the exchange.

PREVIOUS PAGE:
The firing line of the 1st New York *during a fight with a tenacious Alabama regiment.*

Through the winter of 1860-1861 secession fever swept the lower tier of Southern states. By early February, Mississippi, Florida, Alabama, Georgia, Louisiana and Texas had joined South Carolina, forming The Confederate States of America. President James Buchanan, well-meaning but untalented, proved incapable of acting with decision, seeking, on the one hand, to preserve the prerogatives of the Federal government, while not precipitating an open break with the secessionists in the hope that a peaceful solution might be found. Many others, both North and South, shared this hope. But it was futile. Though several last-ditch compromises were proposed, none had much chance of success.

Meanwhile, the seceded states occupied—had to occupy to assert their sovereignty—Federal installations on their territory, so that by the time Lincoln was inaugurated, in early March, the "Stars and Stripes" could be found flying over but three places in the entire South, all isolated posts, Fort Pickens, off Pensacola Harbor, Fort Taylor in the Florida Keys and Ft. Sumter, in Charleston Harbor. And it was at Sumter that the

issue boiled over into war. On 12 April 1861, after over four months of blockade and negotiation and hopes and prayers, Confederate artillery under Brig. Gen. Pierre G.T. Beauregard opened on the small Federal force holding the incomplete fort. Within 48 hours the garrison surrendered with the honors of war.

Fort Sumter proved the tocsin call. The tiny Regular Army, little more than 16,000 strong and losing officers daily as they resigned to "go South," could scarcely muster 4,000 men in one place, at a time when the Confederacy had already some 45,000 men under arms, with nearly 60,000 more authorized. So on 15 April Lincoln issued a call for 75,000 volunteers to put down "combinations too powerful to be suppressed by the ordinary course of judicial proceedings."

Shocked at the threatened use of force against the secessionists, the remaining slaveholding states, hitherto tentatively loyal to the Union, wavered. Most soon threw their lot in with the Confederacy: Virginia on 17 April, followed within weeks by Arkansas, North Carolina and Tennessee, while Maryland,

The Palmetto flag flies over Fort Moultrie after Major Anderson transferred his garrison to the safety of the more formidable Fort Sumter, seen in the distance.

Kentucky and Missouri were held to their loyalty only by extreme measures. North and South, men sprang to arms in the thousands and thousands, all alike desirous of taking part in the glorious adventure which all save a handful believed would be short. In vain did a few suggest that the war would be long and hard, among them old brevet Lt. Gen. Winfield Scott, hero of the Mexican War and general-in-chief of the United States Army.

Over the next few weeks, as men poured into recruiting stations both North and South, fighting began to spread all across the land. It began in small ways. There were relatively bloody riots at Baltimore and St. Louis, and there were virtually bloodless skirmishes at Harper's Ferry, Fairfax Courthouse and Philippi in Virginia. By then the dead from a handful of riots and skirmishes already numbered in the dozens. Meanwhile large forces began to concentrate, notably at Washington and in northern Virginia and in Missouri.

Fighting became more common and more intense. On 10 June the first real battle of the war occurred at Big Bethel in Virginia, a mere skirmish by later standards, but at the time viewed as a great victory for the Confederacy and a disastrous defeat for the Union. It was not until 21 July that the war began in earnest, when, in a confusing, ill-managed, but hard-fought encounter along the Bull Run, a small creek in northern Virginia, a Confederate army under Gen. Joseph E. Johnston and Brig. Gen. Pierre G.T. Beauregard defeated a Union one under Brig. Gen. Irvin McDowell, with nearly 3,000 Union killed, wounded or captured as against less than 2,000 Confederate casualties, appalling losses for the times.

Though Bull Run elated the South and depressed the North, it was but the beginning. In the East both sides pulled back, the Confederates almost as disorganized in victory as the Federals in defeat, each side seeking to strengthen itself for a future effort. Though numerous skirmishes would take place, little of importance would happen in the field through the end of the year, but much in camp and cabinet. A new man came to the helm of the Union forces, Maj. Gen. George B. McClellan, and he began to create a real army out of the inchoate mass of volunteers about Washington, even as, a scant 50 miles away in Virginia, his Confederate counterpart, Gen. Joseph E. Johnston, undertook the same task, the end result being the creation of two armies who's fate and honor would be eternally linked, the *Army of the Potomac* and the Army of Northern Virginia.

In the West it was different. There, the war grew bitter, with major clashes at Wilson's Creek and Lexington in Missouri and scores of little fights in which, by and large, the Union slowly gained the upper hand and secured control of most of the state, while Kentucky, vainly trying to maintain its "neutrality,"

Lincoln's inauguration at the Federal Capitol.

A Baltimore crowd waits to catch a glimpse of Abraham Lincoln on his way to be inaugurated in Washington D.C.. Their expectations would be in vain; warned of a possible assassination attempt, Lincoln slipped through town incognito.

The first shot of the Civil War was either that signalling the start of the Confederate bombardment of Ft. Sumter discharged from a 10 inch mortar at 4:30 a.m. on 12 April 1861 by Lt. Wade Hampton Gibbes, of Capt. George S. James' battery, at Ft. Johnson, or, more accurately, those fired several weeks earlier, on 9 January, when Ft. Moultrie warned off the Federal supply ship *Queen of the West* with a couple of rounds: whichever is preferred, the distinction of firing the momentous round certainly does not belong, as tradition has it, to secessionist fanatic Edmund Ruffin, who may, however, have fired the first round from the batteries on Cummings Point.

found itself being drawn into the struggle.

At sea the United States Navy began, somewhat feebly, to impose a blockade on the South, and even, in August, in cooperation with the army, to essay a successful amphibious operation against Hatteras Inlet, while sustaining the isolated

garrison at Ft. Pickens in Pensacola Harbor.

It was a decisive year, 1861, though not perhaps in terms which most could understand. It was not the issue which was decided, but rather the shape of the war. Though many did not yet see it, the war would be long and hard and bloody.

Northerners gather in New York to demonstrate their devotion to the cause of Union.

Incidents of War

Mrs. Anderson Reinforces Ft. Sumter

The position of Major [Robert] Anderson and his little band [in Fort Sumter], composed of ten officers, fifteen musicians and eighty-five artillerists—eighty in all—was an extremely perilous one. His friends were uneasy; his wife, a daughter of a gallant soldier, General Clinch of Georgia, was in New York City. She knew her husband was exposed to ferocious foes without and possible traitors within, the fort.

In the emergency she remembered a faithful sergeant who had been with her husband in Mexico, but she had not seen him in seven years. His name was Peter Hart. She knew him to be a tried and trusty friend, on whom she could rely in any emergency and she resolved to find him and place him by the side of her husband within the walls of Fort Sumter.

For a day and a half she sought a clew by visiting the residences of the various Harts named in the City Directory. She was an invalid. Her physician protested against her project, as he believed its execution would imperil her life. She would listen to no protests, but found Hart and the two started the next day for Charleston. They traveled without intermission and reached Charleston at the end of forty-eight hours.

The cars were crowded with recruits hastening to join in the attack on Fort Sumter. She neither ate, drank, nor slept and heard her husband threatened with instant death should he fall into their hands. Their language was very violent especially repecting the destruction of the old flag-staff at [Fort] Moultrie, which was considered such an insult to the South Carolinians as might not be forgiven. At the Mills House, Mrs. Anderson met her brother. She found no difficulty in procuring a permit from Governor [Francis] Pickens, who was her father's old friend, to go to Fort Sumter.

The Governor refused one for Hart, saying he could not allow a man to be added to the Sumter garrison. She scornfully asked if South Carolina, claiming to be a sovereign power among the nations of the earth, would be endangered by the addition of one man to a garrison of seventy or eighty, while thousands of armed hands were ready and willing to strike them.

The Governor, seeing the absurdity of his refusal, gave a pass for Hart, requiring from Major Anderson a pledge that he should not be enrolled as a soldier. A small boat carried them to Sumter. On every hand she saw strange banners and warlike preparations. Nearing Sumter, she turned and saw the national ensign floating over the fort, the only one in the whole bay. "The dear old flag!" she exclaimed, and burst into tears.

Reaching the fort, her husband caught her in his arms, whispering, "My glorious wife!"

"I have brought you Peter Hart," she said. "The children are well. I return to-night."

In two hours, Mrs. Anderson was placed in the boat by her husband, and rowed back to the city. The same evening she started for the national capital. Her mission ended, she was utterly prostrate. A bed was placed in the car for her comfort. She was insensible when she arrived in Willard's Hotel, Washington, and after forty-eight hours of suffering from exhaustion, she proceeded to New York and rejoined her children.

This brave woman had done what the government failed to do—she had not sent, but had taken, reinforcement to Fort Sumter.

—The Soldier in Our Civil War (1884)

Of the ten Union officers in Ft. Sumter, six became major generals, three others, including one who resigned after the surrender to "go South," were killed in action early in the war, and one became a colonel.

Maj. Robert Anderson and his noble wife who single-handedly reinforced the besieged garrison at Fort Sumter.

Fort Sumter's 32-pounder and 42-pounder guns return a harmless fire in response to the Southern bombardment on 12 April 1861.

"How I Joined the Army"

Richard A. Pryor, a Virginian on the staff of Pierre G.T. Beauregard, was very nearly the first man to die in the Civil War when, paying a call on Fort Sumter to help arrange its surrender, he took a draught of what he thought was brandy, only to discover that it was iodine, but was saved from this dubious honor by Union Surgeon Samuel W. Crawford—later a major general—who administered a stomach pumping.

FAR RIGHT:
A Confederate view of the type of reprobates enlisted into the Federal army. It was believed that one Southerner could whip seven Yankees.

Northern citizens gather to read the latest war news. In the early months of the Civil War, the Yankees found events somewhat disheartening.

John N. Opie, son of a prosperous Virginia farmer, was 17 when the war began. His wartime experiences were many and varied. He served under Thomas "Stonewall" Jackson and later J.E.B. Stuart before being captured in late 1864, an experience from which he barely emerged alive. After the war he practiced law and served in the Virginia State Senate. His memoirs, *A Rebel Cavalryman with Lee, Stuart, and Jackson* (Chicago, 1899), are lively and amusing, as can be seen from the following excerpts which cover the period from his enlistment through his initiation into military life in the early months of 1861.

My Father, Col. Hierome L. Opie, who was a well-to-do farmer, resided in the beautiful and fruitful County of Jefferson, now West Virginia, until 1856, when, anticipating the impending struggle between the States, he moved up the Valley of Virginia and purchased a farm one mile from the city of Stauton, where we were living at the outbreak of the war. On the 16th day of April, 1861, I, a boy seventeen years of age, was seated in a school room vainly wrestling with a proposition in analytical geometry. Not being able to master my mathematical problem, I was revolving in my mind how I should cut the Gordian knot, when I was informed that my father wished to see me.

I went to the door, and, to my great surprise, he informed me that the volunteer companies were ordered into service, and that, in fulfillment of a promise made a year previous, I could go with them; but it was his wish that I would not go, on account of my youth. I desired very much to please my noble father; but two mighty influences actuated me: one my unsolved mathematical problem; the other, the effect of having just read [the novel] *Charles O'Malley, the Irish Dragoon*, the reading of which induced me to believe that war was a glorious thing; and so I went, with many other thoughtless men and youths, and plunged heedlessly into a long and deadly war, without, at the time, being able to give a reasonable why or wherefore.

If there was any mischief or fun or devilment abroad, I was always implicated. I was a very polite boy, and I believe that, if on my way to Hades, I would bow politely to and exchange greetings with the Devil; but, if his Satanic Majesty desired or sought other than friendly relations, he would surely have been gratified, such was my accommodating nature and disposition.

In war, I ran when it was necessary, fought when there was a fighting chance, burned fence rails when cold, stole when hungry, and was oftentimes insubordinate.

* * *

It was [at Harper's Ferry] that the first Virginia army, which was composed of volunteer militia, assembled.

When we reached the place, where a Government armory and arsenal were located, we found that the small Union force had fled, first setting fire to public buildings. We succeeded, however, in saving most of the machinery and some hundred stand of muskets. Our stay here was spent organizing and drilling. I was detailed to assist Maj. John A. Harmon, afterwards Jackson's quartermaster, my duty being to quarter the troops as they arrived. The Major at first gave me the countersign every evening, until, he remarked to me, "Your father has asked me not to give you the countersign." I replied that, being an enlisted man, I was no longer under his authority. I had, that evening, an engagement, and must have the countersign, so I got my musket; and buckled on my belt, determined not to be circumvented. I took the post at the mouth of an alley, and marched up and down as a sentinel, until, finally, hearing someone advance I brought up my gun to a charge and gave the usual command, "Halt! Who comes there?" "Friend with the countersign." "Advance, friend, and give the countersign." The officer advanced and gave me the countersign, when, returning to the office and divesting myself of gun and accoutrements, I pursued the even tenor of my way. This I continued to do, for several nights, until, at last, one night I heard some one approach, and, upon going through the usual ceremony, I found that I had halted the major himself, who, recognizing me, exclaimed, "You d--- little rascal!" After this he always gave me the countersign. This mode of procuring the countersign I used during the whole war, together with the following plan: When there was a cordon of sentinels around the camp, and there was no possibility of making a new post, I wedged in between two sentinels and walked the beat until I met one, when, having forgotten the countersign, I would ask him for it. He, supposing I was a sentinel, invariably gave it to me.

Southern pickets in a hasty retreat in the face of a Federal advance.

The first man killed in the Civil War was Pvt. Daniel Hough ["huff"] of *Company E, 1st Artillery*, who died as a result of the premature discharge of a cannon being used to fire a salute during evacuation ceremonies after the surrender of Fort Sumter on 14 April 1861.

When a private who had wandered into his quarters at Manassas apologized for appropriating his desk, pen and paper to write a letter, Pierre G.T. Beauregard is said to have replied, "Sit down and finish your letter, my friend. You are very welcome, and can always come in here when you wish to write."

Lt. Manning M. Kimmel of the U.S. *2nd Cavalry* did not "go South" until shortly after serving at the First Battle of Bull Run, and, after a career as a staff officer in the Confederate Army went on to father Husband Kimmel, associated with another national military disaster on 7 December 1941.

On 3 May 1861 the Congress of the Confederate States of America declared war on the United States of America.

The 15 Massachusetts *engaged in the calamitous Union attack at Ball's Bluff. The botched affair would lead to the cashiering and temporary imprisonment of Union Brig. Gen. Charles P. Stone.*

General Cheatham's Escape from the Yankees

One night late in 1861 pickets of the *3rd New York Artillery* took into custody three men in a coach who were proceeding suspiciously through one of the army camps about Washington, only to discover to their dismay that they had arrested the president, the secretary of state and the commander of the *Army of the Potomac*.

In January of 1861 Southern sympathizers in California attempted to establish a "Pacific Republic" by an uprising at Stockton, which was rapidly overcome by loyal citizens.

On the morning of 7 November 1861, Union Brig. Gen. U.S. Grant began advancing a mixed force of over 3,000 men against Belmont, a small Missouri town on the Mississippi. In an effort to see what Grant was up to, Confederate Brig. Gen. Benjamin Franklin Cheatham went out a little in advance of the Confederate lines. As the area was rather wooded, he tarried a little too long beyond Confederate lines. Quite suddenly a small contingent of Union cavalry come upon him as he stood on a country lane. As the Union troopers spotted him almost as soon as he saw them, escape was impossible. Thinking quickly, Cheatham—who, in common with several other Civil War commanders, including Grant, was not what one would term a natty dresser—rode *towards* the column, and the Yankee cavalrymen halted. At a distance of a few yards, Cheatham reined in, asking "What cavalry is this?"

The officer in command replied promptly, "*15th Illinois Cavalry*, sir."

"Oh, Illinois cavalry. All right, just stand where you are."

With an exchange of salutes, Cheatham and his orderly rode on, passing the halted troopers, passing an infantry regiment which halted behind them, and then doubling back through the woods and on to the safety of their own lines.

A recruiting station for the New York Zouaves.

The First to Answer the Call

John T. Hunter of Philadelphia is generally considered the first man to volunteer for the Union. Almost as soon as Gov. Andrew Gregg Curtin of Pennsylvania issued the call for volunteers in response to Lincoln's appeal of 15 April 1861, Hunter telegraphed his willingness to serve. Hunter enrolled in the *Logan Guards*, a militia company from Mifflin, Schuylkill and Berks counties under Capt. John B. Selheimer, which was the first company of volunteers to reach Washington, on 18 April, and the first to be accepted for service by the Adjutant General of the United States Army.

However, Hunter's claim, and that of the *Logan Guards*, is disputed by one Josias R. King and the *1st Minnesota*. It seems that on 14 April, the very day on which Sumter fell, while Lincoln was still composing his appeal, Gov. Alexander Ramsey of Minnesota, who chanced to be in Washington, walked into Secretary of War William Cameron's office and offered 1,000 men for service, which was immediately accepted. Ramsey at once wired St. Paul, where King signed up that very evening, though the regiment was not completed and mustered into Federal service until 29 April.

While the rival claims of Hunter and King cannot be resolved, those of the *Logan Guards* and *1st Minnesota* can. The *1st Minnesota* was accepted for Federal service before the *Logan Guards*, but the latter was mustered into service before the former, so, in a sense, both were the first, depending on how one counts these things. One thing is certain, however, the *27th Pennsylvania*, in which the Logan Guards formed Company A, was the first volunteer unit to suffer a casualty.

The Logan Guards together with four other companies from Pennsylvania, totalling about 460 men, plus one Regular Army company from Minnesota, reached Baltimore at 2:00 p.m. on 18 April. Because there were no through rail connections, the troops—who were not armed—had to march across town to "take the cars" for Washington. As they did, they came under some abuse from secessionist hooligans. Some debris was thrown and Nicholas Biddle, a black freeman serving as an officer's orderly, was struck and injured by a brick-bat, thus becoming the first man injured by hostile action. The troops managed to get through the mob without further injury and reached Washington several hours later, arriving at 7:00 p.m. This took place one day before the more famous attack upon the *6th Massachusetts*, to which the regiment replied with lethal effect, which incident caused the first "combat" deaths in the war, Pvts Sumner Needham, Luther C. Ladd, Addison O. Whitney. and Charles A. Taylor, plus a dozen civilians.

During the West Virginia Campaign in mid-1861, a company of green Illinois volunteers was wearily making its way down a road in execrable marching order until its captain shouted, "Close up, boys! Damn you, close up! If the enemy were to fire on you when you're straggling along that way, they couldn't hit a damn one of you! Close up!", whereupon the troops closed up.

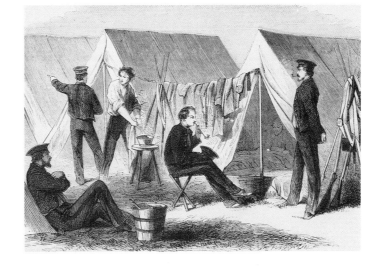

LEFT:
Officers and men of the 7th New York *in camp in April of 1861. The ranks of the* 7th *would yield 606 officers to Federal ranks during the war.*

Soldiers learning their stock and trade, the 2nd New York *at drill.*

When some Southern militia regiments went to war in 1861 the "gentlemen privates" were accompanied by their slave menservants, often wearing the same uniforms as their masters: the 3rd Alabama marched off with about a thousand white rank and file, plus "several hundred" black servants.

Beef cattle executed to provide Yankees with fresh meat.

By the 25th [of July] I had collected all the materials, made my report, and had my brigade about as well governed as any in the army; although most of the ninety-day men, especially the Sixty-ninth [New York Militia], had become extremely tired of the war, and wanted to go home. Some of them were so mutinous, at one time, that I had the battery to unlimber, threatening, if they dared to leave camp without orders, I would open fire on them. Drills and daily exercises were resumed, and I ordered that at the three principal roll-calls the men should form ranks with belts and muskets, and that they should keep their ranks until I in person had received the reports and had dismissed them. The Sixty-ninth still occupied Fort Corcoran, and one morning, after reveille, when I had just received the report, had dismissed the regiment, and was leaving, I found myself in a crowd of men crossing the drawbridge on their way to a barn close by, where they had their sinks; among them was an officer, who said: "Colonel, I am going to New York today. What can I do for you?" I answered: "How can you go to New York? I do not remember to have signed a leave for you." He said, "No; he did not want a leave. He had engaged to serve three months, and had already served more than that time. If the Government did not intend to pay him, he

could afford to lose the money; that he was a lawyer, and had neglected his business long enough, and was then going home." I noticed that a good many of the soldiers had paused about us to listen, and knew that, if this officer could defy me, they also would. So I turned on him sharp, and said: "Captain, this question of your term of service has been submitted to the rightful authority, and the decision has been published in orders. You are a soldier, and must submit to orders till you are properly discharged. If you attempt to leave without orders, it will be mutiny, and I will shoot you like a dog! Go back into the fort *now*, instantly, and don't dare leave without my consent." I had on an overcoat, and may have had my hand about the breast, for he looked at me hard, paused a moment, and then turned back into the fort. The men scattered, and I returned to the house where I was quartered, close by.

That same day, which must have been about July 26th, I was near the river-bank, looking at a block-house which had been built for the defense of the aqueduct, when I saw a carriage coming by the road that crossed the Potomac River at Georgetown by a ferry. I thought I recognized in the carriage the person of President Lincoln. I hurried across a bend, so as to stand by the road-side as the carriage passed. I was in uniform with a sword on, and was recognized by Mr. Lincoln and Mr Seward, who rode side by side in an open hack. I inquired if they were going to my camps, and Mr. Lincoln said, "Yes; we heard that you had got over the big scare, and we thought we would come over and see the 'boys.'" The roads had been much changed and were rough. I asked if I might give directions to his coachman, he promptly invited me to jump in and to tell the coachman which way to drive. Intending to begin on the right and follow around to the left, I turned the driver into a side-road which led up a very steep hill, and, seeing a soldier, called to him and sent him up hurriedly to announce to the colonel (Bennet, I think) that the president was coming. As we slowly ascended the hill, I discovered that Mr. Lincoln was full of feeling, and wanted to encourage our men. I asked if he intended to speak with them, and he said he would like to. I asked him then to please discourage all cheering, noise, or any sort of confusion; that we had had enough of it before Bull Run to ruin any sort of men, and that what we needed were cool, thoughtful, hard-fighting soldiers—no more hurrahing, no more humbug. He took my remarks in the most perfect good-nature. Before we had reached the first camp, I heard the drum beating the "assembly," saw the men running from their tents, and in a few minutes the regiment was in line, arms presented, and then brought to an order and "parade rest."

Mr. Lincoln stood up in the carriage, and made one of the neatest, best, and most feeling addresses I ever listened to, referring to our late disaster at Bull Run, the high duties that still devolved on us, and the brighter days to come. At one or two points the soldiers began to cheer, but he promptly checked them, saying: "Don't cheer, boys. I confess I rather like it myself, but Colonel Sherman here says it is not military; and I guess we better defer to his opinion." In winding up, he explained that, as president, he was commander-in-chief; that he was resolved that the soldiers should have everything that the law allowed; and he called on one and all to appeal to him personally in case they were wronged. The effect of this speech was excellent.

We passed along in the same manner to all the camps of my brigade; and Mr. Lincoln complimented me highly for the order, cleanliness, and discipline, that he observed. Indeed, he and Mr. Seward both assured me that it was the first bright moment they had experienced since the battle.

At last we reached Fort Corcoran. The carriage could not enter, so I ordered the regiment, without arms, to come outside, and gather about Mr. Lincoln who would speak to them. He made to them the same feeling address, with more personal allusions, because of their special gallantry in the battle under Corcoran, who was still a prisoner in the hands of the enemy; and he concluded with the same general offer of redress in case of grievance. In the crowd I saw the officer with whom I had

had the passage at reveille that morning. His face was pale, and his lips compressed. I foresaw a scene, but sat on the front seat of the carriage as quiet as a lamb. This officer forced his way through the crowd to the carriage, and said: "Mr. president, I have cause for grievance. This morning I went to speak to Colonel Sherman, and he threatened to shoot me." Mr. Lincoln who was still standing, said, "Threatened to shoot you?" Yes, sir, he threatened to shoot me." Mr. Lincoln looked at him, then at me, and stooping his tall, spare form toward the officer, said to him in a loud stage-whisper, easily heard for some yards around: "Well, if I were you, and he threatened to shoot, I would not trust him, for I believe he would do it." The officer turned about and disappeared, and the men laughed at him. Soon the carriage drove on, and, as we descended the hill I explained the facts to the president, who answered, "Of course I didn't know any thing about it, but I thought you knew your own business best." I thanked him for his confidence, and assured him that what he had done would go far to enable me to maintain good discipline, and it did.

Mrs. Hancock's Dinner Party

On 15 June 1861 Captain and Mrs. Winfield Scott Hancock gave a farewell dinner party at Los Angeles for several officers who had recently resigned their commissions in order to join the Confederacy. The guest of honor was Col. Albert Sidney Johnston, but lately Acting Commander of the Department of the Pacific, who would later die leading a Confederate army at Shiloh in early 1862. Despite the somewhat awkward circumstances, the evening passed in good spirits and everyone parted on friendly terms. It had been an unusual dinner in many ways, and the aftermath was to be even more so. Years later Mrs. Hancock observed that three of the officers present died at Gettysburg during "Pickett's Charge" against her husband's position along Cemetery Ridge on 3 July 1863. Two of these were the then Capt. Richard B. Garnett and the then Maj. Lewis A. Armistead, who had given Mrs. Hancock a prayer book on that last happy occasion, both of whom led brigades against Hancock's *II Corps*, with the death of the latter marking the instant of the "High Tide" of the Confederacy. Mrs. Hancock could not recall the name of the third, nor has his identity been established with any degree of satisfaction.

The camp kitchen of the 2nd New York.

Rip Van Winkle's Children

During the First Battle of Bull Run there were present in the vicinity of the field at least one governor, six senators and ten representatives, in addition to one president, Yankees all save the last, who was Jefferson Davis.

During the West Virginia Campaign in the spring and summer of 1861 some Union troops penetrated into a forgotten corner of the mountains near Laurel Ridge. As they marched, they came upon a venerable dame sitting in front of a log cabin. One of the men attempted to strike up a conversation with the woman and soon discovered that she was a little hazy as to current events.

Finally the soldier said, "You'll not refuse a 'hurrah' for Old Abe, will you?"

"Who's Old Abe?," asked the confused woman.

The surprised soldier replied, "Why, Abraham Lincoln, the president of the United States."

Stunned, the woman asked, "Why, hain't Genrul Washington president?"

"No! He's been dead for more than 60 years!"

"Genrul Washington dead?" mumbled the amazed woman. Then she suddenly jumped up, and ran into the cabin, crying out "Yeou, Sam!"

From the cabin came a male voice, saying, "What is it mother?", and a moment later the woman emerged with a man of some 50 years or more.

The woman hurriedly informed her son—for such the fellow proved to be—of the earthshaking news, "Genrul Washington's dead. Sakes alive! I wonder what's going to happen next!"

Stonewall Jackson's Railroad Movement

Thomas J. Jackson's campaign in the Shenandoah Valley in the spring of 1861 is widely recognized as a stellar example of the military art, as he successfully out-marched and out-fought less-ably led but greatly superior Union forces, a campaign which has provided inspiration to succeeding generations of soldiers. However, Jackson's earlier tenure in the Valley in mid-1861, is often overlooked, which is unfortunate, for during that period occurred one of the most innovative and clever maneuvers of his career, his rail movements in May and July. It must, of course, be understood that it was not Jackson who was moving by railroad, but rather Jackson who was moving the railroad, or, rather, some valuable pieces of it.

Harper's Ferry, the principal town at the lower end of the Shenandoah Valley, was an important junction in the Baltimore & Ohio Railroad, the most southerly and most direct connection between Washington and Ohio, a link of inestimable value to the Union, if only because it was the principal carrier of coal to Washington and Baltimore. While the iron logic of war dictated that this line be cut, important political considerations dictated otherwise. The B&O was a Maryland railroad and ran mostly through that Border State. Despite swift action by the Lincoln Administration to keep Maryland to her loyalties, it was widely believed in the South that Maryland might yet throw her lot in with the Confederacy, and thus

Lee with his most spectacular lieutenant, Stonewall Jackson. Jackson's death in 1863 was a tragedy for Lee and the Confederacy. (Courtesy Civil War Library and Museum)

66

it was necessary to avoid antagonizing the people of the state. As a result, B&O freight trains were permitted to pass through Harper's Ferry despite the fact that the place was in Confederate hands.

As time went on, it became increasingly clear that Maryland was not going to secede and Jackson began to contemplate action against the railroad. He began in a small way. In mid-May the president of the B&O, John W. Garrett, received an unusual message from Jackson. "The noise of your trains," he wrote, "is intolerable. My men find their repose disturbed by them each night. You will have to work out some other method of operating them." Since Garrett was quite aware that the continued operation of the line depended on Jackson's good

will he acted with commendable speed. Schedules were shortly revised so that trains passed through Harper's Ferry only during daylight hours. But Jackson complained again, for the increased traffic interfered with the daily routine of the troops, who were drilled in the mornings and inspected in the afternoons. Could Garrett make some additional modifications to the schedule? Once again Garrett complied arranging for all traffic to occur from 11:00 a.m. to 1:00 p.m.. Soon the double traced line was "the liveliest railroad in America," for two hours each day as heavily ladened trains carried coal eastbound and empty ones rumbled westwards.

This new arrangement suited Jackson very well. On 23 May he made his move. At 11:00 a.m. Capt. John D. Imboden of

The first great battle of the war, First Bull Run. The Federal defeat there served as grim proof that the great conflict would not end quickly as both sides had anticipated.

Fort Smith, Arkansas. Like all other Federal properties in the South during secession, Fort Smith was seized for Confederate use.

In March of 1862 Jackson, in the course of his brilliant Valley Campaign, chanced to be at Mount Jackson, the western terminus of the Manassas Gap Railroad, at a time when the Yankees were holding the line further down the Valley, thus severing rail communications with the rest of the Confederacy. At Mount Jackson, Stonewall spotted a locomotive and a good deal of rolling stock in the rail yard. He immediately ordered the lot moved overland 50 miles south, to Staunton on the Virginia Central. And once again, it was done.

At the outbreak of the war the Rev. B.C. Ward, pastor of a Congregationalist Church in Genesco, Illinois, attempted to raise an infantry company composed entirely of clergymen.

the Staunton Artillery blocked the eastbound track at Point of Rocks, in Maryland, about 20 miles east of Harper's Ferry, though permitting traffic to continue westwards from that point. Then, at 1:00 p.m. Col. Kenton Harper of the 5th Virginia, cut the westbound track at Martinsburg, about 18 miles west of Harper's Ferry. Altogether 42 locomotives and 386 cars were taken, a valuable prize indeed for the rolling stock-starved Confederacy. Jackson immediately began to send cars south, along the rickety tracks of the Winchester & Potomac. Unfortunately, only four small locomotives could make the run. And since the Winchester & Potomac was a dead end line, the additional rolling stock was of limited use. Limited, that is, until the ingenious Jackson—he would not become "Stonewall" for some weeks yet—got to thinking. At Winchester the locomotives were stripped and taken off the rails. Teams of horses were attached to them and they were hauled over the hard, dry Valley Pike for 20 miles, to Strasburg, on the Manassas Gap Railroad, which connected with the rest of the Southern railroad system. There they were rerailed, refitted and pressed into service. Jackson's clever trap and resourceful movement of the captured locomotives was very valuable to the Confederacy. And within weeks he did it again.

In mid-June, Union forces in southern Pennsylvania began to show signs of moving south, as did those concentrating about Washington. On 14 June Maj. Gen. Joseph E. Johnston, Jackson's newly-appointed superior, ordered him to evacuate Harper's Ferry. Over the next few days Jackson demolished everything of value within miles of Harper's Ferry, including

the rail and road bridges, the rail yards, all remaining rolling stock and the former United States arsenal. Jackson's long arm reached even to Martinsburg, where, in addition to important machine shops, there was considerable rolling stock, including

An example of modern warfare—a train equipped with an armed car for protection.

fourteen big locomotives. Whatever couldn't be evacuated had to be destroyed, but Jackson hesitated over the engines. And decided that what could be done once, could be done twice, and bigger and better at that. He ordered them prepared to be towed overland to Strasburg, 38 miles on the Valley Pike.

It required over 200 men—six machinists, ten teamsters, scores of laborers—with 40 horses to haul one 50-ton locomotive. The work was hard. After a preliminary stripping of all removable parts, each locomotive was jacked up so that the front wheels and all drive rods could be removed. The front end was then lowered onto a heavy wooden truck provided with wide, thick wooden wheels and secured in place, so that the engine now rested on the wooden truck and its rear wheels. The horses were then hitched in place at the end of a 100 foot chain. When all was in readiness, the horses were whipped up and slowly the behemoth began to move.

The movement required four days. The first stage, from Martinsburg to Winchester, was fairly easy, 18 miles of relatively flat going. But the 20 from Winchester to Strasburg was more difficult, as it covered hilly country. It required as many as 200 men heaving on ropes to help the horses haul a locomotive up some of the grades, and as many more to help them

down again. But the work was done, despite the enormous obstacles and some harassment from Union snipers. At Strasburg the engines were rerailed, reassembled and dispatched to Richmond for overhauls. In all, Jackson had added 18 locomotives to the slender rolling stock resources of the South. And then, a couple of days later he turned up at Bull Run.

The idyllic hamlet of Harper's Ferry before war came to the town.

While on picket duty during the West Virginia Campaign a German volunteer in Confederate service chanced to hear his native tongue coming from the Union lines; venturing a call in German, he heard in reply "From what part do you come, countryman?", and responded "Bavaria," which elicited a rifle ball in his direction, sectionalism by no means being an exclusively American problem.

Where Jackson robbed a railroad—the Baltimore and Ohio line running through Western Maryland and West Virginia.

Shortly after the Battle of Belmont (7 November 1861), Yankee Brig. Gen. U.S. Grant and Rebel Brig. Gen. Benjamin F. Cheatham met on a riverboat to negotiate certain technical matters relative to the exchange of prisoners and similar formalities, during which they fell into a discussion of horseflesh, whereupon Cheatham challenged Grant to have a race to decide the war, which the latter, noted for his equestrian ability, declined.

Soldiers of the Army of the Potomac acquire their needs from the "secesh" populace of Virginia during a foraging mission.

FAR RIGHT:

An irritant to Federal pride— a Confederate fort at Munson's Hill only six miles from Washington D.C.

"Self Defense, Sir."

There is a tale which is told of both armies, at various times, in numerous different regiments, but apparently having its origins in the very first months of the war. There are several versions of the story, but all retain the same essential elements, specifically an officer, a private and a pig.

One day a private walked nonchalantly into camp with a rather large, bulky object concealed under his coat. An officer espied the fellow and challenged him.

"What's that you've got there under your coat, soldier?"

"Why, sir, it's a pig," replied the young man.

"Don't you know it's against regulations to take livestock from the local people?"

"Yes, sir, I known that, but I killed the pig in self defense."

"How was that?"

"Well, I was coming down the road just outside of camp when I heard a loud noise. Looking about, I spied this pig charging down on me. Having no choice, I raised my musket and fired, killing him dead."

"Oh, I understand," said the officer, "and, of course, I will have to examine the evidence." Thereupon the private was permitted to go on his way, though with his burden somewhat lightened by that portion of the "evidence" which the officer required.

The Eleven Hour Day

During the Confederate siege of Lexington, Missouri (12-20 September 1861) there was an elderly Texan who served as a free-lance infantryman for the cause. The old gent would arrive at the siege lines each day at 7:00 a.m., dressed in buckskin, toting an old flintlock with a generous supply of ammunition and carrying a full dinner pail. Selecting a good position in the works, he soon settled himself in and then proceeded to bang away at the Yankees. Promptly at noon the gentleman would cease firing for an hour, during which he had his lunch and took a little rest. Then, at 1:00 p.m. he would resume his "work," banging away until six in the evening, when he would knock off for the day, carrying his musket and dinner pail back home, where supper and a good night's rest would ready him for the next day's business.

The Men

Jefferson F. Davis

One of the most influential men in the country long before the Civil War, Jefferson Finis Davis (1808-1889) was born in Christian County, Kentucky, into a family in comfortable circumstances. Though a Baptist, he received his early education at a Catholic school, and then attended both Jefferson College, near Natchez, Tennessee, and Transylvania College, at Lexington, Kentucky, before enrolling in West Point in 1824. Davis' career at the academy was unspectacular, and when he graduated in 1828 he was 23rd in a class of 32. He served as a junior officer of dragoons until 1835, when he resigned to become a planter in Mississippi. That same year he married the daughter of Col. Zachary Taylor, one of the most distinguished officers in the army, but she died of malaria just three months later. Over the next decade Davis built a considerable fortune as a planter, introducing innovative agricultural and management methods: his slaves were governed by an elective body of their own choosing. In 1845 Davis married again, to the considerably younger Varina Howell (1826-1905) of Natchez, who proved an important influence in his life. That same year he entered politics, successfully running for the House of Representatives and immediately establishing a reputation as a champion of "Southern rights." An enthusiastic expansionist, on the outbreak of the Mexican War in 1846 he resigned his seat in the House to serve as colonel of the *1st Mississippi Mounted Rifles*.

In Mexico, Davis served with distinction under his former father-in-law, Zachary Taylor, until severely wounded at Buena Vista. Mexico made him the most popular citizen in Mississippi, and upon his discharge he was elected to the United States Senate. Davis resigned his seat in the Senate in 1851 to make a bid for the governorship of Mississippi. Although he lost, in 1853 Franklin Pierce, who had succeeded to the Presidency upon the death of Zachary Taylor, asked him to serve as secretary of war. Davis proved an excellent secretary, and under his aegis the organization, administration and equipment of the army underwent extensive examination. Several new regiments were added, officers—including Capt. George B. McClellan—were dispatched to observe the British and French military in action during the Crimean War, a new musket was adopted and an experimental camel corps was organized, while military engineers undertook surveys to determine the optimal route for a transcontinental railroad. Meanwhile Davis managed to acquire considerable political influence, and helped secure passage of the Kansas-Nebraska Act, which seriously worsened sectional tensions over slavery. When Pierce left office in 1857, Davis was returned to the Senate by the Mississippi legislature.

On 11 February 1861, Jefferson Davis left his home to journey to Montgomery, Alabama, there to assume the Presidency of the Confederate States, the same day on which Abraham Lincoln was leaving his home to journey to Washington, there to assume the Presidency of the United States.

Jefferson Davis

The first of the 124 generals to die in action during the war was Confederate Brig. Gen. Robert S. Garnett, who fell on 13 July 1861, near Corrick's Ford, on the Cheat River in what is now West Virginia.

FAR RIGHT:
A regiment of Wisconsin volunteers drives against the Confederate line of battle.

Burdened with the hopes of an infant nation, Jefferson Davis accepts the oath of office to become the first and only president of the Confederacy.

Over the next four years Davis became an increasingly strident spokesman for states' rights and slavery, even advocating the reopening of the African slave trade. Despite this, he was viewed by some as a compromise Democratic candidate for president in 1860. But the party split into three parts and Republican Abraham Lincoln was elected. Lincoln's election sparked the "Secession Winter," which seemed to forebode the imminent dissolution of the Union. Mississippi passed an "Ordinance of Secession" on 9 January 1861, the second state to do so. Davis lingered in Washington for a bit, apparently in hopes that a pro-southern "compromise" could be worked out, and then, on 21 January made an eloquent farewell address to the Senate and resigned his seat.

Returning to Mississippi, Davis served briefly as commanding general of the state's military forces before he was elected president of the Confederacy. He served in that post for a little more than four years, guiding the fortunes of the South through one of the most arduous and devastating wars in the history of any English-speaking country.

When chosen president, Davis expressed surprise and regrets at his election. This seems to have been a bit of false modesty. He could not have been so naive as to realize that given his political stature there was no other choice: no Southerner was more popular and none had a greater political reputation, nor did any have superior administrative qualifications. But Davis was, in fact, ill-suited to the task at hand. A stubborn, narrow-minded man, he was usually inflexible, touchy in matters of pride and excessively loyal to the his friends and inveterately hostile to his foes, regardless of circumstances. Moreover, he believed himself to be something of a military genius, a matter which greatly hampered the conduct of the war, and he quarreled with virtually every one of his military commanders. That the Confederacy endured for four years is far more a tribute to the dedication and sacrifice of its people, than to the will, intellect, vision and determination of its president.

When the Army of Northern Virginia was compelled to evacuate Richmond, Davis fled southwards, hoping to join Confederate forces still resisting in the West. On the evening of 10 May he was captured near Irwinville, Georgia, by a Union cavalry patrol. Davis spent two years imprisoned in Fortress Monroe, as various factions in the Federal government tried to figure out what to do with him. In the end, nothing was done. In 1867 Davis was released on bail pending a trial on charges of treason. The charges were eventually allowed to lapse and Davis spent the rest of his life unmolested.

Davis passed his last days quietly. He travelled abroad for a time, and then, in 1877 settled at Beauvoir, his plantation near Biloxi, Mississippi. There he wrote his *The Rise and Fall of the Confederate Government* (New York, 1881), a tendentious, self-exculpatory work of little historical value. Never a beloved man, in his last years he attained some measure of respect and veneration as a symbol of the "Lost Cause," never requesting amnesty nor taking the oath of allegiance to the United States. So in the end, Davis attained a measure of the nobility which eluded him when he needed it most.

Pierre Gustav Toutant Beauregard

Scion of an old and distinguished Louisiana creole family, Pierre Gustav Toutant Beauregard (1818-1893) was the Confederacy's first war hero. Beauregard, second man in the West Point class of 1838, was commissioned in the Corps of Engineers, and sent to help build coast defenses and clear hazards to navigation. During the Mexican War he served with distinction as an engineer on Lt. Gen. Winfield Scott's staff, being twice wounded and earning two brevets. With the coming of peace he returned to more mundane matters. In 1858 he was made chief engineer in charge of the drainage of New Orleans, but devoted most of his time to improving navigation on the Lower Mississippi and supervising the construction of the New Orleans customs house, a white elephant project which

had been dragging on for several decades and continued for several more. In January of 1861 he was briefly Superintendent of West Point, but was relieved for what Southern-sympathizers term "suspicion of disloyalty," which was nevertheless a legitimate charge given that he had informed a Louisiana cadet that he would go with his state should it secede. Louisiana seceded soon afterwards and he tendered his resignation as captain and brevet major.

Within a few days he was appointed a brigadier general in the Confederate Army and sent to Charleston to supervise the investment of Fort Sumter. Sumter made Beauregard's reputation. When he went to Virginia to assume a command under Gen. Joseph E. Johnston, he was given a hero's welcome along

The Union officers holding Ft. Sumter were supplied with cigars and claret through the courtesy of Confederate Brig. Gen. Pierre G.T. Beauregard, who was in command of the investing forces.

While attempting to create an army at Manassas in the first weeks of the war, Pierre G.T. Beauregard discovered that his requisitions for rope to use in wells were being denied at Richmond because all rope was needed for the navy, which at that point had a handful of vessels.

A legion of Mississippians cheer P.G.T. Beauregard while on the march.

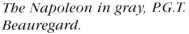

The Napoleon in gray, P.G.T. Beauregard.

Long after he had accepted a brigadier generalcy in the Confederate Army—and while he was commanding Confederate forces facing Ft. Sumter—Pierre G.T. Beauregard was still dunning the United States Army for travel expenses incurred pursuant to his final transfer shortly before he resigned to "go South."

FAR RIGHT:

Brig. Gen. Nathaniel Lyon falls while leading a charge against the Confederate line at Wilson's Creek (10 August 1861). Though the Federal's suffered a major reverse with this defeat, the Confederates failed to follow up their gains and squandered the fruits of victory.

Brig. Gen. Nathaniel Lyon.

the entire route.

Beauregard was in direct command of the Confederate forces during the First Battle of Bull Run (21 July 1861), handing his West Point classmate Irvin McDowell a sound thrashing. As a reward, Beauregard was promoted full general in the Confederate Regular Army. He was not, however, given a command commensurate with his new rank, and ran afoul of Jefferson Davis when he brought up the subject. Davis sent him West to serve under Gen. Albert Sidney Johnston. Beauregard helped plan the Shiloh Campaign, and, when Johnston was killed on 6 April 1862, assumed command. The results of the first day's battle being so favorable, he wired Richmond word of a tremendous victory. The Union riposte on the following day convinced Davis—who bore grudges—that Beauregard was a poor commander. When, several weeks later, Beauregard abandoned Corinth, Mississippi, in the face of superior Union forces (110,000 to 66,000), Davis decided that Beauregard had to go. Rather than act aboveboard, he waited for an opportune moment. A few weeks later Beauregard fell ill and went on sick leave, temporarily turning command of the Army of Tennessee over to Braxton Bragg. Davis pounced. Claiming that Beauregard had abandoned his post without authorization, Davis relieved him of command.

For nearly two years thereafter Beauregard commanded coast defenses in Georgia and the Carolinas. While it was important work, he was probably wasted in such a limited assignment. Finally, in April of 1864 he was sent to the defenses of Petersburg. In the Drewry's Bluff Campaign (4-18 May 1864), Beauregard skillfully met, held, and beat back the initially stronger forces of Union Maj. Gen. Benjamin Butler's *Army of the James*. Several days later his command was merged

into the Army of Northern Virginia and he was again unemployed. Briefly given a hollow theater command in the West, Beauregard ended the war serving with Gen. Joseph E. Johnston in the Carolinas.

After the war Beauregard became quite prosperous in railroading, did some writing and served as adjutant general of Louisiana. Although he became involved in the notorious Louisiana Lottery, he apparently never realized it was crooked: unsold tickets were included in the drawings. His military reputation remaining high, he occasionally considered seeking, and was several times offered, commissions from powers as diverse as France, Brazil, Argentina, Egypt, Romania and Spain.

Beauregard, nicknamed "The Napoleon in Gray," was short of stature, but looked every inch a soldier. He had an enormous military reputation in his lifetime—he was once mobbed by admiring New Yorkers—and much written about him since reflects this high regard. Yet there was little of substance in his career. At neither Sumter nor Bull Run did he demonstrate—nor need—any spectacular military skill. Neither his planning nor his performance at Shiloh were particularly impressive. And his opponent at Drewry's Bluff was one of the most inept in the Union Army. To be sure, his operations after Shiloh demonstrated some skill and he was a fine coast defense engineer. Moreover, he was, with Joseph Johnston, one of the few Confederate leaders to see that a concentration in the Western theater was probably the optimal Southern strategy, a view which, while militarily sound, only got him more deeply into trouble with Jefferson Davis. In the final analysis, it must be said that Beauregard's abilities were never properly tested in the field.

Nathaniel Lyon

A native of Connecticut, the short, slim, redheaded Nathaniel Lyon (1818-1861) graduated from West Point in 1841 and had a fairly typical career in the Old Army: frontier duty, service against the Seminoles, Mexico (one wound and one brevet), and a tour in "Bleeding Kansas." During the "Secession Winter" he was a captain in the *2nd Infantry*, stationed in St. Louis. Secessionists being particularly active in the state, Lyon collaborated with Frank P. Blair to organize a Unionist response. Working behind the back of Lyon's superior, the affable, but Southern-sympathizing and befuddled Brig. Gen.

William A. Harney, the two organized a home guard from loyal citizens and the large German community, pinched arms from the Federal arsenal, which Lyon commanded, and in a clever coup captured the largely secessionist militia while it lay encamped just outside St. Louis. Appointed a brigadier general of state troops in mid-May, Lyon was named brigadier general of volunteers by Lincoln on the 17th. Quickly organizing an army, he led it against the superior secessionist forces of Sterling Price. Lyon conducted a series of operations which largely secured Missouri for the Union, despite his death and

Pierre G.T. Beauregard had the shortest tenure of any Superintendent of West Point, from 23-28 January 1861.

Confederate Brig. Gen. Frank C. Armstrong began his Civil War service as a lieutenant in the Union *2nd Cavalry* at the First Battle of Bull Run, not resigning to "go South" until 13 August 1861, by which time the war was well under way.

RIGHT:
A Federal merchant vessel falls victim to the Confederate commerce raider C.S.S. Nashville.

The captain of the most infamous commerce raider of the Civil War, Raphael Semmes.

the defeat of his forces at Wilson's Creek on 10 August 1861. Lyon was the right man in the right place at the right time. His death in action deprived the Union of a capable soldier willing to take the initiative and not afraid to take responsibility.

Raphael Semmes

The Confederacy's first naval hero, Rafael Semmes (1809-1877) was born in Maryland. Appointed a midshipman in the navy in 1826, he did not actually serve afloat until 1832, by which time he had been admitted to the bar. His career was satisfactory, if largely uneventful save for blockade duty during the War with Mexico, out of which he got two books, one a history of Scott's campaign and the other a personal memoir. Settling in Alabama after the war, Semmes continued in the service, rising to commander in 1855. When Alabama seceded, he resigned from the service and was promptly commissioned in the same rank in the Confederate Navy.

In the tense weeks before Fort Sumter, Semmes was assigned to a procurement mission in the North, purchasing desperately needed supplies for shipment south, during which period he managed to attend Lincoln's inauguration. Briefly in charge of the Confederacy's lighthouse bureau, he was shortly assigned the task of fitting out a raiding cruiser at New Orleans. The 520 ton *C.S.S. Sumter*, was converted from merchant ship to sloop-of-war in about eight weeks, from 18 April 1861 to mid-June.

After playing cat-and-mouse with Federal blockaders for several weeks, Semmes was able to slip out of the Mississippi on 30 June and begin a rather successful career as a commerce raider. Over the next six months, *Sumter* took 18 prizes, several times eluded Union pursuers, and began the near-total disruption of American flag shipping which the war was to cause. Finally, in January of 1862, Semmes put in at Gibraltar hoping to effect some repairs to *Sumter's* increasingly failing engines. Unable to secure assistance—U.S.-British relations were just then in delicate balance—and unable to sortie because three Federal warships (one of them the *U.S.S. Kearsarge*) soon showed up on the horizon, Semmes paid off his crew, sold the ship to a British firm, and made his way overland to England.

In England, a new ship was procured for Semmes, *C.S.S. Alabama.* He took command of the vessel in the Azores in August of 1862, rapidly converted her into a commerce raider, and set out on a devastating career. In the next two years Semmes would take or destroy 69 vessels, including a Union blockader, setting a record for a raiding cruiser never since

equalled. Semmes' activities led to the mass abandonment of the American flag by hundreds of merchant vessels. In June of 1864 he put in at Cherbourg, France, hoping to effect some major repairs. Finding the French government unwilling to cooperate, and with the Union sloop-of-war *Kearsarge* looming on the horizon, Semmes decided to fight it out and actually sent a formal challenge to *Kearsarge.* The two vessels dueled on 19 June, and *Alabama* was struck and sinking after about two hours. Semmes and many of his crew were rescued by a British yacht and landed in England.

Taking a blockade runner home, Semmes was given a hero's welcome, promoted rear admiral, and assigned to command the James River flotilla, a strong squadron which helped keep the Union fleet and army away from Richmond. By this time the war was virtually over. Semmes' sole important act as commander of the flotilla was to order its destruction upon the abandonment of Richmond and Petersburg by the Army of Northern Virginia in early April of 1865. Organizing his men into a naval brigade, Semmes was made an acting brigadier general in one of Jefferson Davis' last official acts. Eluding

immediate capture, Semmes and his men made their way south to join Joe Johnston's Army of Tennessee, with which they surrendered on 18 April.

Although paroled, in December of 1865 Semmes was arrested and charged with piracy, treason and a number of other crimes. After about three months, all charges were dropped. Semmes was briefly a college professor and newspaper editor before returning to Alabama to practice law and write *Memoirs of Service Afloat* and *The Cruise of the Alabama and Sumter*. His younger brother, Paul Jones Semmes (1815-1863), had a distinguished career with the Army of Northern Virginia, serving as colonel of the 2nd Georgia and later as a brigadier general until mortally wounded on the first day at Gettysburg.

On the deck of the Alabama.

Thomas J. Jackson

Among the most successful and the most daring of Civil War commanders, and certainly the most eccentric, the "Gallant Stonewall" (1824-1863) was born in poverty in what is now West Virginia. Raised by an uncle after his parents died, Jackson received a haphazard education, but nevertheless managed to secure an appointment to West Point, where his academic standing increased each year so that it was said of him "if the course had been a year longer he would have come out first."

Graduating in 1846, he served in John B. Magruder's battery during the Mexican War, winning two brevets. After garrison duty in New York and Florida, Jackson resigned in 1851 to become professor of artillery and natural philosophy—physics—at the Virginia Military Institute. In 1859 he commanded a company of cadets at the hanging of John Brown.

On the outbreak of the Civil War, Jackson was promoted colonel in the militia. Soon after appointed a colonel and then

The first Confederate warship to show the flag in a European port was the lightly armed sidewheeler *C.S.S. Nashville*, which landed at Southampton on 21 November 1861.

Ebenezer W. Peirce, a brigadier general of New York militia, was so remorseful about bungling the "battle" of Big Bethel, Virginia, on 10 June 1861, that he shortly afterwards resigned his militia commission and reenlisted as a private, in which capacity he served until discharged three years later.

Thomas J. Jackson, a profoundly religious man, is said to have once refused to use a particular batch of gunpowder because it had been procured on the Sabbath.

Whilst riding in the Shenandoah Valley one day in December of 1861 Thomas "Stonewall" Jackson espied a persimmon tree ladened with fruit, whereupon he halted his staff, climbed up into the branches and ate his fill.

It is said that after a particularly wearing march shortly before the First Battle of Bull Run his men were so exhausted that Thomas J. Jackson posted only one sentry for his brigade, the "Gallant Jackson" himself.

The Civil War was rough on the streets of New York: Gustavus W. Smith and Mansfield Lovell, respectively, the Street Commissioner and the Deputy Street Commissioner, both resigned their posts to take up appointments as major generals in the Confederate Army.

TOP:

The gallant Stonewall Thomas J. Jackson.

BOTTOM:

The 27th New York engaged in the first great battle of the war, First Bull Run.

a brigadier general in the Confederate Army, his first war service was as commander of the brigade which occupied Harper's Ferry. Jackson led his brigade with great distinction at Bull Run on 21 July 1861, earning for it—and himself—the cognomen "Stonewall." Promoted major general early that Autumn, Jackson was shortly sent back to the Shenandoah Valley. Although he was involved in a number of minor operations through the winter, there was nothing, not even his performance at Bull Run, to suggest that he was anything but a rather pedestrian commander. Nothing, that is, until the spring, when he undertook what would become one of the most spectacular campaigns in American history, the Valley Campaign.

Essentially a strategic diversion, Jackson's objectives in the Shenandoah Valley in the spring of 1862 were threefold: to prevent the Union from gaining control of the vital agricultural resources of the fertile Valley, to tie-down Federal forces which might otherwise be committed against Richmond and to act as a reserve for the outnumbered Army of Northern Virginia. All this Jackson achieved with remarkable skill, though himself greatly outnumbered, so that by June, he had neutralized some 50,000 Union troops while bringing nearly 20,000 men to reinforce the Army of Northern Virginia in time for the Seven Days. While his performance during the opening engagements of the Seven Days left something to be desired, Jackson steadily improved as his relationship with Gen. Robert E. Lee grew closer.

After an initially poor start at Cedar Mountain, during the opening phases of the Second Bull Run Campaign, Jackson became Lee's most effective corps commander, entrusted with the most daring missions, culminating in his spectacular envelopment of John Pope's *Army of Virginia* at Second Bull Run and timely arrival at Antietam, which probably saved the Army of Northern Virginia from destruction. Promoted lieutenant general the following October, Jackson led his II Corps at Fredericksburg and Chancellorsville, where he executed the spectacularly successful flank march which resulted in the collapse of Union Maj. Gen. Joseph Hooker's offensive. On the evening of 2 May 1863 Jackson was wounded by some of his own men as he was making a reconnaissance with his staff. Despite the amputation of his left arm, he died on 10 May.

Stonewall Jackson was a remarkable tactician, fearless of vision, bold in execution, daring in the attack and stubborn in the defense. A man of numerous idiosyncrasies—one is almost tempted to suggest that he was not quite sane—he had few, if any, equals as a soldier. A big man, about six feet tall and 175 pounds, Jackson had blue eyes and a brown beard. Extraordinarily religious, Jackson was a devout Presbyterian and did not

smoke, drink, nor gamble, ate sparingly and lived simply. His death was a devastating blow to the Confederacy, Lee himself observing "I have lost my right arm."

George B. McClellan

A native of Philadelphia, George Brinton McClellan (1826-1885) was a child prodigy, who attended the University of Pennsylvania before entering West Point at the age of fifteen. Graduating second in the class of '46, he served as an engineer in Mexico, winning two brevets. Over the next decade he had a varied career, including three years as an instructor at West Point, exploration and survey work in the West and military observer in the Crimean War. As a result of his European tour, he designed the "McClellan saddle" a comfortable and serviceable if clumsy-looking affair which remains the army's official saddle. In 1857 he resigned to become chief engineer of the Illinois Central Railroad, one Abraham Lincoln being counted among the corporation's attorneys.

At the outbreak of the Civil War McClellan was serving as president of the Ohio and Mississippi Railroad. Commissioned a major general of Ohio troops within a fortnight of Sumter, McClellan was extremely active in preparing the state militia for war. On Winfield Scott's recommendation, Lincoln commissioned McClellan—whom he had, rather surprisingly, never met—a major general in the Regular Army on 14 May, making him the second ranking man in the army.

Given command of the upper Ohio Valley, McClellan worked energetically to hold Kentucky and western Virginia for the Union. Taking the field in the latter region, he was credited with securing what would become West Virginia for the Union as a result of the victories at Philippi (3 June 1861) and Rich Mountain (11 July). Though the actions were minor ones, the consequences were considerable and McClellan, who had not actually been present at either fight, rapidly became a major war hero, due partially to the fact that touting his success helped offset the unfortunate experience at Bull Run.

In consequence, McClellan was shortly brought to Washington and given charge of what would become the *Army of the Potomac*. Energetic as ever, he proved a capable organizer and drillmaster, turning a mass of demoralized, ill-trained volunteers into a finely-tuned fighting machine. However, soon after taking command, a certain weakness of character began to manifest itself in a variety of forms. Whatever else his talents, McClellan was also egoistical, argumentative and secretive and had a contempt for the civil authority. Disputes with General-in-Chief Scott—who had gotten him his command to begin with—led to the latter's resignation in November. Despite the fact that he had serious misgivings about McClellan, Lincoln gave him Scott's post. Although Lincoln pressed for a winter campaign, he deferred to McClellan's military opinion: not yet

The sword which the secessionist ladies of Little Rock, Arkansas, awarded Capt. James Totten in February of 1861 for his decision not to defend the U.S. arsenal there when seized by the state, proved immensely useful over the next four years as he rose to become a Union brevet brigadier general.

One of the most tragic figures of the Civil War, George Brinton McClellan. Though a skillful organizer and administrator, McClellan lacked the iron resolve needed to win battles. (Courtesy West Point Museum Collections, United States Military Academy, West Point, New York)

having learned that they were disposable, the president was at this point still in awe of generals.

McClellan devised a brilliant plan of operations for the spring of 1862, one perfectly suited to the strategic situation which confronted him through the winter: with the main Confederate force encamped at Manassas, not 40 miles from Washington, he proposed to make use of Federal sea power to interpose his army between Richmond and Confederate Gen. Joseph E. Johnston's Army of Northern Virginia. But by the time he was ready to move the situation had changed: Johnston had pulled back to a more centrally located position. Despite this reverse—a reverse which McClellan considered a victory secured by "pure military skill"—the "Little Napoleon"

79

FAR RIGHT:

Gen. George B. McClellan is halted by an alert sentry while making his rounds.

RIGHT:

George Brinton McClellan, the "Young Napoleon," at the apex of his career.

Gen. McClellan receives a grand reception at Frederick, Maryland during his attempt to thwart Lee's 1862 Maryland Campaign.

Temporarily on the shelf after the Peninsula, McClellan was recalled to command after the disasters of the Second Bull Run Campaign. Once again demonstrating his abilities, he rapidly restored the morale of the *Army of the Potomac* and at Antietam inflicted a reverse on the Army of Northern Virginia, while letting slip the opportunity to deliver a smashing defeat. McClellan had become increasingly associated with the anti-Lincoln, anti-war elements in the North and there was even some suspicion of disloyalty: certainly McClellan did nothing to discourage anti-democratic and subversive talk among his subordinates. In any case, Lincoln decided to relieve him. On 7 November 1862, McClellan was replaced by Maj. Gen. Ambrose Burnside and told to "await further orders." These never came.

McClellan became politically active, maneuvering to return to command—and indeed he was a better officer than either of his next two successors—and in 1864 he received the Democratic nomination for president. Although verbally committed to the successful prosecution of the war, he was widely regarded as a "peace at any price" candidate and went down to crushing defeat.

McClellan's abilities as a soldier were distinctly mixed. A superb organizer and trainer of men, he was a brilliant commander on paper, but lacked the flexibility, imagination and will to gain smashing victories in the field.

pressed on with his plans. The result was the Peninsular Campaign. Despite the fact that the Confederates were strategically in a much better position to respond to McClellan's movement than at the time the operation was planned, the Peninsular Campaign might well have succeeded, save for McClellan himself.

For all his brilliance and energy and popularity with the troops, McClellan proved less than spectacular on the battlefield. He was too cautious, lacked the ability to grasp the "big picture," proved unable to adequately control his subordinates and took counsel of his fears. And, although he secured several significant victories, he lacked the nerve of a Lee or the killer instincts of a Jackson, and was beaten back from literally the gates of Richmond: the campaign ended in an ignominious retreat. The *Army of the Potomac* would not again get so close to the Confederate capital for two years.

Irvin McDowell

Born in Ohio, Irvin McDowell (1818-1885) was educated in France before attending West Point, from which he graduated in 1838. After a short tour of duty on the frontier, he returned to the Academy as an instructor from 1841 through 1845. As an aide-de-camp to Maj. Gen. J.E. Wool in Mexico he served with some distinction, winning a brevet. After another short tour of duty on the frontier, McDowell was assigned to the office of the Adjutant General and spent many years at head-quarters in Washington.

On the outbreak of the Civil War McDowell was jumped from major to brigadier general for no apparent reason other than that he was well-known to Lt. Gen. Winfield Scott and Secretary of the Treasury Salmon P. Chase. Worse yet, al-though he had never commanded so much as a company, McDowell was assigned to lead the army concentrating about Washington in the spring of 1861. Although his plan for what would become the Bull Run Campaign was sound, it expected too much from the green troops who would have to execute it. Only the fact that the Confederate forces opposing his advance were equally green prevented Bull Run from turning into a decisive disaster.

After Bull Run, McDowell was given a division in the newly formed *Army of the Potomac*. Early in 1862 he was made a major general and given command of *I Corps*, over the objec-tions of the army commander, Maj. Gen. George B. McClellan. McDowell's command went through several name changes, emerging as *III Corps* of John Pope's *Army of Virginia*, which saw service in the Second Bull Run Campaign, during which McDowell clearly did not perform well. Relieved, he demand-ed, and received, a court of inquiry. Although the court found him not culpable of misconduct, he never afterwards com-manded troops in the field. For the balance of the war McDowell served in various administrative capacities.

Continuing in the service after the war, he was promoted major general in the Regular Army in 1872 and retired a decade later to become Parks Commissioner of San Francisco.

McDowell, a big, powerful looking man with a friendly manner, was a perfect example of the kind of officer who rises to high command in peace time. An excellent administrator and able planner, he was a poor commander, and very unlucky.

The senior Jewish officer in the Civil War was Commodore Uriah P. Levy (1792-1862), the owner of Jefferson's Monti-cello—which the Confederacy confiscat-ed as "enemy property"—who retired in 1861, after 49 years of acrimonious—he survived numerous duels, six courts mar-tial and two cashierings—but generally distinguished service in the navy.

For several weeks early in the war Mrs. Robert E. Lee continued to live at Ar-lington, the family home, despite the fact that Union Maj. Gen. Irvin McDowell had made it his headquarters.

Told by William Tecumseh Sherman that he had only requested a colonelcy upon rejoining the army, Irvin McDowell ex-pressed surprise, saying, "What? You should have asked for a brigadier gener-al's rank. You're just as fit for it as I am," to which Sherman replied, "I know it."

Probably the unluckiest general of the war, Irvin McDowell. McDowell (center) was credited for the disaster of First Bull Run and was regarded as partially respon-sible for the loss at Second Bull Run.

Benjamin F. Butler

One of the most prominent and under-rated "political" generals of the war, Benjamin Franklin Butler (1818-1893) was born in New Hampshire, but spent most of his life in Massachusetts. After college he taught in Lowell until admitted to the bar in 1840. The genial, diminutive, stocky Butler rapidly built a successful criminal practice in Lowell and Boston. Entering politics as a Democrat in 1853, he served in both houses of the state legislature. In 1860 he was a delegate to the disastrous Democratic National Convention in Charleston, during which, believing that only a moderate candidate could save the Union, he supported the nomination of Jefferson Davis through 57 consecutive votes. He subsequently took part in the rump convention at Baltimore which nominated the more extreme John C. Breckinridge.

Despite this highly conservative record, Butler proved a staunch Unionist upon the fall the Fort Sumter. A brigadier general of Massachusetts militia, his first war service was early and important. Accompanying the *8th Massachusetts* en route to Washington, he arrived in Philadelphia on the afternoon of 19 April to learn that secessionists in Baltimore had attacked the *6th Massachusetts* earlier that same day. The next morning, as the *7th New York* arrived, he learned that secessionists had burned several railroad bridges, thus isolating Washington from the North. Showing great presence of mind, he took off by steamer for Annapolis, arriving on the 21st, and sent both regiments on to Washington on the 24th, thus reopening communications with the capital. Little more than three weeks later Butler occupied restless Baltimore in a swiftly executed operation on 13 May, thereby insuring rail communications with the North. For his efforts he was named a major general of volunteers, the first such created in the war and was soon transferred to command Fortress Monroe, a Federal toehold on Virginia's Chesapeake shore.

Butler's tenure at Fortress Monroe was acrimonious. Although he was largely responsible for the Union reverse at Big Bethel (10 June 1861), he gained a considerable measure of fame when, unwilling to return fugitive slaves to their so-called masters, he declared them "contraband-of-war," thus bringing the ire of the slaveholding class down upon himself. Lincoln shortly afterwards gave him command of the expedition which seized Hatteras Inlet, an operation which was efficiently executed by the Navy on 27-29 August. Butler received a great deal of credit for the success of the expedition and was authorized to return to Massachusetts and recruit more troops for further coastal ventures. In the spring of 1862 Butler was given a command in the Gulf, with orders to occupy New Orleans.

The occupation of New Orleans was a simple affair, the city having surrendered to David Glasgow Farragut's squadron on 25 April. Butler's troops moved in on 1 May, and he rapidly established a firm grip on the strongly secessionist city. Already a target of Southern wrath, his actions brought still more opprobrium upon his name. William Mumford, a citizen who had defaced the first American flag raised over the city upon its fall, was hanged. Discovering that the Dutch consul had colluded to conceal funds earmarked for the purchase of arms in Europe, he confiscated the entire sum, about $800,000. He hit his stride when he ordered that any female resident of New Orleans who by word or deed showed disrespect to the Union uniform be "treated as a woman of the town plying her avocation," an order which was condemned in newspapers, from pulpits and in legislative houses throughout the English speaking world, and caused Jefferson Davis to order that Butler be instantly executed should he be captured.

Strongly backed from Washington, Butler remained in power, raising some of the first black regiments to muster into Union service, thereby attracting still more Southern vituperation. He was called "Beast Butler" and "Spoons Butler," allegedly for stealing said items from fashionable New Orleans homes: though he did turn a dishonest nickel or two, it was through speculation in cotton, a business in which those who lampooned him took a large part, rather than from loot. Crude tales of his vices, his greed, and his stupidity were widely circulated, many of which he appears to have enjoyed. Despite his reputation, Butler worked tirelessly to care for the hordes of fugitive slaves and impoverished whites who crowded the city, and was solicitous of the welfare of the seriously ill wife of Confederate Gen. Pierre G.T. Beauregard. Not until December of 1862 was Butler relieved.

Fort Monroe.

Held on the shelf for a time, in late 1863 he was returned to Fortress Monroe to command the *Army of the James*. Butler was given a crucial role in Grant's Overland Campaign in 1864: while Grant and the *Army of the Potomac* held Lee's attention north of Richmond, Butler was to advance up the James River, seizing Petersburg, and threatening the Confederate capital from the southeast. It was an undertaking far beyond Butler's capabilities. In the brief Drewry's Bluff Campaign (4-16 May 1864), he bungled a chance to deliver a devastating blow to the Confederacy, and allowed Gen. Pierre G.T. Beauregard's outnumbered forces to bottle up his army at Bermuda Hundred.

His political influence being great, Butler was not relieved, but merely temporarily transferred to other duty. His skill as a "city tamer" being unquestioned, he was detached to New York shortly before the election of 1864 to be on hand should there be a repetition of the rioting which had prostrated the city in the summer of '63. New York remaining calm, Butler was next sent on an expedition to close the port of Wilimington, an endeavor which failed. Though the failure was not entirely Butler's fault—the Navy's David Dixon Porter must share a good deal of the blame—he was relieved at the end of 1864 and told to await orders. Those orders never came.

After the war Butler had an enormously successful career in politics. Elected to the House as a Republican in 1866, he was one of the most enthusiastic supporters of the impeachment of Andrew Johnson. Regularly reelected, he remained in the House until 1875, was reelected in 1877, and in 1879 returned as a Greenbacker. In 1883 he was elected—after trying since 1871—governor of Massachusetts, and in the following year made a bid for the Presidency as a Greenback. From 1884 until his death he lived an uncharacteristically quiet life.

Slaves constituted 25 percent or more of the population of each of the states which seceded from the Union.

Late in 1861 the Hungarian General George Klapka—a very fine commander—offered his services to the Union, expressing a willingness to accept the post of general-in-chief in return for a cash advance of $100,000 plus an annual salary of $25,000, though stipulating that he would serve as chief-of-the-general staff until he learned English.

The attack in Baltimore by a secessionist mob on the men of the *6th Massachusetts* on 19 April 1861 occurred on the 86th anniversary of the day that Bay Staters' grandfathers fired "The Shot Heard 'Round the World."

When Hetty Cary—one of a trio of cousins who were the "prettiest women in Virginia" and outstanding lights of Richmond social life during the war—waved a Confederate flag from her Baltimore window as a Federal regiment marched by, the colonel declined to arrest her because "She is beautiful enough to do as she damned pleases."

LEFT:
In one of the first armed clashes of the Civil War civilians were the casualties. During a riot against Federal troops passing through the city, the 6th Massachusetts opened fire on the violent crowd killing twelve.

Samuel Cooper, the senior general in the Confederate Army, was born in Dutchess Country, New York.

When the Rev. William N. Pendleton (West Point, '30), who eventually became a brigadier general in the Confederate Army, took command of a battery in 1861 he promptly named the guns "Matthew," "Mark," "Luke" and "John."

Butler was unquestionably an incompetent commander. But he was by no means an incapable soldier. He was a fairly good administrator and a firm military governor. In addition, he was far more willing to see value in innovative ideas than were most of the other generals in the war: an early and ardent supporter of the use of black troops, he was also an enthusiast for ballooning and the Gatling gun. Though vilified as an unsuccessful political general, his services to the nation were enormous and precisely political.

Joseph E. Johnston

A native of Virginia, Joseph Eggleston Johnston (1807-1891) graduated from West Point in 1829. He had a busy career in the Old Army, seeing service in the Black Hawk War, the Second Seminole War and on the frontier and then spent 1837-1838 a civil engineer in Florida. Returning to the service, he compiled an impressive record in the Mexican War (five wounds and three brevets), culminating in command of the storming party at Chapultepec Castle. Thereafter he served in the Topographical Engineers, commanded the *1st* (now *4th*) *Cavalry* on the frontier and in Kansas, served as a staff officer during the Utah Expedition and on the eve of the Civil War was an acting brigadier general and Quartermaster General of the Army.

Johnston resigned on 22 April 1861 and entered the service of Virginia as a brigadier general. On 14 May he was named major general in the Confederate Regular Army and assigned to command at Harpers Ferry, where one of his subordinates was Thomas J. Jackson. Shortly appointed a full general, he was placed in command of all Confederate forces in Northern Virginia, but during the Bull Run Campaign permitted Pierre G.T. Beauregard to direct the battle. Meanwhile, Johnston commenced a lengthy bureaucratic squabble with Jefferson Davis and the War Department as to his proper status—in the Old Army he had been senior to the three generals who were now senior to him—a matter which polluted his relations with the president ever afterwards.

Johnston created the Army of Northern Virginia through the autumn and winter of 1861-1862 and led it during the opening phases of the Peninsular Campaign. Severely wounded at Seven Pines, Robert E. Lee replaced him on 1 June 1862. Johnston did not return to active duty for some time thereafter, partially because there as no suitable command for him. Finally, in November, he was placed in overall command of the Department of the West, supervising—but not really permitted to command—the operations of Braxton Bragg in Tennessee and John C. Pemberton in Mississippi. Meanwhile, his feud with

Jefferson Davis resumed, since the latter flatly refused to approve Johnston's proposals for a concentration of Confederate efforts in his theater. As a result, save for Chickamauga, 1863 was essentially a series of devastating reverses for Confederate arms in the heartland: Stones River, Vicksburg, Chattanooga. On 27 December 1863 Johnston was give direct command of the Army of Tennessee.

FAR RIGHT BOTTOM:
The Federal line of battle cracking under the pressure during the Battle of First Manassas.

FAR RIGHT TOP:
Panic stricken soldiers and civilians flee during the disastrous rout of First Manassas.

Joseph Johnston (left) and Robert E. Lee (right). Johnston's exemplary service to the Confederacy included the defense of Richmond in 1862 and Atlanta in 1864. After the war, he maintained a strong friendship with his former adversary, William T. Sherman.

The following year, Johnston led his army with skill, courage and verve in the Atlanta Campaign, managing to slow the greatly superior Union forces of William T. Sherman to a virtual crawl by skilled maneuver, surprise attacks and well-timed retreats. As a result, between 1 May and 17 July, Sherman was able to advance little more than a mile a day, against a foe whom he outnumbered by nearly two-to-one. Such skill was not, however, appreciated in Richmond: Jefferson Davis wanted someone who could fight hammer-blow battles, and so Johnston was replaced by John B. Hood on 17 July. Hood did fight, and Atlanta fell within six weeks, with enormous losses to the defenders.

Because of his feud with Davis, Johnston remained inactive for more than six months, until, in late February of 1865 newly appointed General-in-Chief Robert E. Lee restored him to command of the Army of Tennessee. Johnston led the remnants of this once mighty force with some skill in the hopeless Carolina Campaign. Shortly after receiving news of Appomattox, he concluded an armistice with Sherman on 18 April 1865.

After the war Johnston prospered in the insurance business, served in Congress, wrote and became excellent friends with his erstwhile foemen Sherman and Grant. A small, tough man, Johnston was an outstanding soldier, a master of the strategic defensive, who's abilities did much to sustain the Confederacy, though he was ill-rewarded for his efforts.

War and Society

Army Officer Loyalties in 1861

When, at a meeting in mid-August of 1861, Lincoln heard William T. Sherman state that he had a strong desire to serve in a subordinate capacity, the president expressed immediate agreement with the request, noting that "My chief trouble is to find places for the many generals who want to be at the head of affairs, to command armies, and so forth."

The only Regular Army officer born in the Deep South to remain loyal to his oath was Capt. Benjamin Franklin Davis, a Mississippian, who went on to command the *1st California Cavalry* and later the *8th New York Cavalry* with considerable ability until killed in action at Brandy Station on 9 June 1863.

On the eve of the war the United States Navy had 1,457 officers, warrant officers and midshipmen on duty, of whom 259 line officers and 73 other officers resigned, for a total of 332, or 22.7 percent of the naval officer corps. The Marine Corps, which had 63 officers, lost 22 (34.9 percent) to the Confederacy, one of whom became a general. Of some 200 officers in the Revenue Marine—the precursor of the Coast Guard—and the Coast Survey, about 60 (30.0 percent) resigned, several of whom turned their ships over to the Confederacy, an act which no resigning naval officer emulated. Thus, of about 1,720 officers in the seagoing services, about 404 (23.4 percent) resigned, a figure statistically significantly lower than that for army officers. Unfortunately it is not possible to analyze the regional origins of these officers.

Fed up with the dangers and privations of war, a Confederate deserts his ranks to flee towards Union lines.

The United States Army had 1,080 officers on active duty at the onset of the "Secession Winter." Over the months which followed hundreds of officers left the army. What follows is a series of tables which summarize the professional and regional origins of the officers and look at their loyalties in the crisis of 1860-1861.

It should be noted that in these tables percentage figures given in square brackets refer to the figure appearing in the left hand column. Parenthesized percentages on the "Total" line refer to the "Base" line entry immediately above, while those on subsequent lines refer to the "Total" line entry in the same column.

Origins of the Officers on Duty

	All	West Point	Civil Life
Base/Total	1080 [100.0%]	821 [76.0%]	259 [24.0%]
Of these:			
Northerners	620 (62.0%)	491 (59.8%)	129 (49.8%)
Southerners	460 (38.0%)	330 (40.2%)	130 (50.2%)

On this table, of course, the "Base" and the "Total" are the same, since it is examining the entire officer corps: including slaves, the South had about 35 percent of the population. Note that while Southerners were slightly over-represented in the officer corps, the disproportion was not great. It is, however, interesting to note that Southerners were more likely to have been commissioned from civil life than were Northerners: the ratio of officers commissioned from West Point to those appointed directly from civil life is 3.8:1 for Northerners but only 2.5:1 for Southerners.

Officers Separating from the Army

	All	West Point	Civil
Base	1080 [100.0%]	821 [76.0%]	259 [24.0%]
Total Separating	313 (29.0%)	184 (22.4%)	129 (28.6%)
Of these:			
Northerners	16 (5.1%)	16 (8.7%)	
Southerners	297 (94.9%)	168 (91.3%)	129 (100.0%)

Officers Remaining in the Army

	All	West Point	Civil
Base	1080 [100.0%]	821 [76.0%]	259 [24.0%]
Total Remaining	767 (71.0%)	637 (77.6%)	130 (50.2%)
Of these:			
Northerners	604 (78.7%)	475 (74.6%)	129 (99.2%)
Southerners	163 (21.3%)	162 (25.4%)	1 (0.8%)

Officers of Northern Origins

	All	West Point	Civil
Base	620 [100.0%]	491 [79.2%]	129 [20.8%]
Loyal	604 (97.4%)	475 (96.7%)	129 (100.0%)
Disloyal	16 (2.6%)	16 (3.3%)	

Officers of Southern Origins

	All	West Point	Civil
Base	460 [100.0%]	330 [71.7%]	130 [28.3%]
Loyal	163 (35.4%)	162 (49.1%)	1 (0.8%)
Disloyal	297 (64.6%)	168 (50.9%)	129 (99.2%)

It should be noted that although 313 officers left the army or were expelled as a result of secession, not all of them joined the Confederacy. About 1 percent of the men separated from the service retired to civilian life, being unwilling to either fight for or against the "Old Flag." The Northern men who chose to "go South" were all West Point graduates who had married Southern women. The Southern men who remained loyal were, with one exception, all West Pointers as well, though their marital status is less clear. The only officer of Southern origins commissioned from civil life who did not betray his oath to "support and defend the Constitution of the United States" was Winfield Scott, the general-in-chief and most distinguished American soldier since Washington.

Camp of Confederate marines guarding the approach to Richmond at Drury's Bluff on the James River.

The New York Zouaves parade through New York City on their way to the war. The scene took place when the glorious illusions of combat had not yet been dispelled.

On the eve of the Civil War there were approximately 15,000 enlisted men in the army, 7,600 in the navy plus 1,000 in the Marine Corps, and perhaps 1,200 more in the Revenue Marine and Coast Survey. While the regional origins of these men cannot be determined, it is reasonable to assume that a significant proportion of them were from the South. Nevertheless, very few enlisted men deserted to the Confederacy. Only 26 army enlisted men are known to have gone South, in contrast to the 313 officers. Indeed, at the start of the war there were reportedly a number of army posts which were devoid of officers due to resignations, which nevertheless continued to function under the command of senior non-commissioned officers, the enlisted personnel behaving with greater regard for their oaths than did the officers and gentlemen.

What's in a Name?

As the *3rd Maine* was preparing to depart for the war, the patriotic ladies of Augusta distributed over 50 bushels of doughnuts to their brave boys in blue, roughly 10,000 sinkers in all their infinite variety, including square, long, triangular and round ones, twisted, untwisted and double twisted ones, holed and unholed ones, light risen and hard kneaded ones, with numerous flavors, coatings and fillings.

RIGHT:
The 5th New York Zouaves.

Yankee gunners, working 10-pounders, harass enemy positions across the Potomac River with sporadic fire.

Many of the actions during the Civil War are known by two or even more names. It is not uncommon for a battle to bear both a Northern and a Southern name. The practice began early in the war, on 26 June 1861, with the little action known as Patterson Creek/Kelly's Island, in Virginia, and continued right to the end, in the engagement at Amelia Springs/Jettersville, Virginia, on 5 April 1865. This multiplicity of names persists, sometimes to the confusion of even the most serious student of the struggle.

Writing after the war, former Confederate Lt. Gen. Daniel H. Hill pointed out that the "Union" name for a battle was usually that of a local terrain feature, while the "Confederate" name was frequently that of a town, "In one section the naming had been after the handiwork of God, and in the other section it has been after the handiwork of man." He advanced an elegant explanation for this: Southern soldiers, being mostly from the country, were impressed by man-made features, while their Northern counterparts, being mostly from villages, towns and cities, were more impressed by natural features.

While Hill's observation is accurate enough, his explanation is faulty: most Union troops came from very small towns or rural areas. Moreover, for a number of battles it is the Southern name which refers to a geographic feature and the Northern one which refers to a place, as in the case of Olustee/Ocean Pond. And in any case, battles are not usually named by the common soldiers. For a better explanation one must look elsewhere.

In the Middle Ages the heralds of the opposing armies would meet after a battle to decide upon an appropriate name. In modern times the two sides rarely communicate and so

battles are named by generals, politicians, historians and common usage. There are sound reasons for differences in the naming of battles, not just during the Civil War, but during any war. Frequently, the name of a battle is drawn from that of the most prominent locale on the field or in the immediate vicinity behind friendly lines. It is thus perfectly possible for a different place or geographic feature to catch the fancy of one side and the other. As a result, at least 24 of the major actions of the war have two names, including some of the most famous, such as Shiloh/Pittsburg Landing and Antietam/Sharpsburg. Now this is relatively easy to understand. More difficult

by far, is the fact that at least a dozen important battles have three names, at least three have four name, four have five and one glories in seven: White Oak Swamp/Frazier's [or Frayser's] Farm/Glendale/Charles City Cross Roads/Nelson's Farm/Turkey Bend/New Market Cross Roads, fought on 30 June 1862.

Fortunately, time has eliminated most of these. They had their origins in the use of different names by officers making reports, by newspapermen filing dispatches and even by political leaders making public pronouncements.

The problem of names extends, of course, even to that of the struggle itself, for the name preferred in different parts of the country is still largely a matter of opinion. Although "Civil War" had some usage in the South in the early years of the conflict, no genuinely Southern name emerged until some years after Appomattox, when "The War between the States" gained favor. In the North "The War of the Rebellion" was fairly common at the time, and is, indeed, the official name by Congressional fiat, but it gradually gave way to "The Civil War". Other names for the conflict are numerous: one researcher enumerated 120 of them, and he clearly missed a few. Some of the more popular have been:

The War for Separation
The War of the Sections
The War for Constitutional Liberty
The Confederate War
Mr. Davis' War
Mr. Lincoln's War
The Southern Rebellion
The Great Rebellion

The War for Southern Rights
The War of Northern Aggression
The Reb Time
The Late Unpleasantness
The War for Abolition
The War for Southern Liberty
The Second American Revolution
The War of Yankee Arrogance
The War of Southern Arrogance
The War of the 1860s

None of these were quite satisfactory, and in common usage "The War between the States" and "The Civil War" have had no competitors for nearly a century now, despite the fact that they both refer to the same events, and that neither is particularly accurate. A civil war is, of course, a dispute over control of the state, which was not at all the issue, since—aside from some genuinely extreme fanatics—the South did not wish to take control of the United States but merely to secede from it. Similarly, "The War between the States", aside from being grammatically poor, makes equally little sense unless one subscribes to the Southern political view of the conflict. Superior names exist. "The War for Southern Independence" is certainly accurate and had some popularity in the South in the late nineteenth century, while "The War of the Slaveholders Rebellion" is also accurate and once found some favor in the North. However, neither of these are entirely satisfactory to all concerned. There is, of course, a perfectly accurate, and politically neutral name which has never found much favor, the "War of Secession."

To provide for the enormous number of troops in Washington in the early months of the war a huge bakery was installed under the west front terrace of the Capitol where 16,000 loaves of bread were baked each day in mid-1861.

During the first winter of the war, patriotic Quaker ladies in Pennsylvania attempted to do something for the boys in blue by providing some "non-lethal" supplies in the form of mittens, which, alas, were of only marginal use since the good ladies refrained from putting trigger fingers on them.

A guerrilla band is formed to fight irregular warfare not only against enemy armies, but civilians as well.

The Units

The Louisiana Tigers

RIGHT:

This black and white photo does not do justice to the brilliant crimson uniforms of these soldiers of the 55th New York. The outlandish Zouave costume was favored by soldiers in both Union and Confederate armies.

A South Carolinian serving in the ranks of McClellan's Zouaves.

The "Louisiana Tigers" or "Wheat's Tigers," one of the toughest combat forces of the Civil War, was formed from the "lowest scrapings of the Mississippi and New Orleans" by Chatham R. Wheat (1826-1862). Born in Virginia of an old Maryland family, "Rob" Wheat, son of an Episcopal minister, had an extraordinary career. Graduating from the University of Nashville in 1845, he was reading law in Memphis when the Mexican War broke out. Wheat promptly volunteered and served with some distinction, emerging as a captain. Back in civilian life, he opened a law practice in New Orleans, while dabbling in politics and serving in the state legislature. Growing bored, he threw it all up to become a soldier of fortune, serving in Cuba, Mexico, Nicaragua and Italy from 1850 to 1860.

Still abroad on the outbreak of the Civil War, he hurried home to lend a hand. Upon his return to New Orleans, Wheat began to raise an infantry battalion. Meanwhile, one Alex White was raising a company from among the sweepings of the local prisons, with which he was intimately familiar. White, who had managed to convince a wealthy citizen to foot the bill to equip his company as *zouaves*, offered his company for service with Wheat's battalion. Wheat happily incorporated White's "Tiger Zouaves" into his battalion, which was mustered into Confederate service as the 1st Louisiana Special Battalion, with Wheat as its major and White numbered among the captains.

The rowdy "Louisiana Tigers" were certainly a showy outfit, with baggy blue-and-white stripped trousers, red shirts, brown jackets and tasseled scarlet skullcaps, Bowie knives hanging from their belts as they trotted along in the peculiar quick-step gait popular among the French-inspired *zouave* regiments both North and South. Shortly after mustering into service the battalion went East to join the army just then concentrating in northern Virginia. When it left New Orleans, there were allegedly serving in its ranks three women, all alike uncharitably described as "women of no status," one ostensibly serving as a lieutenant and two as color bearers, carrying Louisiana's Pelican flag and the regimental banner, which ironically depicted a

lamb and the slogan "As Gentle As." The battalion arrived in Virginia without these "ladies" but in time for First Bull Run.

Assigned to Col. Nathan G. Evans' provisional command, the Tigers played a crucial role early in the battle by helping to hold the left of the Confederate line as it fell back on Henry House Hill under considerable pressure from stronger Federal forces, and later joined in the counterattack which threw the

Union troops back in disorder. This action gained them a reputation for considerable tenacity under fire, and unusual ferocity in the attack: they were alleged to have thrown down their muskets and charged the Yankees with their Bowie knives. Wheat himself was seriously wounded at Bull Run, a ball passing through both of his lungs. Informed that the wound was fatal, Wheat replied "I don't feel like dying yet" and proceeded to recover nicely.

In the reorganization of the Confederate forces in Virginia following the Bull Run Campaign, the Louisiana Tigers were brigaded with four other Louisiana outfits, the 6th, 7th, 8th and 9th Louisiana Volunteer Infantry Regiments, to form the Louisiana Brigade, under Brig. Gen. Richard Taylor, one of the Confederacy's finest combat leaders. This brigade was shortly incorporated in Maj. Gen. Richard S. Ewell's division which was sent to support Stonewall Jackson's operations in the Shenandoah Valley in early 1862. The Tigers took part in Jackson's series of victories at Front Royal, Winchester, Cross Keys and especially Port Republic (20 May-9 June 1862), where it spearheaded a desperate attack against the Union left.

After the briefest of rests, the Tigers were shortly transferred, along with the rest of Jackson's command, to support the Army of Northern Virginia against the *Army of the Potomac*, which was advancing up the Virginia Peninsula.

Hotly engaged at Gaines' Mill on 27 June, the Louisiana Tigers took heavy casualties, most notably Wheat himself, who was mortally wounded. With Wheat, whom they worshipped, gone the spirit went out of the Louisiana Tigers. Worse still, without Wheat to keep them in line, the troops lost all discipline. Although the battalion served to the end of the Peninsular Campaign, it performed its duties in a perfunctory fashion, desertions soared—even a major went over the hill—and the troops proved extremely unruly. In August the 1st Louisiana Special Battalion was broken up, its men being distributed among the four regiments of the Louisiana Brigade. But if the battalion died, its spirit did not. Wheat's veterans, who together proved such poor soldiers without him, separately imparted some of their style and dash to their new comrades, no poor soldiers to begin with. And the Louisiana Brigade shortly acquired the nickname "Louisiana Tigers."

The Confederacy's 1st Louisiana probably holds the record for the most cosmopolitan outfit in the war, with 37 different nationalities represented in its ranks, although several New York regiments probably came close to matching this record.

Although the *7th New York Militia* was one of the first Federal regiments to reach Washington, it suffered not a single battle death in its 150 days of service during three separate wartime enlistments. But of the 991 men on the rolls in April of 1861 fully 603 (60.9 percent) went on to become officers in other regiments, 58 dying in the service.

The Meagher Guards of Charleston, composed of Irish volunteers for the Confederacy, became the Emerald Light Infantry shortly after Sumter fell, when it was learned that Irish nationalist hero Thomas F. Meagher ["marr"], after whom the company was named, had raised a company for the Yankee *69th New York*.

Raw recruits serving in Union ranks as men answered Lincoln's call for volunteers.

The 39th New York

Four regiments raised in Philadelphia in the spring of 1861 were for a time known as the *1st, 2nd, 3rd* and *5th California*, since Sen. James A. McDougall of the "Golden State" helped foot the bill for their recruiting: later redesignated the *71st, 72nd, 69th*—an Irish outfit which wanted the same number as New York's famed Irish regiment—and *106th Pennsylvania*, the regiments went on to distinguish themselves as the *Philadelphia Brigade*, among other things holding The Angle at Gettysburg.

The *5th Pennsylvania Cavalry Regiment* appears to have the distinction of being the largest unit in the history of the United States Army to be composed primarily of Jewish personnel.

Many regiments, both North and South, may have had a more distinguished battlefield record than did the *39th New York*, but certainly few were more colorful. The regiment was raised by a remarkable military adventurer, Frederick D'Utassy. Born Frederick Stasser, possibly in Vienna, D'Utassy appeared in New York during the 1850s, claiming to have been a veteran of the Hungarian Revolution of 1848-1849. For a time he made his living as a language teacher, while involving himself in various emigre circles and the city's social whirl.

In May of 1861 D'Utassy raised a regiment of European exiles with himself as colonel and two of his brothers serving as company officers. The *Garibaldi Guard* was a polyglot outfit, incorporating such diverse volunteer units as the *Italian Legion*, the *Polish Legion*, the *Netherlands Legion*, the *Hungarian Regiment* and the *German 1st Foreign Riles*, the regiment is alleged to have included men of fifteen different nationalities. As organized, four companies, including one of Swiss volunteers, spoke German, three spoke Hungarian, one Italian and one French and one was half Spanish and half Portuguese. As a result, orders were regularly given in seven languages—English plus these six—though Spanish and Portuguese were usually omitted from recruiting posters.

The regimental uniform was loosely based on that of the famed Piedmontese *Bersaglieri*, being blue with red and gold trim, topped by a broad "Garibaldi" hat trimmed with green cock feathers, however for fatigue duties the men wore a loose red shirt with a broad belt similar to that popularized by Garibaldi and his famed "Red Shirts," and a few men wore the uniforms of their original ethnic volunteer outfits. Since it was composed of European personnel, the regiment had several *vivandieres*. As a result, the *39th New York* cut a brave figure on 4 June 1861, when it headed off to war, with the men lustily singing "Les Marseillaise" as they marched down Broadway behind an Italian flag which had flown from the battlements of Rome during Garibaldi's heroic defense of the city in 1849. It was a glorious beginning for what was perhaps the most romantic of the hundreds of regiments mustering North and South in 1861. But like most outfits which served in the war, although the *Garibaldi Guard* had a interesting record, it had but few moments of glory.

Accepted for state service on 27 May 1861, the regiment was mustered into Federal service at Washington on 6 June, to date from 28 May. At First Bull Run, the *39th New York* was part of Col. Louis Blenker's brigade in the reserve and performed well in helping to cover the retreat of the Union troops on that disastrous afternoon. In the reorganization of the

Members of the Garibaldi Guard *during a skirmish with Confederate troops during an engagement near the Potomac.*

Federal forces about Washington which resulted in the creation of the *Army of the Potomac*, the regiment was incorporated into by then Brig. Gen. Louis Blenker's division. Like the *39th New York*, this division was a polyglot outfit composed mostly of middle European volunteers.

In March of 1862, Blenker was ordered to take his division to the Shenandoah Valley. What resulted was one of the most mismanaged marches of the war, with the troops taking six weeks to make a movement of little more than 100 miles, amid considerable privation and contingent depredations on the part of the hungry troops. The division, and the *39th New York*, nevertheless reached the Valley in time to take part in the Union defeat at the hands of Stonewall Jackson, fighting at Cross Keys (8 June 1862).

When Blenker's division was shortly afterwards broken up, the regiment was transferred to the garrison at Harper's Ferry, where it passed the next few months. Meanwhile, the regiment began to lose some of its European character, the *bersaglieri* uniforms giving way to Uncle Sam's standard issue and the *vivandiere's* gradually losing their zest for military life. D'Utassy assumed command of a brigade comprising the *111th*, *115th* and *125th New York*, green outfits all, as well as the *39th*, which

passed temporarily to the command of Maj. Hugo Hilde-brandt. Unfortunately the garrison commander at Harper's Ferry, Colonel Dixon Miles, proved highly inept. Neglecting the most elementary precautions, he allowed himself to be encircled and invested there by Stonewall Jackson on 12 September 1862, in the opening stages of the Antietam Campaign. Although most of his subordinates—D'Utassy among them—were inclined to attempt an escape—and one regiment did elude the trap—Miles demurred and surrendered after a brief siege. The angry D'Utassy concealed the regimental colors in his personal baggage and ordered his men to smash their weapons before surrendering. The entire brigade was almost immediately paroled, being sent to Camp Douglas, Illinois and was shortly thereafter formally exchanged and sent to Washington, to form part of the garrison there. Although by the spring of 1863 the regiment had been but lightly engaged, in its two years of service it had lost heavily from disease and desertion.

In May of 1863 the regiment, which numbered little more than 300 men, was reorganized, forming four companies. Meanwhile D'Utassy was removed from command and eventually sent to Sing Sing Prison in New York, having been tried

In August of 1861 the *79th New York Highlanders* mutinied when the army decided to take away their kilts, but were quickly brought to their senses when higher authorities presented an irrefutable argument in the form of a Regular Army battery.

Grand parade of a volunteer regiment in the streets of Washington D.C.

When organized in October of 1861, the *6th Pennsylvania Cavalry* was equipped as lancers, toting 9-foot pig-stickers and pistols into action, rather than sabers and carbines: despite the near-total inutility of the regiment's armament, "Rush's Lancers" were not re-equipped as a proper cavalry regiment until June of 1863, possibly because they looked good on parade.

and convicted of a variety of charges, most notably of having been skimming a little off the top.

In late June of 1863 the *39th New York*, now under Col. Augustus Funk, an Old Army man, was incorporated, along with its brigade mates into *II Corps* of the *Army of the Potomac*, just in time for the Gettysburg Campaign. The *39th New York* was hotly engaged for all three days of Gettysburg, its greatest moment being on the evening of 2 July, when, in a furious charge, it drove the 21st Mississippi back from a captured battery, retaking all six pieces and capturing three Rebel flags: during the three days the regiment lost 35.3 percent of the 269 men it brought into action, 95 men being killed or wounded, including six field officers. After Gettysburg the regiment was gradually brought up to strength, an additional six companies being added over the next few months. As a result, when, in May of 1864 the regiment's enlistment expired, these six companies remained with the colors, absorbing those veterans of

'61 who wished to reenlist, and a seventh company was shortly added.

The *39th New York* served in *II Corps* from the Wilderness to the end of the war and was present at Appomattox. But by that time the regiment had lost its European character, the ranks being filled up with drafted men. Funk became a casualty in the Wilderness, and was temporarily replaced by Maj. Joseph Hyde, who was in turn replaced by Capt. David A. Allen, before the colonel returned to service. When mustered out in July of 1865 some 200 men were still with the colors. Of the 2,110 men who had passed through the ranks, 115 men had been killed in action, 163 had died of disease, and over 1,000 had been wounded, disabled by disease, or missing. Like most regiments whether Union or Confederate, the *Garibaldi Guard* rendered hard service, but garnered little fame. In the end Gettysburg was the *39th New York's* moment of glory.

Lee's cannoneers. The gunners of the Washington Artillery.

The Washington Artillery

The most famous artillery outfit of the war was undoubtedly the Confederacy's Washington Artillery of Louisiana. This distinguished organization was formed at New Orleans in 1838 as the "Native American Battery" and was comprised of the finest and richest young men of the Crescent City's Creole society. When the Mexican War came, the battery reorganized as infantry and served as *Company A* of Persifor Smith's *1st Louisiana Volunteers*. Returning in glory to its' native city, the company was reorganized in 1852 and renamed the "Washington Artillery."

On the outbreak of the war the battalion, probably one of the most skilled militia outfits in the country, acquired a good deal of equipment with the seizure of the Federal arsenal at Baton Rouge. Volunteering for service in the Confederate Army, the battalion mustered in on 26 May 1861. One company, the 5th, was detached from the battalion and sent to serve with the Army of Tennessee, but the other four went East together and joined the Army of Northern Virginia.

When it went to war, the Washington Artillery went in style. As was common in the early days of the war, a lot of unnecessary luxuries and personnel accompanied the battalion into the field. Its uniforms alone were estimated to have cost $20,000. The first commanding officer, Maj. James B. Walton—a wholesale grocer who helped found the outfit in 1838, went on to command the *1st Louisiana* in Mexico after Smith's promotion, and would later rise to Inspector General of Field Artillery in the Army of Northern Virginia—brought along his German-born major-domo, while the latter's wife accompanied the battalion as a *vivandiere*. M. Edouard, the chef of the famous Victor's of Carrollton, came along as well, to provide proper meals for the troops and brought along his pet fox. But if the men of the battalion liked luxury, they also knew how to fight.

The Washington Artillery compiled the most distinguished record an artillery outfit could possibly have in the war. The first four companies were engaged in every battle of the Army of Northern Virginia from First Bull Run—before there even was an Army of Northern Virginia—to Appomattox, and served with particular brilliance at Fredericksburg and at Chancellorsville: so heavily engaged was the battalion that at Gettysburg it could muster but eight guns for four batteries. The 5th Company was with the Army of Tennessee throughout the war, from Shiloh to the Carolinas. In addition, James Dearing, a West Point drop-out who joined the battalion as a lieutenant in 1861, rose to brigadier general by the war's end: one of only three Confederate gunners to become a general.

The Washington Artillery was as distinguished in camp as in the field. The battalion had one of most famous amateur theatrical troupes in the Confederate Army. It was noted for elaborate and professional productions, to the extent that for one performance while in camp near Fredericksburg in January of 1863 a special train was run up from Richmond so that various dignitaries from the capital could attend. Robert E. Lee himself once sent formal regrets at having to miss a performance.

At the end of the war the Washington Artillery was officially disbanded. However the veterans maintained an informal association with each other until, after a year or so, they were permitted to incorporate as "The Washington Artillery Veterans Charitable and Benevolent Association," a name which belied their true purpose, to keep alive resistance to Reconstruction. With this object in mind, the veterans held secret infantry drills and acquired arms. The veterans of the Washington Artillery—and not a few new recruits—took part in a number of the demonstrations and riots which attended the overthrow of carpetbagger government in Louisiana, once even appearing in the streets with two small brass cannon! With the end of Reconstruction in 1876 the veterans association was recognized as a unit of the state militia, later becoming part of the National Guard. As such, the Washington Artillery served in Cuba and in both world wars.

Soldiers of the Fifth Company of the Washington Artillery in their pristine uniforms before they endured a true taste of war.

Of 500 men raised in San Francisco who were enrolled as the *California Battalion* of the *2nd Massachusetts*, fully 10 percent eventually became officers.

A late night parade in honor of the commander of the Army of the Potomac, *George B. McClellan.*

The Ways of War

The Flags of the Confederacy

The events of the "Secession Winter" saw Old Glory replaced by the state flag in South Carolina, Georgia, Florida, Alabama, Mississippi, Louisiana and Texas. With the formation of the Confederacy at Montgomery, Alabama, in February of 1861, the question of a flag for the new nation was of pressing concern.

While there was some sentiment for the so-called "Bonnie Blue Flag," with it's one white star on a blue field, enthusiastic citizens from all over the South were not hesitant in submitting ideas. Most of the suggestions were essentially variants on "Old Glory," for there was much affection for the flag of Washington. Indeed, some Southern leaders, such as Jefferson

The Stars and Bars, the first Confederate flag adopted before the war broke out on 4 March 1861. (Courtesy Civil War Library and Museum)

FAR RIGHT TOP:
The banner adopted by the Confederacy in 1863. At times it could be taken for a flag of surrender. (Courtesy Civil War Library and Museum)

RIGHT:
Perhaps the most famous symbol of the Confederacy, the Confederate Battle Flag. (Courtesy Civil War Library and Museum)

FAR RIGHT BOTTOM:
Adopted almost belatedly on 8 March 1865 as defeat seemed inevitable, this flag was the last standard of the Confederacy. (Courtesy Civil War Library and Museum)

Davis, believed the Confederacy should co-opt the old flag entirely, to suggest that it, rather than Yankeedom, was the true heir to the Republic. One delegate to the Provisional Congress actually submitted a bill to insure that the new flag be "as similar as possible to the flag of the United States." These proposals, however, did not find favor among more ardent secessionists and slavocrats. Observing that the "Stars and Stripes" had inspired the flags of both Liberia and Hawaii, South Carolina's William P. Miles, chairman of the committee on heraldic devices, remarked that it would be improper to use "what had been pilfered and appropriated by a free negro community and a race of savages." Nevertheless, the influence of the old flag persisted in the design which the committee adopted on 4 March, even as Lincoln was preparing to take the oath of office in far-off Washington.

The new flag was to be a rectangle in the ratio of 1.5:1, with three stripes of red, white and red, and a blue canton on which were arranged a circle of seven white stars, one for each Confederate state at the time, the famed "Stars and Bars." A sample was hastily put together and was hoisted over the capitol at Montgomery that very afternoon by a granddaughter of John Tyler, the only ex-president living in the Confederacy. The new flag was soon seen everywhere in the South, and was often displayed by secessionists in the then still-loyal "Upper South" and Border States. However, when the new flag was used in battle its similarity to the old one caused problems, particularly at a distance. At First Bull Run—by which time the "Stars and Bars" had eleven stars—Confederate troops almost fired on Brig. Gen. Jubal Early's brigade as it marched up because they could not at first discern which flag it bore. As a result, when Brig. Gen. Pierre G. T. Beauregard approached Gen. Joseph E. Johnston and suggested that the Confederacy needed a battle flag as distinct from the "Stars and Stripes" as possible, the latter expressed enthusiastic agreement. With the help of some staff officers they soon came up with a unique design.

The proposed flag was square, having a blue field charged with a red St. Andrew's cross on which were placed the stars representing the states. After some quibbles about heraldic propriety the field was changed to red and the cross to blue. The enthusiastic generals submitted their design to the Congress. Since the Congress took no action on the matter, the generals then went to the War Department. The result was that on 1 October 1861 the new design was approved for military use. Thus was born the famed Confederate battle flag.

The first Confederate battle flags were made by the vivacious and beautiful Cary girls, the sisters Hetty and Jennie of Baltimore and their cousin Constance of Alexandria, Virginia. Alas for romance, the flags were not made from their dresses nor from their undergarments: as Constance later observed, they had no "apparel in the flamboyant colors of poppy red and vivid dark blue required," and, in fact, they had trouble securing materials of the proper colors, with the result that the red silk which she obtained for her flag was of such poor quality she had to use an interlining to provide proper stiffening. On 28 November the new flags were given to the three most prominent Confederate commanders at the time, Hetty's to Joseph E. Johnston, Jennie's to Pierre G.T. Beauregard and Constance's to Earl Van Dorn: when Van Dorn was murdered in mid-1863, his flag was returned to Constance, who, along with the other girls, had by then become prominent in the social life and war work in the Confederate capital. Use of the battle flag greatly reduced confusion on the battlefield.

Meanwhile, of course, the debate over the "Stars and Bars" continued. A Richmond newspaper effectively expressed the dissatisfaction when it observed " . . . we took, at rough calculation, our share of the stars and our fraction of the stripes, and put them together and called them the Confederate flag." Although the Confederate Congress had more pressing business, it was constantly bombarded with suggestions for a new flag to replace the "Stars and Bars." The proposed designs were numerous and varied. Many different symbols and color combinations were proposed, including snakes, horses and the sun. One suggestion anticipated Australia a bit by incorporating the Southern Cross, which was nowhere visible in the Confederacy. And one had a white field with a black bend, which its designer—ignorant of heraldry—claimed symbolized the eternal truth of the white race dominating the black. None of these received serious consideration.

On 1 May 1863 the Congress adopted a new design, a white flag of 2:1 dimensions with the battle flag in the canton. This new flag proved even less satisfactory than the old. Unless there was a stiff breeze, the new colors could not be distinguished from a flag of truce. Moreover, it was remarkably difficult to keep clean. So the Congress went back to work. Not until 8 March 1865—when the matter was rapidly becoming academic—was a new design approved, and this merely a stop-gap expedient which added a broad red panel at the fly and returned the dimensions to 1.5:5. In any case, the white flag was the last Confederate flag to be displayed in an official capacity, being worn by the cruiser *C.S.S. Shenandoah* at the time of her surrender to British authorities in November of 1865.

The Confederacy's search for a flag is a good example of failing to see what was right under one's nose. The obvious flag for the Confederacy was the battle flag, which like Britain's Union Flag, readily could have been adapted to a wide variety

At the outbreak of the Civil War Samuel F.B. Morse, artist and inventor of the "Morse Code", had something to say on the subject of flags. He suggested that "Old Glory" be divided in half diagonally, from the upper hoist to the lower fly, with the upper half to be used by the North and the lower by the South, each side replacing the missing portion with a white field, thus symbolizing the sundering of the old nation and expressing hope for its eventual reunification. This, and several other proposals to remove the "seceded" stars from the "Stars and Stripes," were all quashed by Lincoln, who pointed out that the states had never left the Union.

Rejecting Lincoln's first call for troops in April of 1861, Gov. Henry M. Rector of Arkansas said "The people of this Commonwealth are freemen, not slaves," and began to press for immediate secession, conveniently overlooking the fact that over 25 percent of the people of Arkansas were slaves.

Confederate Lt. James E. Hanger, who lost a leg as a result of wounds incurred at Philippi (3 June 1861), in what is now West Virginia, an action sometimes called the first battle of the war, devised for himself an artificial limb so superior to existing devices that he founded a firm for their manufacture which still exists.

According to Article 2, Paragraph 5, of the Confederate Army regulations, if two officers of the same rank had the same date of commission and no prior United States or Confederate military service, questions of seniority were to be decided by a lottery.

of uses. But if the Confederate Congress failed to act, history and the Southern people did, and the battle flag today symbolizes the Confederacy far more effectively then the three successive national flags which were adopted. While the national colors are largely forgotten, the battle flag is widely displayed throughout the South and at Ku Klux Klan rallies as well.

Service and Rank in the Civil War

One of the more confusing aspects of the Civil War is the matter of branches of service and rank. One can best understand this by looking at the Union forces. There were four different branches of the land forces and as a result it was possible for an officer to have several different ranks. A man might have one rank in the militia, another in the Regular Army, yet another in the volunteers, and possibly still another in the state troops.

The militia, of course, were the part-time forces which each state could muster from its own population. A rank in the

Federal cannoneers of the 1st New York Light Artillery.

militia did not necessarily have any value outside the borders of one's own state, though in emergencies the militia of one state was known to serve in another, such as when 13,000 New York militiamen went to help hold the line of the Susquehanna during the Gettysburg Campaign. At the height of the war there were some 200,000 active militiamen in the loyal states.

The Regular Army was the permanent land force maintained by the Federal government, a small band numbering little more than 16,000 at the start, and no more than about 50,000 during the war. Normally the regulars and the militia were responsible for the defense of the country. However, militia terms of service were rather short, and they served under state control. As a result, there was also the Volunteer Army.

The Volunteer Army was usually recruited by states, often drawing men from the militia, but served under Federal terms of enlistment. Some states over-filled their volunteer quotas and chose to retain the surplus troops at their own expense as permanent, standing force for territorial defense. These were the state troops, maintained by several states, the most notable of which were the famed *Pennsylvania Reserves*, thirteen regiments recruited and maintained at state expense which later passed into the Volunteer Army and proved to be among the best Union outfits: there were perhaps 50,000 troops maintained on active duty by various of the loyal states at the height of the war. Since militia and state regiments might sometimes volunteer for Federal service, some regiments had two designations, such as the *83rd New York Volunteers* which was also the *9th New York Militia*, or the *11th Pennsylvania Reserves*, which was also the *40th Pennsylvania Volunteers*.

The situation in the Confederate Army was simpler, but only marginally so. On paper there existed a Regular Army, authorized to recruit a number of infantry and cavalry regiments, none of which were ever completed. As a result, the Volunteer Army, known as the "Provisional Army," represented virtually the whole of the national forces, supplemented by the militia and the state troops of those states which maintained such, notably Georgia. There was another way in which the Confederate differed from the Union Army. After the fighting got serious all Confederate troops were in for the duration, a fact which many one-year volunteers resented when they found their enlistments extended in early '62. In the Union Army enlistment was in the form of a personal contract. As a result troops were enlisted for 30-days, 90-days, three months, 100-days, six months, nine months, one year, two years, or three years, a matter which greatly complicated operations: time-expired regiments sometimes marched off on the eve of battle.

In general, Civil War literature refers to regiments merely by number and state, so it is sometimes difficult to tell what type of outfit is meant, though on both sides most of the fighting was done by volunteer regiments. This plethora of branches of the service complicated the rank structure. Under prevailing terms of service, a man might be a lieutenant in his state militia, serving as a major in a volunteer regiment. Or he might be a captain in the Regular Army serving as a brigadier general of volunteers, or a Regular Army captain, a major of volunteers, and a colonel in the state troops. Only one's Regular Army rank counted towards permanent time-in-grade for purposes of post-war retention and promotion in the regulars. As if this were not confusing enough, there was also *brevet* rank.

A brevet was an honorary promotion, awarded for distinguished service. Thus, a major of volunteers might also have a brevet as a colonel of volunteers. Brevet rank conferred some prestige on an officer and did make him technically senior to another officer of equal rank under certain circumstances, such as when serving on courts martial or when in detachments composed of elements of several arms, but brought few other benefits. One could hold several brevets, for example in both the volunteers and the regulars. The Union awarded brevets with a lavish hand, including 1,700 brevet generalships, a matter which did much to discredit the practice, which gradually passed into disuse. In any case, as a result of the complicated inter-relationships of rank and service, it was at least theoretically possible for a Union officer to have eight ranks, one substantive rank and one brevet in each branch of the service—the militia, the regulars, the volunteers and the state troops—though this does not actually ever seem to have occurred.

The rank situation in the Confederacy was somewhat simpler. Save for a list of mostly senior officers, there was very little in the way of a Regular Army. An officer might be, as in Union service, a captain in the Regular Army and a colonel in the Provisional Army but the former rank was of no consequence. Moreover, the Confederacy was far more generous with rank than the Union, giving out the real thing rather than brevets to deserving officers. It was a better reward for excellent service and given the precipitous decline in the value of Confederate currency, didn't cost much.

The experience of the Civil War caused the practice of awarding brevets to be discredited. As time went on fewer and fewer were awarded, the last being during World War I, when Maj. Gen. Trasker Bliss was made a brevet general so he could hob-knob on a fairly equal footing with the marshals of the Allied Supreme War Council. But the duality of ranks between the wartime and peacetime army continued right down into World War II: at the time that Dwight D. Eisenhower was wearing four stars as commander of the largest army in the history of the Republic, his Regular Army rank was colonel.

The first naval officer to be killed in action was Cdr. James H. Ward, U.S.N., who died on 27 June 1861, whilst leading an effort to dislodge some Confederate batteries covering the lower Potomac from Mathias Point, Virginia.

The first Regular Army officer to die in the war was Lt. J. T. Greble of the *2nd Artillery*, who fell by his guns at Big Bethel on 10 June 1861, which was also the occasion of the first non-fatal wound to be received by a Regular Army officer, Capt. Judson Kilpatrick of the *5th New York*, who later became a major general of volunteers.

Southern commanders, a group of Confederate officers. The legendary military skill of many Rebel commanders prolonged the life of the Confederate States by several years.

Civil War Military Organization

Given that the military leadership on both sides was drawn largely from among West Point graduates it is not surprising that there was considerable similarity between the organization of the two armies. The basic formation was the infantry regi-ment. Both armies consisted largely of infantry: artillery and cavalry will therefore be treated elsewhere.

In the Old Army, regiments were on paper composed of twelve companies organized in three battalions, but in practice had only ten companies in one battalion. As it was rare for an entire regiment ever to be in one place at one time, this was not a particular problem. Militia regiments, and the quality and strength of the militia varied considerably from state to state, were usually on a ten company basis, two of which were

"flank" companies, technically trained for skirmishing and oth-er special duties. As a result, when war came, virtually all infantry regiments in both armies were composed of a head-quarters and ten companies, lettered from "A" through "K" omitting the "J," and, at least in the early period of the war, usually a regimental band as well.

Occasional regiments had a somewhat different organiza-tion, particularly at the start of the war. Thus, in April of '61 the *7th New York* had only eight companies, plus a pair of howitzers, an engineering platoon, a band and a drum corps, for a total of 991 officers and men, while the *56th New York* (the *"Tenth Legion"*) had ten line companies, a sharpshooter company, two light artillery companies and two lancer com-panies, with only a few more hundred men and the *2nd Massa-chusetts* 13 companies, with some 1,200 men. In both armies there were some separate battalions as well, usually of four companies designated "A" through "D", though in Confeder-ate service often as many as seven companies, "A" through "G". Several new Regular Army regiments were raised early in the war which theoretically had three battalions of eight com-panies each, a pattern which was also used when a number of heavy artillery regiments were converted to infantry.

A Confederate regiment had a colonel, a lieutenant colonel, and a major at headquarters, plus two captains to deal with quartermaster and subsistence matters, a first lieutenant as adjutant and a second lieutenant as ensign or color bearer. In addition there was a surgeon major and an assistant surgeon, ranking as a captain. Noncommissioned staff comprised a ser-geant major and three sergeants, one each to deal with quarter-master, commissary and ordnance matters. Each company had a captain, three lieutenants, five sergeants, four corporals and from 80 to 112 privates.

A Federal regiment was very similar, with a colonel, lieuten-ant colonel and major, plus a quartermaster captain, a lieuten-ant serving as adjutant and a chaplain. There was, in addition, a surgeon ranking as a major or captain and two assistant sur-geons ranking as captains or lieutenants. The noncommis-sioned staff included a sergeant major, quartermaster sergeant, commissary sergeant, hospital steward and two musicians, plus, later in the war, the ambulance sergeant and his staff of 12, who were not normally counted on the rolls of the regi-ment. Each of the companies had a captain, a first and a second lieutenant, a first sergeant and four other sergeants, eight corporals, two musicians and a wagoner, plus from 64 to 80 privates and, while in camp, four washerwomen.

1 8 6 1

FOR EVER

O.K. HOUSE

DINING
SALOON
FREE FOR
VOLUNTEE

HOT COFFEE AND REFRESHMENT FREE FOR THE UNION VOLUNTEERS

WATER WATER WATER WATER

The first Union victory at sea oc-curred in June of 1861, when William Tillman, the young black cook of the schooner *S.J. Waring*, single-handedly recaptured the ship from a prize crew off the Confederate privateer *Jeff Davis*, kill-ing three and capturing three, for which feat, which he is said to have accom-plished in little more than seven minutes, Congress awarded him $6,000 in prize money.

Uniformed officers of the Army of the Potomac. Many commanders, such as Grant, dispensed with such pompous attire during cam-paigns in the field.

had four direct subordinates, one for each corps, plus J.E.B. Stuart for the cavalry, and only nine infantry divisions and the cavalry division, thus giving him far fewer people to supervise. So superior was the organization of the Army of Northern Virginia, that in preparation for the Campaign of 1864, Lt. Gen. Ulysses S. Grant restructured the Army of the Potomac,

so that it emerged with but four corps, plus the cavalry, artil-lery reserve and headquarters assets, thus greatly easing the burden of command.

In general, by the middle of the war both sides had achieved a fairly satisfactory system of organization, albeit with minor problems which would be refined as time went on.

Drummer Boys

Until well into the nineteenth century armies regularly recruited young boys for service as drummers. This was not merely to provide music. As with bugles—called "trumpets"—drums formed an important part of the battlefield communications system, with various rolls signalling different commands. Recruiting boys for the work freed men for combat duty. As the boys got older they could regularly enlisted in the ranks. Drummer boys were usually treated as something of a mascot by the troops, and often entrusted to the good offices of the regimental chaplain. Since they had few military duties to perform, the life of a drummer boy was not particularly onerous and appeared rather glamorous. As a result, boys of all ages tried to enlist, often running away from home. Officially there were age restrictions, but these were often ignored, and boys as young as ten were occasionally found beating the "long roll" which called the men to action.

Needless to say, drummer boys—in Confederate regiments they were sometimes black—were often in the thick of the fighting, becoming casualties on a regular basis. Many lie in unknown graves, such as the heroic boy who fell at the head of Confederate Col. James C. Tappan's 13th Arkansas in an unnamed skirmish along the Arkansas River.

A number of drummer boys greatly distinguished themselves in action, and several became rather well known. The most famous drummer boy of the Civil War was undoubtedly John Clem (1851-1937), who added "Lincoln" as a middle name in 1861. At the age of ten little Johnny ran away from home in Newark, Ohio, and tried to enlist in various regiments, until the *24th Ohio* took him on. He served at Shiloh, earning the nickname "Johnny Shiloh" for his steadiness. Later transferring to the *22nd Michigan*, Clem drummed the long roll at Chickamauga—where he acquired the nickname "The Drummer Boy of Chickamauga"—and at Chattanooga and several other battles, occasionally finding the time to lend a hand with the fighting as well. After the war he attempted to win an appointment to West Point, but, having been otherwise occupied when most children his age were in school, he was a little weak academically. With the support of President Ulysses S. Grant, in whose army he had drummed at Shiloh, and Maj. Gen. George "The Rock of Chickamauga" Thomas, for whom he had drummed on that disastrous occasion, Clem was given a direct commission into the army as a second lieutenant in 1871, retiring 45 years later as a major general, the last Civil War veteran on active duty.

Willie Johnson, from St. Johnsbury, Vermont, was a drummer boy in *Company D* of the *3rd Vermont*. His service during the "Seven Days" retreat in the Peninsular Campaign was exemplary, and he was the only drummer in his division to come away with his instrument, by no means a trivial accomplishment. As a result, he was awarded the Medal of Honor on the recommendation of his division commander, thereby becoming the youngest recipient of the highest decoration, being then just 13 years old.

Drill instructors were in such short supply at the onset of the war that 13-year old cadets from places such as Virginia Military Institute were pressed into service to drill men old enough to be their fathers and grandfathers.

A drummer boy who served throughout the war in the ranks of a Virginia regiment.

John McClaughlin, a native of Lafayette, Indiana, enlisted as a drummer in the *10th Indiana* in 1861, being then "a little over ten years of age." McLaughlin had numerous adventures. During the Henry-Donelson Campaign he put aside his drum to take up a musket and join the firing line. Subsequently transferring to a Unionist Kentucky cavalry regiment, he fought as a trooper at Perryville, where he took a wound in his leg and took part in the pursuit of Col. John Morgan, during which he received a saber cut in the same leg. His wound proving serious, he was discharged. Although he recovered only partial use of his leg, he fought the discharge, appealing to Lincoln. After a private interview with the president, McLaughlin was enlisted as a bugler in the Regular Army.

"Little Oirish" was a Kentucky lad of about eleven who enlisted in the Confederacy's famed "Orphan Brigade." At Shiloh he is credited with stemming a rout by grabbing the colors and rally elements of the brigade which were in danger of breaking under a Federal assault.

Artillery pieces were in such short supply in the Confederacy in 1861 that some batteries received British 3-pounders, 6-pounders and 8 inch howitzers captured in the War of 1812.

During the Battle of Carrick's Ford, in West Virginia (13 July 1861), an Indiana Methodist preacher not only battled mightily for the Lord, but also for the Union, appending to each shot the line "And may the Lord have mercy on your soul!"

FAR RIGHT:
Obtained from England and smuggled through the blockade, this breech-loading Whitworth was used by Confederate gunners.

A battery of 12-pound Napoleons stationed near Washington. The Napoleon was a favorite among gunners and was quite common in the ranks of both sides.

Field Artillery

During the early nineteenth century there were significant improvements in artillery. However, as a result of the existence of the new rifled small arms, artillery service was both more difficult and more dangerous than in the past. Most artillery pieces were direct fire weapons, so the gunners had to see their targets in order to hit them. As recently as the Mexican War (1846-1848) it had been possible to site batteries within 500 yards or less of enemy formations, but this was now highly dangerous, given that rifle-armed infantry could deliver voluminous and accurate fire at such ranges, cutting down gunners and horses alike.

In an attack artillery was used to soften up the defenses, showering them with explosive shell and solid shot, inflicting casualties and destroying the cohesion of the defenders. This was most effectively done at relatively short ranges, to insure accuracy. Unfortunately, this put the gunners within range of enemy rifle-men. As a result, unless the guns could be put under cover of woods, fire had to be delivered at rather long range. At Gettysburg, for example, the Confederate batteries which fired the preparatory bombardment on 3 July were mostly sited in the woods atop Seminary Ridge, at ranges of between 1,200 yards and 2,200 yards away from the Union lines. This was one reason why the two-hour bombardment, involving perhaps 5,000 rounds, was ineffective. At such ranges, gunners were unable to observe the fall of shot and tended to overestimate the range. As a result, a substantial proportion of their fire fell behind the Union lines, rather than on them.

When it was possible to deliver a preparatory bombardment from massed batteries at closer range, as James Longstreet's batteries did during the same battle on the afternoon of 2 July against the Union *III Corps* or as Alpheus Williams' did on the morning of 3 July against the Confederate forces on Culp's

Hill, the results could be effective. In these cases, of course, the guns were firing from cover, which permitted such close work.

Artillery could also be used to bring enemy artillery under fire. However, although opposing artillerymen often engaged each other in such personalized gun-duels, counter-battery fire was relatively ineffective. The guns all used black powder, which generated lots of thick white smoke. As a result, after a few rounds, the guns were literally shrouded in great clouds, making it difficult to observe one's targets. Continuing to fire in such circumstances was merely a waste of ammunition. It was for this reason that most artillerymen preferred not to return fire during a preliminary bombardment: there was no point in wasting ammunition which could be put to better use in meeting an infantry attack.

As with the infantry rifle, it was in defense that artillery was particularly useful. A single well-handled battery could often hold up the advance of thousands of troops. And massed batteries could be particularly devastating, especially if the attackers had to cross wide stretches of open ground, as at Malvern Hill on 1 July 1862 or Gettysburg on 3 July 1863. An attacking formation could be brought under fire at ranges upwards of 2,000 yards, albeit with low effectiveness. As the troops drew nearer, effectiveness increased. Solid shot could bowl swathes through the attacking ranks and explosive shell could burst in the midst of the troops, both alike causing great slaughter. When the enemy was within 300 yards the gunners would switch to canister, which were giant shotgun shells capable of tearing a man to pieces. At the very last moment, the guns could be double-loaded with canister, which could be discharged right into the faces of the enemy as they reached the muzzles. Consider a charge against a battery of six 12-pounder Napoleons:

**Volume of Fire Delivered
Against Troops Attacking at 1,500 Yards**

Attacker	Time*	Type of Projectile Fired			
		Shell	Ball	Canister	Total
Cavalry	4.9 min	42	12	12 +	66 +
Infantry	16.9	120	42	66 +	228 +

[*Time required for the attackers to reach the battery at prescribed attack rates.]

As can be seen, even cavalry, which charges at a much faster rate than infantry, would receive an enormous volume of fire. Given that the attackers would also be receiving increasingly accurate rifle fire as they closed with the defenses, it is not difficult to see why frontal attacks were costly.

Field Artillery of the Civil War

Type	Bore	Weight	Round (pds)		Range	Notes
	(in)	(pds)	Proj	Chg	(yds)	
Howitzer						
12-Pdr U.S. 1841	4.62	788	8.9	.75	1072	A
24-Pdr U.S. 1841	5.82	1318	18.4	2.00	1322	A
Gun-Howitzer						
12-Pdr U.S. 1857	4.62	1227	12.3	2.50	1680	B
Guns						
3″ U.S. Ri 1861	3.00	820	9.5	1.00	2788	C
6-Pdr U.S. 1857	3.67	884	6.1	1.25	1523	D
10-Pdr Parrott Ri 1863	3.00	890	9.5	1.00	2970	E
12-Pdr Blakely Ri BL 1859	3.10	700	12.0	1.50	1760	F
12-Pdr Whitworth Ri BL 1860	2.75	1100	12.0	1.75	8800	G
14-Pdr James Ri 1857	3.67	875	12.0	0.75	1700	H
20-Pdr Parrott Ri 1861	3.67	1750	20.0	2.00	4400	I

This table includes the specifications for the most commonly used field artillery pieces of the Civil War. Type indicates that the piece was a *Howitzer*, able to use high angle fire to drop explosive shells behind obstacles, or a *Gun*, designed for a flat trajectory, and able to fire shells or solid shot to long ranges, or a *Gun-Howitzer*, theoretically capable of being fired in either mode. The designation given a piece is the official one, with the year normally that of introduction, though sometimes that of design. *Ri* indicates a rifled piece, all others being smooth bores. *BL* indicates a breech loading-piece, all others being muzzle loaders. Bore is the diameter of the tube, in inches.

The largest warships under construction in America in 1861 were the 5,610 ton broadside ironclads *Re d'Italia* and *Re di Portogallo*, laid down at the Webb shipyard in New York in November and December of that year under contract from the Royal Italian Navy.

In the foreground is a formidable James Rifle used to guard the Union capital from attack.

On the outbreak of the Civil War the Confederacy had 3,549 miles of coastline, with 189 ports, harbors and other navigable inlets.

When a brave Texan rode out to retrieve a flag which had fallen between the lines at the Battle of Wilson's Creek (10 August 1861) the men of the Union *1st Iowa* held their fire, calling out to the troops on either side to likewise honor a gallant enemy.

The 5th Ohio Battery attempts to withstand a charge from advancing Confederate ranks during the conflagration of the Hornet's Nest at Shiloh.

Weight is the total weight, in pounds, of the piece, with carriage, but exclusive of limber, caisson, and ammunition. *Round* is the weight, again in pounds, of the *Projectile* and the propellant *Charge*; for howitzers the projectile weight is for shells, for other pieces for solid shot. Note that official pounder designations were not usually a reliable indication of actual projectile weight. *Range* is the maximum range in yards, that at which it could project rounds, though not necessarily with any accuracy; for guns the range given is for solid shot: when using explosive shell this was about 25 percent less. Effective range, that at which most of the rounds fired reached the vicinity of the target, was usually about 60 percent of maximum range. *Notes* refers to the lettered paragraphs below.

A. The standard U.S. howitzers of the pre-war period, both models, plus a lighter mountain version of the 12-pounder were widely used early in the war, but were soon phased out by both sides in the major theaters, due primarily to their short range and the difficulty of observing their fire with any accuracy. A

less serious problem, that of properly setting fuzes, was shared with all artillery pieces able to fire shell. Howitzers could also fire canister. They were made of gun metal, normally called "brass," but actually a bronze of about 10 percent tin plus some other minor alloying ingredients. Cast solid, the tubes were then bored out on a lathe.

B. The famed "Napoleon," this was actually an American version of the field piece designed by Napoleon III in 1853. Though heavy and short-ranged, it was the most commonly used artillery piece of the war. A great favorite with the troops, who considered it highly reliable, the Napoleon could fire all types of ammunition, but was particularly effective firing canister in support of defending infantry. At least theoretically it could fire both as a gun and a howitzer, though rarely employed in the latter role. As with the howitzers, Napoleons were cast in gun metal, and bored out, though some Confederate versions were made of weaker cast iron, with a reinforcing jacket at the breech and were consequently much heavier.

C. Variously referred to as the "Ordnance Rifle" or "Gun", or as the "Rodman Gun" or "Rifle," or as the "Griffen Gun" this was, after the Napoleon, the most reliable piece in service and in numbers, eventually used by all Union horse artillery and many field batteries as well. The piece was so good that the 10-Pounder Parrott guns were converted to take the same ammunition. Like all rifles, however, the 3″ gun was not really good at firing canister, since the latter scoured the inside of the barrel, damaging the rifling. The piece was made by welding together wrought iron strips which had been wound in a spiral around a solid core, which was then drilled out and seven rifling grooves cut into the tube.

D. The light field gun version of the Napoleon. Little used in the Eastern Theater by the middle of the war, it remained with the troops in the West rather longer.

E. Designed by Robert P. Parrott, Superintendent of the West Point Iron and Cannon Foundry, both armies made considerable use of this reliable gun, which had been designed originally with a 2.9″ bore but was rebored to take the same ammunition as the 3″ Ordnance Rifle in 1863. It was made of cast iron, poured solid and then bored out, and was reinforced at the breech by a wrought iron band which was shrunk on. Since Confederate attempts to duplicate the gun were not successful—the end products weighing nearly 70 percent more than the originals—the Rebels relied on captured stocks.

F. A small number of these highly unusual guns were obtained in England by the Confederacy. Although impressive enough in performance, and very suitable for horse artillery due to their lightness—indeed, Wade Hampton actually imported a battery at his own expense—they had a terrific recoil, making relaying difficult. The guns were made of cast iron poured solid and drilled out. The shells had flanges which fit the rifling grooves in the barrel.

G. Designed by Sir Joseph Whitworth, small numbers were imported by the Confederacy and a single battery by the Union. They fired a 9.6″ long hexagonal shaped bolt up to five miles. However, the peculiar shape of the projectile precluded the development of an effective explosive shell, thereby restricting its use to solid shot. Although satisfactory in service, with remarkable accuracy and hitting power, the piece was a disappointment for no system existed by which the fall of shot could be observed and corrected at such ranges. The Whitworth was made out of cast steel, poured solid and drilled out in the desired diameter.

H. Invented by Charles James of Rhode Island, the James rifle proved unsatisfactory in service, due to unstable projectiles. Indeed, James himself was mortally wounded by the accidental detonation of one of his shells in 1862. Most James guns were cast in gun metal, but a few seem to have been made of high grade cast iron. Very few James rifles were actually produced, however, though numbers of existing cannon were experimentally converted to the James system and referred to as "James" guns.

The first drill manual issued by North Carolina upon its secession was printed at "The Institute for the Deaf and Dumb, and the Blind".

An artillery battery goes into position in the face of an explosive battle.

I. This was a heavier version of the standard Parrott field gun, and the heaviest normally carried into the field. It was substantially similar to the 10-Pounder version.

Infantry Tactics

The infantry was the principal arm of both armies in the Civil War. The overwhelming majority of the combat casualties were suffered, and inflicted, by infantrymen. In the generation before the Civil War the old smooth bore, muzzle loading musket which had been first introduced some two centuries earlier had passed from the scene. These weapons were highly inaccurate, extremely slow firing and of very short range. As a result, battles were fought with the troops lined up shoulder-to-shoulder, firing coordinated volleys at very short ranges against enemy troops similarly arrayed, which could be devastatingly effective. This was all perfectly satisfactory for well over a century. Both organization and tactics were based on the use of these weapons.

It had long been known that the smooth bore musket was decidedly inferior to the rifle, a weapon which had shallow grooves cut into the barrel which imparted a spin to the projectile, thus helping to stabilize it in flight, thereby greatly enhancing range and accuracy. But the existing rifles were even clumsier than the smooth bore, with an even lower rate of fire, for it required very careful loading. As a result the rifle was rarely used by armies.

In 1848 a French officer, Capt. Claude Etienne Minie, invented a practical rifled musket. What Minie actually invented was a more practical bullet for the rifled musket. The so-called "minie-ball" was a cylindro-conoidal (i.e. "bullet-shaped") lead projectile with a hollow base, cast to a somewhat smaller diameter than the musket barrel. When the piece was fired the rapid generation of gas expanded the soft, hollow base of the

cult of the bayonet persisted. Attacks in waves, with skirmishers to the fore were tried, to better effect, but these were by no means widely successful. Attempts were also made to attack with troops advancing by rushes in open order, again with mixed results. The best way to conduct any attack was to avoid the enemy's strength, to use maneuver and surprise to strike where he was weakest, on an exposed flank or at a thinly held position or against a poorly deployed formation, or one already badly battered by infantry and artillery fire. In these circumstances, going in with the bayonet was possible, though most of the fighting was still by fire, the principal effect of the bayonet being psychological. It was precisely this sort of attack which Lee effected at Chancellorsville (1-4 May 1863). However, such an attack required considerable tactical skill. Even if successful, one had to pay the price, for even in highly adverse situations the tactical defensive was enormously strong and anyone undertaking an offensive, even against poorly organized opposition, had to be willing to take losses. Thus, at Second Bull Run and Chantilly (27 August-2 September 1862) the Army of Northern Virginia lost nearly 20 percent of its strength in defeating the *Army of Virginia* and the *Army of the Potomac*, which lost about 13 percent. This was one reason why the Union suffered repeated defeats during the earlier period of the war, Union forces were more often on the offensive. It also helps explain why Confederate losses were often enormous, for Rebel generals had a predilection for the tactical offensive even when on the strategic defensive. So fine a commander as Lee himself fought only one purely defensive battle, when, at Fredericksburg on 13 December 1862, he held Marye's Heights in strength and accepted the repeated frontal attacks of the *Army of the Potomac*. Both absolutely and statistically Union casualties were almost double his own, whereas when he won by a tactical offensive his casualties were almost invariably statistically greater than his opponent's.

Certainly by mid-1863 the effectiveness of entrenched infantry defending against frontal assaults had been fairly clearly established. Nevertheless, the temptation to try precisely such an assault seems to have been overwhelming. Certainly it is extremely difficult to understand such attacks as "Pickett's Charge" at Gettysburg on 3 July 1863, Grant's assault at Cold Harbor on 3 June 1864 and Hood's at Franklin on 30 November 1864, all against strong forces well posted and all resulting in enormous losses to no purpose. Perhaps in the end, the Napoleonic ideal was stronger than reality.

Union troops shake fists and hurl venomous insults against Confederate captives brought into camp.

Army Life

Vivandieres

One of the more unusual phenomena of warfare in the nineteenth century was the *vivandiere*. An eighteenth century French military development, the *vivandiere* was, in effect, a paid camp follower properly enlisted on the rolls of a regiment, to serve as den mother, nurse and mascot, with eminent respectability, frequently being the wife or daughter of one of the men. Since the French were reputedly the finest soldiers in the world, the practice was widely imitated.

A number of *vivandieres* served in the early part of the Civil War, on both sides, primarily in French-style zouave regiments or in outfits with large numbers of foreigners. Like nurses, who also often served in the field, the "job description" of *vivandieres* was a non-combat one, but it at least implicitly included service under fire. These women were often up on the firing line in some of the hottest battles of the war, and a few seem to have taken at least a small part in the fighting. Three women who gained particular distinction in the role of *vivandiere* were Kady Brownell, Annie Etheridge and Bridget Divers.

Kady Brownell (1842-??), was born in Africa, the daughter of a British soldier. By most accounts an expert with pistol and saber, she enlisted at age 19 as a *vivandiere* in her husband's regiment, the *1st Rhode Island*, a 90-day outfit and carried the regimental colors at First Bull Run. When her husband reenlisted, in the *5th Rhode Island*, Kady went with him, although not carried formally on the rolls this time. She stayed with the regiment for nearly two years, often serving as color bearer under fire. On at least one occasion she saved the regiment from the fire of another Union outfit by running out into the line of fire with colors in hand. Her husband was severely wounded at New Berne on 14 March 1862. Kady spent 18 months nursing him back to health, whereupon he was discharged and they both left the service forever. Her subsequent life is obscure.

Annie Etheridge (1844-??), a some-time resident of both Wisconsin and Michigan, enlisted as a nurse-*vivandiere* in the *2nd Michigan*, later passed over to the *3rd Michigan* and in 1864 reenlisted in the *5th Michigan*, serving throughout the war. Said to have been very brave under fire, she served in most of the battles of the *Army of the Potomac*, being in the thick of things on numerous occasions, such as at Gettysburg on the second day. She was wounded only once, a graze across one hand, despite numerous bullet holes in her clothing, and at Spotsylvania was credited with rallying retreating troops in the face of the enemy. Known to the troops as "Gentle Anna" and "Michigan Annie," Phil Kearny was said to be planning to make her a sergeant-major at the time of his death, and Daniel Butterfield, his successor as division commander, awarded her a Kearny Cross. After the war she received a government job in lieu of pension.

Bridgett Divers (??-??) joined the *1st Michigan Cavalry* as a *vivandiere* when her husband enlisted in 1861 and served in numerous engagements. She subsequently worked as an agent for the Sanitary Commission. During the war she had many adventures, and was twice almost captured. On two separate occasions "Irish Biddy" was credited with rallying her regiment under fire, and was several times reported to have taken up a musket and joined the firing line. After the war she followed her soldier-husband into the Regular Army, serving as a regimental laundress for many years on the frontier.

Ms. Sally L. Tompkins of Richmond was made a captain of cavalry—becoming the only woman ever to hold a commission in the Confederate Army—by Jefferson Davis on 9 September 1861 because a hospital which she had established after First Bull Run proved to have a remarkable recovery rate.

At a meeting for the families of the *1st Vermont* early in the war, one woman arose to say how proud she was that she could do something for her country by having two sons in the ranks, and regretted only that 20 years earlier she had not had the foresight to provide more.

Women of the South sew uniforms for the troops in the field.

Uniform Expenses

Confederate Army regulations specified that uniform trousers were to be "sky blue," but, though well-heeled officers and regiments occasionally sported such in the early part of the war, there is no record of them ever being issued to the troops.

The Bowie knives, with which many volunteers equipped themselves early in the war, were later found to be worthless in battle but enormously useful for "carving beef and pork."

A group of Confederates who found themselves in Union hands. Evidence of the incapacity of the Southern government to adequately clothe its soldiers can be found in the diverse uniforms of these men.

On the outbreak of the war both armies had elaborate uniform regulations, the Confederacy adopting virtually unchanged the prewar regulations of the United States Army. For a Union soldier a full uniform cost about $40.00, while for his counterpart in gray the price was rather higher, about $62.00, reflecting the relative shortage of manufactured goods in the Confederacy. On this basis, uniform costs for an infantry regiment were about $40,000 for the Union and about $62,000 for the Confederacy. In addition, there were equipment costs, including blankets, knapsack, haversack, canteen and the like, which added an additional $10.00 to the bluecoats' outfitting costs and, although this is less certain, perhaps $15.00 to that of his graycoated foeman, which brings regimental outfitting costs up to about $50,000 for the Union and $77,000 for the Confederacy. Then consider the price of arms. A complete stand of arms—musket, bayonet and accoutrements—seems to have run about $30.00 for the Yankee, more for the Rebel, though how much more being impossible to calculate. This brings the cost of outfitting a Union regiment of about 1,000 men up to about $80,000, without considering the cost of such necessary items as mess pans (at $0.17 a piece), camp kettles ($0.48), axes ($0.66), spades ($0.56), picks ($0.57), bugles ($2.82), fifes ($0.45) and drums ($5.58), nor regimental colors nor supply wagons nor medical equipment, and certainly not officers kit, equipment and mounts, which they themselves had to supply. So a single regiment of infantry probably cost Uncle Sam about $100,000 in the first year or so of the war. What it cost "Uncle Jeff" is conjectural, but certainly more, even considering that the Rebels often marched off to war with a lot less than the Yankees.

Prescribed Annual Uniform Allowances Union and Confederate Armies, 1861

Year of Service:	1st	2nd	3rd
Hat	1		
Caps	2	1	1
Cap Cover	1	1	1
Coat	2	1	1
Trousers	3	2	2
Shirts	3	3	3
Blouse	1		
Drawers	3	2	2
Shoes, pair	2	2	2
Stockings, pair	2	2	4
Stock [tie]	1		
Great Coat	1		
Woolen Blanket	1		
Rubber Blanket	1		

In addition to these items, mounted troops—cavalrymen, artillery drivers and wagoners—were issued a stable frock each year while engineers and ordnance men received a set of fatigue overalls every other year. Theoretically each year's allotment of uniform items was divided into two batches, one for issue in the spring and one in the fall.

Initial Uniforming Costs, 1861

	Number Issued	Unit Cost	
		Union	Confederate
Hat	1	1.98	?
Caps	2	$0.63	$1.00
Cap Cover	1	.25	.38
Coat	2	6.71	8.00
Trousers	3	3.03	4.00
Shirts	3	.88	1.00
Blouse	1	2.15	?
Drawers	3	.50	1.00
Shoes, pair	2	1.94	3.00
Stockings, pair	2	.26	.50
Stock [tie]	1	.25	.25
Great Coat	1	7.20	25.00
Woolen Blanket	1	3.50	7.50
Rubber Blanket	1	1.00	?

At the beginning of the war there were many variations in the kit issued to newly mustered troops. Many militia regiments, both North and South, which were mustered into the service often had their own very elaborate uniforms and kit: the *7th New York* and the Washington Artillery come readily to

WH.SHELTON

mind, with their camp stools and tents and other bric-a-brac. On the other hand many newly raised regiments found themselves only partially outfitted, or outfitted in a fashion other than that prescribed in regulations, due to shortages in the availability of uniforms and equipment. It was rare, for example, for Union volunteers ever to receive a hat and blouse, which were dress uniform items. A typical example is that of the *7th Wisconsin*, outfitted at state expense, which was mustered into Federal service in August of 1861.

Initial Uniform Allotment
7th Wisconsin Infantry

	Number	Unit Cost
Cap & Cover	1	$1.00
Winter Coat & Trousers	1	9.50
Summer Coat & Trousers	1	4.63
Shirt	2	1.38
Shoes, pair	1	1.87
Stockings, pair	2	.30
Great Coat	1	7.50
Woolen Blanket	1	3.50
Rubber Blanket	1	1.00

The differences between what the state supplied and what the Federal government prescribed were eventually made good, though there was an unpleasant exchange of notes between the two jurisdictions as to who owed what to whom. Of course, the Federal supply situation grew steadily better as the war went on. Moreover, as time went on the troops found that they could manage with a lot less than the prescribed allotments of uniform and kit: the knapsack, for example, was discarded early. For Confederate troops this was making a virtue of a necessity, since their quartermaster department was never up to the task of outfitting them according to regulations anyway. They frequently made do with captured Union uniforms, eked out by civilian clothing and occasional bits and pieces of their prescribed uniforms.

No one knows whether it was a Yank or a Reb who made one of the most monumental discoveries of the war, but the troops of both sides very quickly learned that the barrel of a musket could hold nearly a pint of whiskey.

Westerners of the 4th Michigan serving with the Army of the Potomac *in the East. A brigade composed solely of Westerners was one of the toughest units in the* Army of the Potomac, *the* Iron Brigade.

Architecture of a Federal camp between campaigns. At times camps seemed to take on the appearance of primitive towns with streets and avenues.

War and the Muses

The Bonnie Blue Flag

On 6 March 1861, at a time when the United States Army totalled but 16,000 men, Jefferson Davis, president of the Confederacy, issued a call for 100,000 volunteers to serve for one year.

Francis Scott "The Star-Spangled Banner" Key's entire family supported secession.

In September of 1861 a New Orleans song writer, Harry McCarthy, an immigrant from Britain, wrote "The Bonnie Blue Flag" to fill a hole in a theatrical program which he was directing, with music adapted from an old Irish air by Jacob Tannenbaum, a German immigrant. The song was an instant hit, running through eleven editions during the war, and was soon popular second only to "Dixie" throughout the Confederacy. Unlike many other songs of the war, it was not popular in the North, due to its blatantly secessionist sentiments and its reference to slavery in the line "Fighting for the property we gained by honest toil." When Union forces occupied New Orleans in the spring of '62 a silly effort was made to ban it, with little success, despite a $25 fine. The song endured, though it lost some popularity when its writer abandoned the Confederacy for the North.

The Bonnie Blue Flag

We are a band of brothers, and native to the soil,
Fighting for the property we gained by honest toil;
And when our rights were threatened, the cry rose near and far:
Hurrah for the bonnie Blue Flag that bears a single star!
  Hurrah! hurrah! for the bonnie Blue Flag
  That bears a single star.

As long as the Union was faithful to her trust,
Like friends and like brothers, kind were we and just;
But now when Northern treachery attempts our rights to mar,
We hoist on high the bonnie Blue Flag that bears a single star.

First, gallant South Carolina nobly made the stand;
Then came Alabama, who took her by the hand;
Next, quickly Mississippi, Georgia, and Florida—
All raised the flag, the bonnie Blue Flag that bears a single star.

Ye, men of valor, gather round the banner of the right;
Texas and fair Louisiana join us in the fight.
Davis, our loved president, and Stephens, statesman are;
Now rally round the bonnie Blue Flag that bears a single star.

And here's to brave Virginia! the Old Dominion State
With the young Confederacy at length has linked her fate.
Impelled by her example, now others must prepare
To hoist on high the bonnie Blue Flag that bears a single star.

Then here's to our Confederacy; strong we are and brave,
Like patriots of old we'll fight, our heritage to save;
And rather than submit to shame, to die we would prefer;
So cheer for the bonnie Blue Flag that bears a single star.

Then cheer, boys, cheer, raise the joyous shout,
For Arkansas and North Carolina now have both gone out;
And let another rousing cheer for Tennessee be given,
The single star of the bonnie Blue Flag has grown to eleven!
  Hurrah! hurrah! for the bonnie Blue Flag
  That bears a single star.

Confederate cannoneers at rest.

Musically inclined Confederate troops during the opening days of the war.

When a pompous young lieutenant answered his challenge by calling out "Ass!", a sentry is said to have responded, "Advance, ass, and give the countersign."

Although flogging was abolished by the Union Army in August of 1861 and by the Confederates the following April, the practice was not entirely eliminated until after the war.

Maryland! My Maryland!

James Ryder Randall, an expatriate Baltimorean serving as a professor at Pydras College, in Pointe Coupee Parish, Louisiana wrote "Maryland! My Maryland!" soon after hearing of the bloody clash between the 6th Massachusetts and a secessionist mob in Baltimore on 19 April 1861. Shortly after the poem was published in the New Orleans Delta it came to the attention of Jennie Cary, one of the redoubtable Cary Cousins. Miss Cary set the words to the music for "Lauriger Horatius," more familiar as the tune of the Christmas carol "O Tannenbaum," and performed it at a patriotic rally. The song caught on rapidly and became a favorite Southern marching song in the early years of the war, losing little of its popularity as the state clung to the Union. Later adopted as the Maryland state song, it's avowedly secessionist verses are a constant irritant to the state's black population.

Maryland! My Maryland!

The despot's heel is on thy shore,
  Maryland!
His torch is at thy temple door.
  Maryland!

Avenge the patriotic gore
That flecked the streets of Baltimore,
And be the battle-queen of yore,
  Maryland, my Maryland!

Nearly one-third of the 2,952 Union men killed or injured at First Bull Run were from New York City.

Hark to an exiled son's appeal,
   Maryland!
My Mother State, to thee I kneel,
   Maryland!
For life and death, for woe and weal,
Thy peerless chivalry reveal,
And gird thy beauteous limbs with steel,
   Maryland, my Maryland!

Thou wilt not cower in the dust,
   Maryland!
Thy beaming sword shall never rust,
   Maryland!
Remember Carroll's sacred trust,
Remember Howard's warlike thrust,
All thy slumberers with the just,
   Maryland, my Maryland!

Come! 'tis the red dawn of day,
   Maryland!
Come with thy panoplied array,
   Maryland!
With Ringgold's spirit for the fray,
With Watson's blood at Monterey,
With fearless Lowe and dashing May,
   Maryland, my Maryland!
Come! for thy shield is bright and strong,
   Maryland!
Come! for thy dalliance does thee wrong,
   Maryland!
Come to thine own heroic throng,
Stalking with Liberty along,
And chant thy dauntless slogan-song,
   Maryland, my Maryland!

Dear Mother, burst thy tyrant's chain,
   Maryland!
Virginia should not call in vain,
   Maryland!
She meets her sisters on the plain,—
''Sic semper!'' 'tis the proud refrain
That baffles minions back amain,
   Maryland, my Maryland!
I see the blush upon thy cheek'
   Maryland!
For thou wast never bravely meek,
   Maryland!
But lo! there surges forth a shriek
From hill to hill, from creek to creek,-
Potomac calls to Chesapeake,
   Maryland, my Maryland!

Thou wilt not yield the Vandal toll,
   Maryland!
Thou wilt not crook to his control,
   Maryland!
Better the fire upon thee roll,
Better the blade, the shot, the ball,
Than crucifixion of my soul,
   Maryland, my Maryland!

I hear the distant thunder-hum
   Maryland!
The old Line's bugle, fife, and drum,
   Maryland!
She is not dead, nor deaf, nor dumb;
Huzzah! She spurns the Northern scum!
She breathes! She burns! She'll come!
   She'll come!
      Maryland, my Maryland!

A way station for Federal political prisoners, Fort Lafayette.

The John Brown Song

The origins of what is more commonly known as "John Brown's Body" of "John Brown's Song" are obscure. The tune seems to have been adapted from an old Negro spiritual, "Say, Brothers, Will You Meet Us?" by William Steffe in 1852 and was used for several songs over the next few years. The words are attributed to one Thomas B. Bishop. The two were somehow combined shortly after the war began, reputedly by two Massachusetts men, Messers Gilmore and Greenleaf, and soon became a favorite Union march, possibly the most popular of the war, particularly in the early days. As with all genuine folk songs, there were many variations. In early 1862 the most enduring and powerful version was written, "The Battle Hymn of the Republic."

The John Brown Song

John Brown's body lies a-mouldering in the grave;
John Brown's body lies a-mouldering in the grave;
John Brown's body lies a-mouldering in the grave;
    His soul goes marching on!

Glory, halle—hallelujah! Glory, halle—hallelujah!
    Glory, halle—hallelujah!
    His soul is marching on!

He's gone to be a soldier in the army of the Lord!
He's gone to be a soldier in the army of the Lord!
He's gone to be a soldier in the army of the Lord!
    His soul is marching on!
    Chorus
Glory, halle—hallelujah! Glory, halle—hallelujah!
    Glory, halle—hallelujah!
    His soul is marching on!

John Brown's knapsack is strapped upon his back!
John Brown's knapsack is strapped upon his back!
John Brown's knapsack is strapped upon his back!
    His soul is marching on!
    Chorus

Glory, halle—hallelujah! Glory, halle—hallelujah!
    Glory, halle—hallelujah!
    His soul is marching on!

His pet lambs will meet him on the way;
His pet lambs will meet him on the way;
His pet lambs will meet him on the way;
    As they go marching on!
    Chorus
Glory, halle—hallelujah! Glory, halle—hallelujah!
    Glory, halle—hallelujah!
    As they go marching on!

They will hang Jeff Davis to a sour apple tree!
They will hang Jeff Davis to a sour apple tree!
They will hang Jeff Davis to a sour apple tree!
    As they march along!
    Chorus
Glory, halle—hallelujah! Glory, halle—hallelujah!
    Glory, halle—hallelujah!
    As they march along!
Now, three rousing cheers for the Union!
Now, three rousing cheers for the Union!
Now, three rousing cheers for the Union!
    As we go marching on!

Glory, halle—hallelujah! Glory, halle—hallelujah!
    Glory, halle—hallelujah!
    Hip, hip, hip, Hurrah!

A solitary Federal sentry maintains a lonely watch no doubt wondering when the cruel war would finally end.

The first battlefield monument commemorating a Civil War hero was that to Confederate Col. Francis Bartow of the 8th Georgia, erected in September of 1861 on the spot where he had fallen whilst commanding a brigade on the previous 21 July, during the Battle of Bull Run.

Campsite of the 8th New York, a three months regiment which served at Bull Run before being mustered out. At the beginning of the war, many outfits on both sides had distinctive uniforms. The gray clothes of the 8th New York led it to be confused for the enemy in combat.

Out of the war for the moment, Confederates spend their time leisurely in a Yankee prison camp.

122

All Quiet Along the Potomac

Ethel Lynn Eliot Beers, a sensitive young woman from New York, was moved to poetry by the newspaper headline, "All Quiet Along the Potomac," which appeared frequently in the autumn of 1861, usually followed by a subhead dealing with some minor incident or other. One day the subhead read "A Picket Shot." The incongruity of the headline, which suggested nothing of importance, and the subhead, which reported a personal tragedy of devastating consequence, prompted Beers to write a sad poem, "The Picket Guard." By some accounts first published in an unidentifiable newspaper on 21 Oct 1861, the poem certainly appeared in *Harper's Weekly* for 30 Nov 1861, signed "E.B.", for "Ethelyn Beers." The poem shortly came to the attention of John H. Hewitt, a noted journalist, poet and musician, serving as an officer in the Confederate Army, who set it to music as "All Quiet Along the Potomac."

Hewitt credited the words to Lamar Fontaine of Texas, which the latter did not dispute. Indeed, Fontaine claimed to have written them in August of 1861 and to have circulated handwritten copies among his comrades at the front. When Mrs. Beers' claims were advanced, Fontaine argued that she must have obtained a copy from a Yankee who had looted the body of a dead Confederate. While Lamar's father, an Episcopal rector, swore that his son was telling the truth, the latter was a notorious liar: among other tales, he claimed that he had lived four years among the Comanche while a child, that he had served in the Crimea and that he had been wounded 67 times during the Civil War while taking part in 27 battles and 57 skirmishes. Mrs. Beers' authorship seems probable. The song became rather popular with the troops on both sides, dealing, as it did, with the pain and suffering caused by war.

When the *55th Illinois* mustered into Federal service in 1861 there were 91 pairs of brothers among its 1,056 men: in four years of service, 58 of the brothers died in battle, over a third of the regiment's combat deaths.

Rebels massacre fleeing Yankees attempting to flee to safety across the Potomac during Ball's Bluff (21 October 1861).

All Quiet Along the Potomac

"All quiet along the Potomac to-night!"
   Except here and there a stray picket
Is shot, as he walks on his beat, to and fro,
   By a rifleman hid in the thicket.

'Tis nothing! a private or two now and then
   Will not count in the news of a battle;
Not an officer lost! only one of the men
   Moaning out, all alone, the death rattle.

All quiet on the Potomac to-night!
   Where the soldiers lie peacefully dreaming;
And their tents in the rays of the clear autumn moon,
   And the light of their camp-fires are gleaming.

A tremulous sigh, as a gentle night-wind
   Through the forest leaves slowly is creeping;
While the stars up above, with their glittering eyes,
   Keep guard o'er the army sleeping.

There's only the sound of the lone sentry's tread,
   As he tramps from the rock to the fountain,
And thinks of the two on the low trundel bed,
   Far away, in the cot on the mountain.

His musket falls slack, his face, dark and grim,
  Grows gentle with memories tender,
As he mutters a prayer for the children asleep,
  And their mother—"may heaven defend her!"

The moon seems to shine forth as brightly as then—
  That night, when the love, yet unspoken,
Leaped up to his lips, and when low-murmured vows
  Were pledged ever to be unbroken.

Then drawing his sleeve roughly over his eyes,
  He dashes off the tears that are welling;
And gathers the gun closer up to his breast,
  As if to keep down his heart's swelling.

He passes the fountain, the blasted pine-tree,
  And his footstep is lagging and weary;
Yet onward he goes, through the broad belt of light,
  Towards the shades of the forest so dreary.

Hark! was it the night-wind that rustled the leaves?
  Was it the moonlight so wondrously flashing?
It looked like a rifle: "Ha! Mary, good-by!"
  And his life-blood is ebbing and splashing.

"All quiet along the Potomac to-night!"
  No sound save the rush of the river;
While soft falls the dew on the face of the dead,
  And the picket's off duty forever!

Their state under Federal occupation, Marylanders cross the Potomac to join Confederate forces in Virginia.

124

*"All quiet on the Potomac"—
a Federal Picket falls dead
from a snipers bullet.*

*The Army of Northern Virgina
fords the Potomac to engage
in Lee's 1862 campaign in
Maryland. The Confederate
defeat at Antietam would
force the Confederates to
recross the river in the
opposite direction.*

III.

1862

I propose to move immediately upon your works.
—Ulysses S. Grant

We must this day conquer or perish.
—Albert Sidney Johnston

Come on! Come on! Do you want to live forever?
—Unknown Confederate Colonel

If we have lost today, we have yet preserved our honor.
—George B. McClellan

Fight, fight—be whipped if you must, but fight on.
—Edwin M. Stanton

The enemy may win a victory, but we must make it a victory that will ruin him.
—Edwin V. Sumner

It is well war is so terrible, we should get too fond of it.
—Robert E. Lee

During the hottest part of the Battle of Fair Oaks (31 May-1 June 1862), two men of the *2nd Connecticut* "got at loggerheads with each other, threw down their muskets and fell to at fisticuffs—had it out, picked up their arms and pitched into the Rebels again."

Of 583 Union generals, 188 (32.3 percent) had no military experience prior to the Civil War, while of 425 Confederate generals, 153 (36 percent) also lacked such training.

PREVIOUS PAGE:
The bloody fight in the Hornet's Nest on the field at Shiloh. The tenacious stand of the Union troops that held this position bought Grant the time he needed to shore up a defensive position to save the rest of his embattled army and avoid disaster. (Courtesy Civil War Library and Museum)

FAR RIGHT:
Federal and Confederate positions around the city of Fredericksburg during Burnside's failed campaign there in December of 1862.

The Federal rear at Shiloh. After hours of attempting to hold off Albert Sidney Johnston's Confederates, Union soldiers, their bodies ripped and torn by shot and shell, are carried to safety.

128

Both sides prepared for 1862 with enormous energy, for it was generally expected that it would be the decisive year. Great armies had been raised and each side believed it had the ability to win. The Union adopted a realistic strategy: to strangle the enemy with a naval blockade, to send armies down the Mississippi River to cut the Confederacy in two and to attempt to seize Richmond, capital of the rebellion. In a sense the Confederacy adopted no strategy at all, counting on winning by being able to avoid defeat, which required that Federal forces be beaten back wherever they appeared.

In the West, the new armies were concentrated in Missouri and Tennessee and along the Ohio River, while in the East they were concentrated in Virginia and Maryland and around Washington. And when the armies began to move in early 1862, the troops were still but half-trained, led by generals as ill-prepared as themselves. It began in the West, where Union Brig. Gen. Ulysses S. Grant conducted a successful mid-winter offensive. In cooperation with a small naval flotilla, his 20,000 men seized the critical Confederate positions at Forts Henry (6 February) and Donelson (16 February), with some 12,000 prisoners. This had the effect of clearing Kentucky and Central Tennessee of Confederate forces. Advancing southwards up the Tennessee River, Grant, with some 35,000 men, was surprised by Confederate Gen. Albert Sidney Johnston with some 40,000 men at Shiloh on 6 April. After a brutal two-day fight

by the still largely green armies, Grant threw back the enemy, having lost 13,000 men while inflicting some 10,000 casualties, including Johnston himself, who fell at the head of his troops. Soon after, on 25 April, a Federal naval squadron under Flag Officer David Glasgow Farragut boldly swept up the Mississippi to seize New Orleans. This meant that the Union controlled both ends of the river, making it a logical avenue for an advance which would cut the Confederacy in two. It was an opportunity for which Grant immediately began to prepare.

The key to Confederate control of the Mississippi lay at Vicksburg, a well-fortified city high above the river. In the late summer and early autumn of 1862 Grant undertook several offensives in Northern Mississippi. A series of battles, raids and skirmishes resulted in which Confederate Maj. Gen. Earl Van Dorn demonstrated that an overland advance was unprofitable. Grant altered his strategy. In late December his able subordinate Maj. Gen. William Tecumseh Sherman advanced down the Mississippi, with the object of taking Vicksburg by storm. The effort failed. Rather than withdraw Sherman's 32,000 men back up river, Grant left them in position on the Mississippi in Northern Louisiana, just across from Vicksburg, supplying them by river and there they settled down for the winter. Meanwhile, great battles were being fought in the heartland of the Confederacy.

When a pro-Confederate Englishwoman visiting his studio in Florence, Italy, asked American sculptor Thomas Powers if he had ever executed a bust of Jefferson Davis, he replied "No madam, but I hope that before long, an artist of another profession than mine will have the pleasure of executing him."

When asked by the secretary of war if he had organized a regiment of "fugitive slaves," Union Brig. Gen. David Hunter, serving on the Carolina coast, replied that he had not, but that he did have "a fine regiment of persons whose late masters are 'fugitive rebels'."

The proud capital of the Confederacy, Richmond, Virginia during the war.

Brig. Gen. U.S. Grant's army storms the ramparts of the Confederate garrison at Fort Donelson under the command of Brig. Gen. John B. Floyd. It was here that Grant issued his famous demand for unconditional surrender.

In the summer of 1862 Confederate armies under the general direction of Gen. Braxton Bragg undertook an invasion of Kentucky, primarily as a strategic diversion to draw Federal attention from the vulnerable line of the Mississippi. Considerable maneuvering resulted, as Union forces sought to pin Bragg down and destroy him. Union Maj. Gen. William S. Rosecrans, with 45,000 men, finally ran Bragg to earth at Murfreesboro, Tennessee, on 29 December. Bragg, who had about 35,000 men, attacked. A tough fight followed, which lasted on and off for three days (31 December 1862-2 January 1863) after which Bragg drew off southwards, each side having incurred about 12,000 casualties. The months of maneuvering had basically restored the situation as it was before Bragg's offensive.

Meanwhile, the armies in the East had not been idle. After Bull Run, there was a long lull in the East as the armies were made ready. Confederate forces in Virginia were commanded by Gen. Joseph E. Johnston and concentrated north of Richmond, with the intention of defending the city against an advance from Washington. Union forces concentrating about Washington were under Maj. Gen. George McClellan. A talented, energetic and brilliant planner and organizer, McClellan created the *Army of the Potomac*, but·lacked the instincts and will to lead it into battle, despite the great confidence which he publicly and repeatedly expressed. As the spring of 1862 approached, anticipation of a Federal offensive rose. McClellan dithered, demanding yet more men and yet more equipment. Taking counsel of his fears, he argued that he was greatly outnumbered, when, in fact, overall Union forces available for offensive operations were about twice those of the Confederacy (150,000 to 75,000). After much prodding he made his

move, in a brilliantly conceived amphibious operation. He placed some 112,000 men on the peninsula between the James and the York Rivers on the coast of Virginia in early April, intending to advance on Richmond before the Confederate forces in Northern Virginia could be properly redeployed. Then he lost his nerve, frittering away a month in unnecessary siege operations.

McClellan thus gave Johnston time to shift his forces and turn what could have been a spectacular Union victory into a dismal and disappointing failure. While Brig. Gen. Thomas "Stonewall" Jackson covered his exposed rear by a brilliant campaign in the Shenandoah Valley, Johnston held McClellan away from Richmond, though two efforts to inflict a major defeat on the Union forces were frustrated by inexperience, a rather confused Confederate command structure and some remarkably hard fighting on the part of the Union troops. Wounded, Johnston was replaced by the very able Gen. Robert E. Lee on 1 June. While McClellan lapsed into inactivity not ten miles outside Richmond, Lee laid his plans. Then on 26 June, having recalled Jackson from the Valley, he undertook a brilliant series of successful, though costly, counter-attacks known as the "Seven Days Battles." By their end, McClellan's *Army of the Potomac* had been forced back into a fortified camp up against the James River, from whence it could draw supplies. During much of this fighting McClellan had performed poorly, though his conduct of the retreat to the James was superb and he remained remarkably popular with the troops. Wars, however, are won neither by retreats nor by popularity.

Faced with apparent disaster in the Peninsular Campaign, Lincoln attempted to recover the situation with an advance by the forces remaining in the Washington area. On 26 June, even

Albert Sidney Johnston's army takes U.S. Grant's Yankees by surprise at Pittsburg Landing or Shiloh. Many underfed and poorly clad Confederates chose to loot abandoned Federal camps during the course of the battle.

The 12,000 Union troops taken prisoner by Stonewall Jackson at Harper's Ferry on 15 September 1862 was the largest surrender of troops in the history of the United States Army until the Japanese took 40,000 men on Bataan on 9 April 1942.

Soldiers attend to the grim task of burying the dead at Antietam (17 September 1862). 23,000 Americans became casualties during the battle making it the bloodiest day in this nation's history.

as Lee began his counter offensive, Lincoln ordered the creation of the Union *Army of Virginia*, placing it under Maj. Gen. John Pope, a mildly successful commander from the western theater who happened to be junior in rank to his subordinates.

Pope advanced south from the Washington area with 45,000 men on 14 July. Lee, alert to the threat to his rear, dispatched Jackson northwards with 24,000 men. Jackson dealt Union Maj. Gen. Nathaniel Banks, commanding Pope's leading army corps, a crushing blow at Cedar Mountain on 9 August. Pope fell back towards Bull Run, while being reinforced by sea from the Army of the Potomac. On 28 August, Lee, with some 55,000 men, boldly undertook an envelopment against Pope's 75,000. In the series of battles which followed (Groveton, Second Bull Run, Chantilly), Pope conducted Union forces so ineptly that by 1 September they had suffered 21 percent (c. 16,000) casualties as against the enemy's 19 percent (c. 9,200). Confederate leadership had again proven itself superior.

However, these Confederate victories had been won by forces on the strategic defensive. In order to secure genuine victory and independence from the Union, the Confederacy would have to demonstrate an ability to carry the war to the enemy. On 4 September 1862 Lee took the 55,000 men of the Army of Northern Virginia across the Potomac into Maryland. By 7 September he was concentrated about Frederick, in Western Maryland, from whence he could threaten both Washington, some 40 miles to the southeast, or Baltimore, some 50 miles to the east. Desperate, Lincoln re-appointed McClellan to the command of the *Army of the Potomac*. McClellan advanced cautiously westward with his 85,000 field troops. He missed an opportunity to cut Lee's army in two on 13 September, when he captured a copy of Lee's orders, but managed to keep his army well concentrated. A series of small battles resulted. Lee began to fall back. On the evening of 16 September he held an ambiguous position around Sharpsburg in Western Maryland. While the terrain tended to favor the defense, and Antietam Creek partially covered his front, he had his back to the Potomac. Moreover, some 13,000 of his available 40,000 men were several miles to the south of the Potomac, over which there was but one available crossing. Lee had placed himself in a trap. Confronted by an abler foe than McClellan, he would have paid dearly for his error. McClellan, however, was true to form. In the Battle of Antietam, fought on 17 September, he appears to have had no overall plan of attack, but merely threw in army corps after army corps, in ill-coordinated, poorly supervised and piecemeal attacks which did not take advantage of his superiority in numbers and which permitted Lee to shift his slender resources from one part of his front to another as the situation dictated. For all that, Union forces almost won a smashing victory, but Lee's situation was saved in a powerful counterattack delivered by his last arriving division. McClellan received some reinforcements during the night and, given Lee's precarious situation, could have renewed the fight on the next day with excellent chances of securing a crushing victory over his foe. Ever cautious, he failed to do so. The armies faced each other throughout 18 September. That night Lee slipped back across the Potomac to Virginia. The battle had been a remarkable defensive success for Lee. Nevertheless, he had been forced out of Maryland with nothing to show for his efforts save a considerable casualty list (c. 13,700). Union performance had been poor, with casualties high (c. 12,400), but a strategic success could be claimed, for the Army of Northern Virginia had been thrown back into the South. This success was sufficient to give Lincoln the opportunity to more clearly define Union war aims in the form of the Emancipation Proclamation.

On 17 September 1862 Yankee Col. John T. Wilder, an amateur soldier, commanding Union forces besieged in Munfordville, Kentucky, was uncertain as to protocol in such situations and so asked Confederate Maj. Gen. Simon Bolivar Buckner for advice, which the latter honorably refused to give, though he did permit Wilder to inspect the investing forces, whereupon Wilder said "I believe I'll surrender" and did.

The Army of the Potomac *slugs its way through the Chicka-hominy Swamp on its way to the gates of Richmond. McClellan's ranks not only faced the wrath of Confederates, but mosquitos, oppressive heat and disease.*

After Antietam both armies withdrew to recuperate. The Army of Northern Virginia was heavily reinforced, underwent a major reorganization which saw the introduction of proper army corps, and was partially re-equipped. McClellan put the *Army of the Potomac* through much the same drill, while feuding by telegraph with his superiors in Washington, who wished him to advance at the earliest opportunity. There was some maneuvering on the part of both armies in late October, but nothing decisive resulted. Finally, thoroughly exasperated with McClellan's "slows", Lincoln replaced him with the reluctant Ambrose E. Burnside on 7 November. Burnside was apolitical, had a number of successes under his belt, and had not performed noticeably worse than anyone else. But he lacked confidence in himself and said so. Nevertheless, he almost immediately undertook an offensive, commencing a series of maneuvers which by 17 November saw his forces begin to concentrate on the north side of the Rappahannock River, across from Fredericksburg, on Lee's right flank. He planned to effect a crossing and then strike against Richmond in Lee's rear, but a shortage of pontoons delayed the crossing,

The Federal position at the Battle of Perryville (8 October 1862). Though the fight was effectively a draw, Braxton Bragg was forced to give up his invasion of Kentucky.

133

giving Lee time to gather his own forces. Burnside got much of his 110,000-man army across on 11-12 December in the face of light resistance. The next day he ordered a series of frontal attacks against Lee's 75,000 well-entrenched troops. The result was a one-sided Confederate victory (some 12,000 U.S. casualties to about 5,000 C.S.). Burnside withdrew.

Thus ended 1862. For the Confederacy it had seemed a successful year. Despite some losses in the West, the Union armies had repeatedly been beaten back in the East. For the Union, the year seemed disastrous, for the victories in the West appeared small alongside the failures in the East. Yet the West was far more decisive a theater than most realized, and the performance of the Federal armies there had demonstrated that it was not the troops who were at fault but their leaders. The men on both sides had performed splendidly. The key to the outcome of the fighting in the East lay in the fact that the Confederate forces were better led than those of the Union. And so the armies went into winter quarters for the second time.

Because a newspaper story mentioned that he was smoking a cigar during the Confederate breakout attempt at Fort Donelson, patriotic citizens in the North sent Ulysses S. Grant 10,000 stoges in all their infinite variety.

As night began to fall at the Battle of Perryville on 8 October 1862, a Union officer who was bringing his troops into action, spotted a general and said "I have come to your assistance with my brigade, sir," and went to identify his outfit, whereupon Confederate Lt. Gen. Leonidas Polk replied "There is some mistake about this. You are my prisoner."

FAR LEFT:
Brig. Gen. Samuel R. Curtis' command receives a smashing attack from Earl Van Dorn's army of Southerners and pro-Confederate Indians at Pea Ridge (7-8 March 1862). Though Van Dorn was able to provide the Federals with reason for concern, his attack was uncoordinated and sputtered out when supplies ran low.

The indecisive yet extremely sanguinary Battle of Stones River (31 December 1862 - 2 January 1863). Stones River displayed the irregular talents of Confederate Maj. Gen. Braxton Bragg who failed to follow up his successes during the first day of the battle.

Incidents of War

Espying an ill-dressed soldier swaying badly on the back of a horse, a thirsty Confederate straggler asked, "Where did you get your liquor from? Give me some!" only to discover that the man in question was Thomas "Stonewall" Jackson, who, although the most careless dresser and the worst horseman in the Confederate Army, was also the most abstemious.

A Valley Bivouac

Late in December of 1861 Thomas "Stonewall" Jackson undertook an expedition to destroy the Chesapeake and Ohio Canal. It was bitterly cold in the Shenandoah Valley that winter, and the troops crumbled mightily as they marched and camped in the ice and snow. One morning early in January, near the town of Bath, a group of Jackson's troops woke up to find themselves covered with snow, for it had snowed once again while they slept. As the men got up, shook out their snow-covered blankets, and started to get into the routine of the day, they cursed Jackson roundly for the miseries of their lives.

While this was going on, no one noticed one slug-a-bed curled up in his blanket under a nearby tree. Shortly, the man stirred, crawled out of his blanket and, shaking off the snow, stood up. The troops were shocked into silence, for it was Jackson himself and they braced themselves for a blast of general's ire. But the gallant Stonewall, who had ridden up in the night, made a smiling remark to a couple of the men, shook out his blanket and was soon away.

An army comes to life as dawn arises over a military camp.

Looking for missing friends, soldiers make their way through the darkness and horror of a nighttime battle field.

"Go to your right"

William F. Jenkins, a 17-year old private in the 12th Georgia, was severely wounded and left on the field during the Second Battle of Bull Run (29-30 August 1862). Soon after nightfall, two of his comrades came looking for him. By good fortune they located Jenkins, gave him what help they could, and then proceeded to carry him off to a field hospital. Making their way through the darkness they heard a challenge.

"Who goes there?"

"Two men of the 12th Georgia," they replied, "carrying a wounded comrade."

A Yankee sentry appeared, "Don't you know you're in the Union lines?"

"No," said the startled Rebels.

"Well you are," said the Yankee, adding "Go to your right." As the bluecoat faded back into the darkness, one of Jenkins' buddies called out, "Man, you've got a heart in you," and they continued on their way.

In the darkness which engulfed the field at Perryville on the night of 8 October 1862, Confederate Lt. Gen. Leonidas Polk rode up to a colonel and angrily admonished him for firing into friendly troops, only to discover that he had blundered into the Yankee lines, whereupon he ordered the regiment to cease fire and rode slowly down the line until he could make his escape.

Butler Recruits a Black Brigade

Maj. Gen. Benjamin Butler, an amateur general of little ability in the field but much political influence, commanded the Union forces occupying New Orleans in 1862. Butler was one of the first senior officers to see the value of recruiting black troops for the Union. His account of how the first black regiments were mustered into his army is taken from Butler's Book (Boston, 1892).

. . . the rebel authorities in New Orleans had organized two regiments from the free Negroes, called "Native Guards, Colored." When [Maj. Gen. Mansfield] Lovell ran away with his troops these men stayed at home. The rebels had allowed the company officers to be commissioned from colored men—colonels, lieutenant colonels and majors, and the staff officers—they were white men.

I found out the names and residences of some twenty of these

One of the first black regiments mustered into Federal service was the *1st Louisiana Native Guards*, originally organized—but rejected—for Confederate service by the free blacks of the state at the onset of the war.

When, in late 1862 the Union commander at New Orleans, Maj. Gen. Benjamin F. Butler—nicknamed "Beast" by Southerners for his lack of noble qualities—learned that Caroline Beauregard was seriously ill, he offered her husband, Confederate Gen. Pierre G.T. Beauregard, a pass through Federal lines so that he might visit her, an offer which the latter declined: when Mrs. Beauregard died early the following year, the Union provided a steamboat to carry her remains to her native parish.

colored officers, and sent for them to call on me. They came, and a very intelligent-looking set of men they were. I asked them if they would like to be organized as part of the United States troops. They unanimously said they would. In all bodies of men there is always a spokesman, and while many of my guests were of a very light shade, that spokesman was a Negro nearly as dark as the ace of spades.

"General," he asked, "shall we be officers as we were before?"

"Yes; every one of you who is fit to be an officer shall be, and all the line officers shall be colored men."

"How soon do you want us to be ready."

"How soon can you give me two regiments of a thousand men each?"

"In ten days."

"But," I said, "I want you to answer me one question. My officers, most of them, believe that Negroes won't fight."

"Oh, but we will," came from the whole of them.

"You seem to be an intelligent man," said I, to their spokesman; "answer me this question: I have found out that you know just as well what this war is about as I do, and if the United States succeed in it, it will put an end to slavery." They all looked in assent. "Then tell me why some Negroes have not in this war struck a good blow somewhere for their freedom? All over the South the men have been conscripted and driven away to the armies, leaving ten Negroes in some districts to one white man, and the colored men have simply gone on raising crops and taking care of their women and children."

The man's countenance lightened up. He said: "You are General here, and I don't like to answer that question."

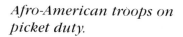
Afro-American troops on picket duty.

138

Fanciful depiction of the Battle of Shiloh (6-7 April 1862). Though the Confederates were able to catch Grant's army by surprise, the Federals managed to hold on until reinforcements arrived and then launched a smashing counterattack on the second day of the battle.

At the Battle of Pea Ridge (7-8 March 1862) some Confederate Indian troops, having captured a Union cannon, put its carriage to the torch, with consequent casualties when the loaded piece blew up spectacularly.

"Answer it exactly according as the matter lies in your mind, and I pledge you on my honor, whatever the answer may be it shall harm no one of you."

"General, will you permit a question?"

"Yes."

"If we colored men had risen to make war on our masters, would not it have been our duty to ourselves, they being our enemies, to kill the enemy wherever we could find them? and all the white men would have been our enemies to be killed?"

"I don't know but what you are right," said I. "I think that would be a logical necessity of insurrection."

"If the colored men had begun such a war as that, General, which general of the United States army should we have called upon to help us fight our battles?"

That was unanswerable.

"Well," I said, "why do you think your men will fight?"

"General, we come of a fighting race. Our fathers were brought here slaves because they were captured in war, and in hand-to-hand fights, too. We are willing to fight. Pardon me, General, but the only cowardly blood we have got in our veins is white blood."

"Very well," I said, "recruit your men and let them be mustered into service at"—I mentioned a large public building—"in a fortnight from to-day, at ten o'clock in the morning. Report, and I will meet you there. I will give orders that the building be prepared."

On that morning I went there and saw such a sight as I never saw before: two thousand men ready to enlist as recruits, and not a man of them who had a white "biled shirt" on.

General Lew Wallace and the Great Sioux Uprising

In late 1862, the Santee band of the Sioux Indians of Minnesota, "unreasonably" resentful over the fact that white settlers had stolen 90 percent of their land, driven off most of the game, plundered their burial places and generally subjected them to abuse, went on the war path. Although the nation was just then engaged in the Civil War, the army reacted swiftly and overwhelming force was rapidly concentrated.

Among the troops ordered to proceed to Minnesota were the paroled prisoners-of-war being held at Camp Chase, near Columbus, Ohio, pending formal exchange. Since both the troops, and their commander, Maj. Gen. Lew Wallace, had enlisted to fight Rebels, not Indians, they were not inclined to depart for Minnesota. As a result, Wallace began a series of bureaucratic maneuvers designed to avoid this unpleasant duty.

To begin with, Wallace observed that conditions at Camp Chase were abominable, and that there were numerous sick and debilitated men in his charge. Permission was sought, and granted, to relocate the men to a more salubrious site in preparation for their eventual movement to Minnesota. This done, a matter which occupied several days, he then requested that the troops be paid before being transferred. Thus ensued several more days of paper-shuffling, culminating, when the local paymaster refused to issue the monies in question, in Wallace's arresting the fellow and seizing the funds at gun-

point. Now, of course, the troops had to be properly organized, outfitted and equipped, which caused several more days' delay.

Finally, of course, there were no more dodges available. The men would have to move. But Wallace had one more trick up his sleeve. He paraded the men and made a grandiloquent speech announcing that they were shortly to depart for Minnesota, where they would fight Indians, warning them not to try to desert, even though they had all that money in their pockets. That night he posted guards. Much to his surprise, the next morning he discovered that the guards had deserted. He again paraded the troops and once again warned them against desertion. That night he doubled the guard, only to find that they too deserted. He repeated this performance for two or three more nights, until virtually all the parolees were gone. Then he wired the War Department, explaining that most of his men had deserted, but recommended that no charges be made against them, as they would probably all shortly report to their original regiments.

Perhaps because Wallace proved to be correct, the War Department took no further action in the matter. In any case, neither Lew Wallace nor any of the parolees were involved in the disgraceful slaughter of the Santee which followed.

Indians serving as scouts for the Confederate armies in the West.

"The Angel of Marye's Heights"

On the night after the Battle of Fredericksburg (13 December 1862), thousands of Union troops lay dead and wounded on the cold ground before the Confederate lines on Marye's Heights. The piteous cries of the wounded could be heard throughout the night. Finally, as the new day dawned, Confederate Sgt. Richard R. Kirkland, a 19-year old from South Carolina, could bear it no more. Kirkland asked permission to succor the wounded. His superiors demurred, but the young man pressed them and finally the brigade commander assented.

Carrying a number of canteens, Kirkland climbed over the low stone wall which ran along the crest of the heights and had formed the mainstay of the Confederate lines. No one fired on the young soldier as he went to a wounded Yankee and, kneeling, gave him a drink of water and a few words of comfort. For over an hour Kirkland went from man to man, giving them water and trying to make them more comfortable, as the amazed men of both armies looked on. He spread his overcoat to cover one man, and bundled up one that he found on the field to pillow the head of another man. In the end, as he walked back to his own lines, the watching Union troops cheered him for a gallant enemy.

Kirkland died at Chickamauga on 20 September 1863, but the memory of his brave and compassionate deed lives on.

When Union troops captured Fort Pulaski, Georgia, on 11 April 1862, the newly appointed commander Col. Alfred H. Terry of the *7th Connecticut* summoned his Confederate predecessor, a Colonel Olmstead, and lent him $50.00 to tide him over any inconvenience which might occur while he was a prisoner-of-war.

The slaughter at Marye's Heights—Lee's troops mow down advancing legions of Yankees during Burnside's doomed attack on the position. All told, the Federals lost some 12,000 men for no purpose.

The situation at the surrender of Ft. Donelson on 16 February 1862 was so confused that Confederate Brig. Gen. Bushrod R. Johnson was able to escape merely by walking calmly through the Yankee lines.

Captain Newsham at Fort Donelson

During Grant's Henry and Donelson Campaign in early 1862, Capt. T. L. Newsham was Assistant Adjutant General on the staff of Brig. Gen. Charles F. Smith. During the heavy fighting at Fort Donelson on 15 February, Newsham's duties caused him to ride several times back and forth along the Union front. Since he was mounted on a splendid white horse, he very quickly attracted the attention of the enemy. Among those who spotted Newsham was Brig. Gen. Simon Bolivar Buckner, ablest of the three Confederate generals in the fort.

Buckner personally ordered several of the most experienced gunners in the garrison to let fly at the officer on the white horse, but Newsham never received so much as a scratch despite a considerable volume of ammunition being expended

at him. Among the rounds aimed at Newsham were six shots from a six pounder, several more from a ten pounder, and at least one charge of grapeshot. Several of the rounds came close, including a couple which passed between his body and his horse's head, one which passed over the horse's back and the grapeshot, which passed between the horse's legs, leaving nought but a few scratches. The most unusual piece discharged at Newsham was a hand-crafted Turkish rifle of .75 caliber, of fine damascus steel, with inlaid bands of silver, gold and ivory, worth about $1,000. The owner of this piece, a Captain Naughton, claimed to have loosed eleven rounds at Newsham to no avail.

When Fort Donelson surrendered on the 16th, Newsham

met Buckner outside his headquarters. Spotting the white horse, the general inquired as to whether Newsham was the same officer whom he had observed on the previous day. When Newsham replied in the affirmative, Buckner told him "Then you certainly bear a charmed life." As for Captain Naughton, he gave his rifle to Newsham.

The 8th Missouri *and the* 11th Indiana Zouaves *engaged during the siege against the Confederate held Fort Donelson.*

"What Did You Do?"

During one of his battles in the West, it is said that an officer rode furiously up to U.S. Grant as he stood with his staff. Touching his cap in salute, he addressed the general in a heavy German accent, "Dscheneral, I vants to make vun report; Schwartz's battery is tooken."

"How was that?" said Grant.

"Vell, you see, Dscheneral, die sczessionists come up in die front of us, und die sczessionists come up in die flank of us, und then die sczessionists come up in die rear of us, und Schwartz' battery vas took."

"Well, sir," inquired the General, "you of course spiked the guns?"

"Vat!," cried the officer, "schpike die guns, schpike die new guns! —no, it vould schpoil dem!"

With a sharp look, Grant asked, "What did you do?"

"Do? Vy, we took dem back again!"

Among the many prisoners taken when Confederate Brig. Gen. Nathan Bedford Forrest's troopers captured Holly Springs, Mississippi, on 20 December 1862 was Julia Grant, the wife of Union Maj. Gen. Ulysses S. Grant, who was shortly passed through the lines.

Vidette Duty

During the Peninsular Campaign there was some skirmishing around Lee's Mills, Virginia, in April of 1862. It is said that one particular morning, a Georgian and a Down-Mainer chanced to be on vidette opposite each other, each well ensconced behind a stout old tree. As the two ineffectively traded shots, they kept up a steady stream of conversation and became rather friendly. After a while the business grew tedious. Finally, the Georgian called out, "Give me a show," meaning that the other fellow should expose himself a bit and give him a chance for a hit. As was perfectly natural, the Bluecoat stuck his head out a little, and of, course, the Georgian let fly, but the ball went wide. "Too high," shouted out the Mainer, "Now give me a show." The Georgian obligingly poked out his head and the Yankee squeezed one off. Again the ball went wide. "Too low," called out the Rebel, "My turn again." And so, in this fashion the two swapped a few more rounds. Then, by chance, the Yankee sent a ball into the tree, barely clearing the Rebel's ear.

"Cease fire," called out the Georgian.

"Cease it is," said his opponent.

"Look here," said one to the other, "we have carried on this business long enough for one day. S'pose we adjourn for rations?"

"Agreed," replied the other.

And so, after an exchange of good wishes, the two marched off in different directions, one allegedly whistling "Yankee Doodle" and the other "Dixie."

FAR RIGHT:
Rather inaccurate depiction of the assault across Burnside's Bridge by the IX *Corps during the Battle of Antietam. The entire attack was a fiasco in which a handful of Georgians managed to delay the advance of thousands of enemy troops.*

RIGHT:
Federal sharpshooters engaged at Malvern Hill in the epic battles during the Seven Days.

Colonel A.K. Johnson's hair raising experience.

The Kentuckians at Stones River

Gallant charge of the 55th and 60th Virginia Regiments against a Federal battery at Fraysers Farm. The Confederates engaged the Yankees in a hand-to-hand contest to win the guns.

During the Battle of Stones River/Murfreesboro (31 December 1862–2 January 1863), as Maj. Gen. William S. Rosecrans' Union *Army of the Cumberland* battled Gen. Braxton Bragg's Confederate Army of Tennessee, there is alleged to have occurred an incident which could have only happened in a civil war.

The battle opened at dawn on 31 December, when Bragg's left, under Maj. Gen. William J. Hardee fell upon Rosecrans' right, under Maj. Gen. Alexander McCook. The Union troops put up a tough fight, but were forced back by Hardee's troops.

After about two hours, the Union line began to stabilize. Bragg strengthened Hardee for one more try and at about 1:00 p.m. Hardee essayed another attack. As his troops advanced, his 3rd Kentucky found itself confronting the *23rd Kentucky*, a Union regiment recruited from men of the very same county. As if by mutual consent, these former friends and kin and neighbors ceased firing and are said to have begun to berate each other with fearsome curses and insults. This went on for some minutes in the midst of the great battle which raged about them.

Suddenly, someone on one side said something which caused someone on the other side to really get angry. Muskets were once more brought into play and the firing grew heated. Then the two regiments clashed in an intense hand-to-hand struggle with knives, clubbed rifles, fists, bayonet and pistols, as rough-and-tumble a fight as ever occurred anywhere. Gradually the Rebel Kentuckians began to gain the upper hand, but then, quite suddenly some of their erstwhile friends and neighbors managed to get athwart their flank and began pouring fire into their ranks. The 3rd Kentucky fell back, bringing with them not a few of their former friends and neighbors as prisoners. Just then the Union *9th Ohio* came into action, charging

into the 3rd Kentucky in time to liberate most of the Union men while bagging many of the Rebel ones. Hardee's attack had been halted.

Meanwhile, the Unionist Kentuckians discovered that a number of their Confederate counterparts had fortuitously brought whiskey in their canteens, rather than less potent stuff. The canteens in question began to pass from hand to hand. Soon, the two groups of Kentuckians, who had some minutes earlier been striving mightily to massacre each other, were renewing old friendships, inquiring about mutual associates, laughing, joking and talking together, getting into the spirit of the New Year as it were.

When a Yankee Kentuckian chanced to be captured by his Rebel brother during the Battle of Shiloh, he admonished the latter to take care not to fire at a particular Union officer since "that's father."

Embroiled in the effusion of blood at Perryville, the 78th Pennsylvania *displays incredible elan as it drives off the* 26th Tennessee *to take a Confederate battery.*

The Men

David Glasgow Farragut

Within a year of the start of the war, Confederate Gen. Pierre G.T. Beauregard's black hair had turned almost completely white, a development which his friends attributed to the pressures of war but less charitable—and more accurate—folks suggested was because the Federal blockade had cut off the supply of dye.

Edward C. Stockton had perhaps the most unusual military career of anyone in the Civil War: graduating from Annapolis in 1850, he was shortly after expelled from the Navy and engaged in various civilian pursuits until the war broke out, whereupon he became successively a lieutenant in the South Carolina State Navy in early 1861, a second lieutenant in the Confederate States Marine Corps from May through September of that year, then a captain in the 21st South Carolina from January through April of 1862 and thereafter an officer in the Confederate States Navy, rising to lieutenant.

FAR RIGHT:
Farragut's fleet runs past enemy ships and forts during his daring cruise up the Mississippi which led to the capture of New Orleans, one of the history's most spectacular naval victories. (Courtesy Civil War Library and Museum)

Lithograph showing Adm. David "Daring Dave" Farragut as well as his spectacular victories such as New Orleans and Mobile Bay. (Courtesy Civil War Library and Museum)

150

The nation's first admiral, David Glasgow Farragut (1801-1870), was born in Tennessee. The son of naval hero George Farragut (1755-1817), David G. Farragut was adopted by Commodore David Porter, father of the nation's second admiral, David Dixon Porter. Commissioned a midshipman at the age of nine, Farragut served with Porter during the War of 1812, and at the age of twelve was made master of the prize *Frolic*, thus becoming the youngest person ever to command a ship in the United States Navy, and was briefly a prisoner-of-war. After the war he rose steadily through the ranks, while serving in the Mediterranean, the West Indies, the South Atlantic and in the Mexican War. During his long career he established the Mare Island Navy Yard in California and acquired fluency in several languages.

A captain on the outbreak of the Civil War, Farragut was a resident of Norfolk, Virginia, and immediately removed to the North. Although he encountered some difficulties because of his southern background, in December of 1861 Secretary of the Navy Gideon Welles gave him command of the West Gulf Squadron with orders to maintain the blockade and capture New Orleans. Displaying considerable skill as an organizer, Farragut put together a powerful expeditionary force, and proceeded to take New Orleans by running his fleet up the Mississippi past the Forts Jackson and St. Philip, which had been subject to the attentions of a mortar flotilla under his adoptive brother Cdr. David Dixon Porter, on 24 April 1862, earning for himself the thanks of Congress and a promotion to rear admiral.

During the Summer of 1862, Farragut operated his oceanic fleet on the Mississippi, twice running the defenses of Vicksburg, but failing in his efforts to take the place by riverine power alone. Returning with his squadron to the Gulf, Farragut tightened the blockade, assisted in the army's operations on the lower Mississippi, most notably against Port Hudson, and tried to interest Washington in the capture of Mobile.

Finally given permission to take Mobile, Farragut boldly steamed into Mobile Bay 5 August 1864, uttering the famous line "Damn the torpedoes! Full steam ahead!" after the monitor *Tecumseh* sank after hitting a mine. Although the city itself did not fall, Farragut's operation effectively closed the port, for which Congress promoted him to vice admiral.

Soon after Mobile ill-health put Farragut on the beach until early 1865, when he assumed command in the James River, in time to be present at the surrender of Richmond. After the war he was promoted to full admiral and died on active duty.

Farragut was an excellent administrator, fine seaman, and a bold tactician who cared little for his own safety, preferring to view the action from a perch in the rigging—where he was once joined by his cabin boy—than from the relative safety of the deck of his flagship, the sloop-of-war *Hartford*.

Robert E. Lee

Lee's three sons all saw service in the Confederate Army: George Washington Lee and William Henry Fitzhugh Lee rising to major generals, while his youngest, Robert E. Lee, Jr., enlisted as a private and rose to a captaincy in the artillery. His brother, Sydney Smith Lee, became a captain in the Confederate Navy, while his nephew, Fitzhugh Lee, became a lieutenant general in the Confederacy. Several cousins served the Union, notably Samuel P. Lee and Roger Jones, who were naval officers, and William R. Terrill, who fell as a brigadier general, as did his brother, James, though he fought for the South.

Born on a plantation in Virginia, Robert Edward Lee (1807-1870) was the son of Revolutionary War cavalry hero Henry "Light Horse" Harry Lee—whose spendthrift ways resulted in the family living in genteel poverty for many years—and the nephew of two signers of the Declaration of Independence. Lee graduated from West Point 2nd in the class of 1829. An engineer, he served in garrison, on various civil and military engineering projects, and in Mexico with notable brilliance, being once wounded and receiving three brevets. Meanwhile he found time to marry Martha Washington's granddaughter by her first husband. Lee was superintendent of West Point from 1852 to 1855, at a time when his son and his nephew

The grand Confederate warrior, Robert E. Lee, poses with Gen. G.W.C. Lee and Colonel Walter Taylor.

were cadets. He was then acting commander of the *2nd Cavalry* (renamed the *5th* in 1861) in Texas and Utah from 1857, on the "Mormon Expedition." In Washington on leave in 1859, Lee commanded the detachment of Marines which captured John Brown at Harper's Ferry.

General-in-Chief Lt. Gen. Winfield Scott apparently offered Lee command of the Federal armies on 18 April 1861. However, although a Unionist and opposed to both secession and slavery, Lee would not serve against his state. He declined the offer and on 20 April resigned his commission, entering Virginia's service as commanding general of state forces. On 14 May he entered Confederate service as a brigadier general and was promoted full general one month later.

Lee's first wartime command was in West Virginia, where he displayed little talent as a field commander. He was shortly transferred to command Confederate forces on the Georgia and Carolina coasts, and was then called to serve as military advisor to Jefferson Davis in March of 1862. He helped plan Jackson's famed Valley Campaign and the Peninsular Campaign. Upon the wounding of Gen. Joseph E. Johnston, Lee was given command of Confederate forces defending Richmond on 1 June. From then on his career and reputation were inextricably bound up with the Army of Northern Virginia.

Almost from the moment he assumed command, Lee displayed remarkable skill as a tactician, beating back McClellan's *Army of the Potomac* from the gates of the city during the Seven Days Battles (26 June-2 July). He went on to lead the Army of Northern Virginia with considerable success during the balance of the Peninsular Campaign, and in the Second Bull Run,

Antietam, Fredericksburg and Chancellorsville Campaigns, the last of which was his most brilliant tactical success. During the Gettysburg Campaign he did not perform up to his own standards, failing to properly coordinate the actions of his subordinates and possibly fighting an unnecessary battle. After Gettysburg he continued to lead the Army of Northern Virginia in the long, grinding defensive battles of the Campaigns of 1864 and 1865, during which his health deteriorated seriously. In February of 1865 he was made general-in-chief of all Confederate forces, much too late to influence the course of the war. His surrender at Appomattox on 9 April of that year is generally considered to mark the end of the war.

After the war Lee served as president of Washington College—now Washington and Lee University—until his death. One of the finest soldiers in American history, Lee, who always managed to appear immaculately dressed, regardless of circumstances, looked every inch the great commander he was. Immensely loved by his troops, who called him "Marse Robert" and "Bobbie Lee," Lee was essentially a tactician and a good defensive strategist on a theater level. He failed to rise above local professional concerns and view the war as a whole, displaying little interest or understanding of the overall strategic situation, demonstrating a predilection for Virginia—and Virginians—to the exclusion of all other theaters. More seriously, he never realized that it was he who was the real soul of the Confederacy and not Jefferson Davis. Nevertheless, it is difficult to believe that the war would not have taken a different course had he been named general-in-chief sooner.

During one of the many campaigns in '62, a weary Robert E. Lee took a nap by the side of a road, down which came a division of his doughtiest warriors, who, seeing their beloved commander at rest, hushed their voices and lightened their tread lest they disturb him.

The "Gray Fox," Robert E. Lee at the height of his fame.

Nathaniel P. Banks

Born in Massachusetts, Nathaniel Prentiss Banks (1816-1894) rose from relatively humble origins to become one of the most influential men in the nation. He had little formal education, at an early age going to work in a cotton mill which his father managed. At 23 he was admitted to the bar. Banks built a successful law practice while attempting to engage in politics, making seven tries for a seat in the Massachusetts legislature before actually securing one. His political career took off from there. He was shortly elected speaker of the Massachusetts House of Representatives, presided over the state constitutional convention of 1853 and was elected to Congress. In 1856 Banks became Speaker of the House of Representatives on the

133rd ballot, and proved an effective voice for compromise in a period when sectionalism and slavery were becoming increasingly heated issues. Elected governor of Massachusetts in 1858, Banks resigned his seat early in 1861 to offer his services to Abraham Lincoln, who promptly named him a major general of volunteers.

Banks proved himself an inept field commander. Sent to the Shenandoah Valley in late 1861, he was roughly handled by Stonewall Jackson. Given a corps in John Pope's *Army of Virginia*, he was again badly handled by Jackson at Cedar Mountain, in mid-1862.

After briefly commanding the defenses of Washington, he

The beginning of the Peninsular Campaign, Federal troop steamers depart from Alexandria.

FAR RIGHT:
Federal troops engaged on the ground of slaughter around the Dunker Church during the Battle of Antietam on 17 September 1862.

When, during the Battle of Murfreesboro, Confederate Maj. Gen. Benjamin Cheatham shouted "Forward, boys, and give 'em hell, boys," his superior, Lt. Gen. Leonidas Polk, agreeing in principal, but, as an Episcopal bishop, unwilling to utter profanity, shouted "Give 'em what General Cheatham says, boys! Give 'em what General Cheatham says!"

When the *3rd Wisconsin* broke at the Battle of Winchester (25 May 1862) Maj. Gen. Nathaniel Banks called out "Stop men! Don't you love your country?", whereupon one of the fleeing men replied "Yes, by God, and I'm going back to it just as fast as I can."

was transferred to command in Louisiana. Banks proved himself an able and—perhaps most importantly—an honest military governor and administrator, but once more bungled operations in the field, making costly and unnecessary assaults on Port Hudson in mid-1863 and embarking on the almost disastrous Red River Campaign in 1864. Relieved, Banks remained inactive until mustered out in August of 1865.

After the war Banks reentered politics, serving six terms in the House of Representatives—five as a Republican and one as a Democrat—at various times, while at other times serving again in the state legislature and as United States marshal for Massachusetts. Although his political services were considerable, Banks was one of the least successful amateur generals of the war.

Philip Kearny

The "most gallant officer in the United States Army," Philip Kearny (1815-1862) was born into one of the wealthiest and most prominent families in New York City. Shortly after graduation from Columbia in 1833, he was admitted to the bar and travelled widely. Inheriting a million dollars in 1836, he gave up the law to enter the army the following year, securing a direct commission in the 1st Dragoons (now the 1st Cavalry), commanded by his uncle, Col. Stephen W. Kearny. Kearny attended the French Army Cavalry School at Saumur in 1839 and got his first taste of combat with the Chasseurs d'Afrique in Algiers in 1840.

Returning to the United States, he was shortly appointed an aide-de-camp to Maj. Gen. Alexander Macomb, the general-in-chief, and was retained in this position by the latter's successor, Winfield Scott. Kearny resigned early in April of 1846, but returned to active duty six weeks later, on the outbreak of the Mexican War. At his own expense Kearny recruited a troop of cavalry which Scott made his personal escort during the Mexico City Campaign. Kearny himself served with considerable distinction, losing his left arm at Churubusco, for which action he was brevetted major.

After the war, he served for a time in California. Resigning his commission in 1851, Kearny travelled extensively, married, and settled in New Jersey. On the outbreak of the Italian War in 1859, Kearny joined Napoleon III's *Garde Imperial* and, according to tradition, took part in every cavalry charge at Magenta (4 June) and Solferino (24 June), holding the reins in his teeth, for which he became the first American to win the Cross of the Legion of Honor.

Still abroad when the Civil War broke out, Kearny immediately returned to the United States. Made a brigadier general of volunteers, he was given a brigade of New Jersey troops. Kearny served with great ability during the Peninsular Campaign, rising to command a division and securing promotion to major general. Commanding part of the rear guard during the Second Bull Run Campaign, he accidentally rode into the Confederate lines at Chantilly on the night of 1 September 1862. Challenged by some sentries, he attempted to escape but was killed instantly. A small, dashing looking man, Kearny was a superb officer with a genuine zest for combat, who was greatly mourned by both sides.

When, after the Battle of Chantilly (1 September 1862), the body of a Union major general was brought to him, Stonewall Jackson took one look at the dead man's face, and, lifting his hat, said, "My God, boys, you know who you have killed? You have shot the most gallant officer in the United States Army. This is Phil Kearny, who lost his arm in the Mexican War."

The Union line of W.F. Smith's division serving as a rear-guard during the fight at White Oak Swamp.

The "Kearny Patch"

Philip Kearny was responsible for the invention of one of the most enduring American military traditions, the unit patch. As the story has it while commanding the *3rd Division* of the *III Corps* during the Peninsular Campaign, Kearny came upon some officers loitering by the side of a road. He gave them a severe dressing down, and then, much to his embarrassment, discovered that they were not from his command. Shortly thereafter he ordered all the men in his division to sew a red diamond patch to their caps. Inspired by his idea, in the spring of 1863 Daniel Butterfield designed similar badges for the rest of the *Army of the Potomac*, and the practice soon spread to the rest of the Union Army.

The Italian Wars

Phil Kearny was not the only man in the Civil War who had served in the Italian Wars of Independence. Col. Philip St. George Cooke of the *2nd Dragoons* was in Italy in 1859-1860 as an official observer, later becoming a Union brigadier. The future Confederate Maj. Gen. James J. Pettigrew was a volunteer observer with the Sardinian Army at San Martino (24 June 1859). Two former French regular officers rose to brigadier generalships in the Union service, Alfred Napoleon Alexander Duffie, who served as a cavalry officer at Solferino, and Gustave P. Cluseret, who commanded the French volunteers fighting with Garibaldi and was wounded at the Volturno (1 October 1860), while Chatham R. Wheat, who later raised the famed "Louisiana Tigers" served with Garibaldi's English volunteer legion. Former Sardinian cavalryman Luigi di Cesnola, who served in the Italian War of 1848-1849, rose to command the *4th New York Cavalry* and briefly led a brigade in the *Army of the Potomac*, before becoming one of the founders of the Metropolitan Museum of Art. In the Spring of 1862 veteran Italian artilleryman Capt. Achille de Vecchi obtained a year's leave, during which he organized and commanded the *9th Massachusetts Battery*, which served with distinction in the *Army of the Potomac*.

An unusually distinguished veteran of the Italian Wars was Robert d'Orleans, the *duc de Chartres*, who had served as a 16-year old junior officer in the Piedmontese Nizza Light Cavalry Regiment in 1859, earning a decoration for gallantry from, of all people, Napoleon III. Together with his brother, the Comte de Paris, the Bourbon pretender to the throne of France and the Prince de Joinville, young Chartres served as an aide-de-camp to McClellan in 1862.

Perhaps the most interesting veteran of the Italian Wars to turn up in the Civil War was Frank Vizetelly, an artist/correspondent for *The Illustrated London News*, who had covered the 1859 war and the expediton of Garibaldi and "The Thousand" in 1860. On the outbreak of the Civil War he came to the United States, covering events from behind the Union lines in 1861-1862, and then slipping over to the other side for 1862-1865.

There was very nearly an even more impressive veteran of the Italian Wars in Union service, for Lincoln made a tentative offer of a commission to Giuseppe Garibaldi, which the latter tentatively accepted. But Garibaldi would serve only on condition of immediate emancipation, a move which Lincoln found politically inopportune early in the war. And in any case, Garibaldi had other fish to fry.

One of the most fearsome of Federal generals, Philip Kearny.

LEFT:
A depressing sight for any soldier, wounded being brought into camp for care after a skirmish with the enemy.

James Ewell Brown Stuart

"Jeb" Stuart (1833-1864) was born in Virginia and graduated from West Point 13th in the class of 1854. Most of his career was spent on the frontier, where he was wounded. From 1855 he was with the *1st Cavalry* (renamed the *4th* in 1861). He was in Kansas during the pre-statehood dispute over slavery and was with Robert E. Lee when John Brown was captured at Harper's Ferry in 1859.

Stuart resigned as a captain on 3 May 1861 and was made a lieutenant colonel by Virginia. He entered Confederate service soon after and was named colonel of the 1st Virginia Cavalry, with which he served in the Shenandoah Valley and during the Bull Run Campaign with great distinction. He was promoted brigadier general in September and further distinguished himself commanding a brigade of cavalry in various skirmishes through the winter of 1861-1862.

During the Peninsular Campaign Stuart demonstrated remarkable abilities in reconnaissance, raiding and screening, and once rode entirely around the *Army of the Potomac*. In July of 1862 he was given command of the Cavalry Division of the Army of Northern Virginia and made a major general. He led his command, later elevated to the status of a corps, thereafter until his death, serving with great skill in the Second Bull Run, Antietam and Fredericksburg. During the Chancellorsville Campaign, in May of 1863, he demonstrated some ability for higher command, when he temporarily led II Corps after Stonewall Jackson and Richard Ewell had both been wounded.

During the Gettysburg Campaign Stuart proved relatively ineffective. Taking advantage of some ambiguity in his orders he embarked on an unnecessary and unprofitable raid. This foray, undertaken primarily to restore his reputation after the unusual success of the Union cavalry at Brandy Station in June, effectively deprived Lee of the "eyes" of his army and had much to do with the disastrous failure which resulted. Nevertheless, Stuart performed well during the retreat, and in numerous skirmishes and engagements along the Rappahannock line in the winter of 1863-1864.

During the attack on the Confederate forts guarding Hatteras Inlet on 28 August 1862 a Union warship, believing it was bombarding enemy cavalry, decimated a herd of beef cattle.

During a burial truce after the Battle of Mundorsville in September of 1862, Union Col. John Thomas Wilder of the *17th Indiana* lent Confederate Brig. Gen. James R. Chalmers shovels so that he could dispose of his dead.

One of the legendary figures of the Civil War, cavalry man J.E.B. Stuart.

RIGHT:
Riding ahead of his troopers is one of the most famous and flamboyant cavalrymen of the Civil War, J.E.B. Stuart.

During the Second Bull Run Campaign (August-September 1862), Confederate cavalryman J.E.B. Stuart chanced to "capture" Union Maj. Gen. John Pope's dress coat, while the former's best plumed hat fell into the hands of the latter, with the result that Stuart proposed, and Pope accepted a formal exchange of prisoners.

He led his corps ably during the Battles of the Wilderness and Spotsylvania in the Campaign of 1864, and was mortally wounded by Union cavalrymen at Yellow Tavern on 11 May, attempting to block Maj. Gen. Philip Sheridan's raid on Richmond. He died the next day, greatly mourned.

Heros von Borcke, Stuart's Prussian aide and himself one of the unique characters of the war, wrote that Stuart was "a stoutly built man, rather above average height, of a most frank and winning expression." One of the finest cavalrymen in American history, Stuart had a remarkable ability to gather information, screen operations and conduct raids, but he was overly sensitive about his reputation, and perhaps a bit too aggressive, with the result that he had to be issued careful instructions lest he go off on his own, which is precisely what happened in the Gettysburg Campaign. Stuart, who wore a beard to hide a receding chin, was the son-in-law of Brig. Gen. Philip St. George Cooke, a fellow-Virginian who remained loyal to the Republic, despite the fact that his sons and son-in-law "went South".

Ambrose E. Burnside

Although born in Indiana, Ambrose E. Burnside (1824-1881) came from Southern stock, his father having been a slaveholder in South Carolina before moving northwards and freeing his bondsmen. After completing primary school, Burnside ran a tailor shop for a time until he secured an appointment to West Point through his father's political connections. Graduating in 1847, he served on occupation duty during the Mexican War and was subsequently on the frontier, where he was wounded in a skirmish with the Apaches. Resigning from the army in 1853, he went into the firearms business in Rhode Island, attempting to manufacture a breech-loading rifle of his own design. Although the venture was only moderately successful, Burnside became active in state politics, serving in Congress and receiving an appointment as a major general of militia. A close friend of George B. McClellan, the latter secured for him an appointment as treasurer of the Illinois Central.

On the outbreak of the Civil War, Burnside organized the *1st Rhode Island*, which was among the first regiments to reach Washington. He commanded a brigade with some ability at Bull Run and was shortly made a brigadier general. Having attracted the eye of President Lincoln, in October of 1861 Burnside was entrusted with command of an expedition to the

Carolina Coasts. He carried out this operation with considerable success, earning a promotion to major general. From February through June of 1862 Burnside inflicted several defeats on the opposing forces, capturing New Bern and a number of other minor ports, establishing a firm grip on the coast of North Carolina.

Recalled in early July, he joined the *Army of the Potomac* as a corps commander—it is generally believed he was offered, and refused, command of the army at this time. Although he did moderately well commanding his *IX Corps*, Burnside did poorly when entrusted with the Union left wing at Antietam, although the Union failure to destroy Lee at this battle was more directly McClellan's failure to exercise close control of the battle than Burnside's poor handling of his part of it. Again offered command of the *Army of the Potomac*, Burnside attempted to refuse, but was pressured into accepting by most of the other corps commanders, who did not want Joseph Hooker to get the job.

Burnside's modest opinion of his abilities was well founded and his tenure in command of the army was disastrous, culminating in an unnecessary and bloody reverse at Fredericksburg in December of 1862. Although allowed to remain in com-

Coming upon an abandoned gun during the Battle of Antietam, Confederate Maj. Gen. James Longstreet and his staff proceeded to put it into action, serving the piece until a less exalted crew could be gotten together.

A badly chafed heel forced Confederate Maj. Gen. James Longstreet to fight the Battle of Antietam wearing a pair of "clumsy carpet slippers."

As a result of a "personal encounter" with Union Brig. Gen. Jefferson C. Davis on 29 September 1862, Union Maj. Gen. William Nelson died of a bullet in the chest, for which Davis was never brought to account.

Gen. Ambrose Burnside in command during the Federal disaster at Fredericksburg. Though the Confederate position outside of the town was almost impregnable, Burnside ordered costly attacks which only swelled Union casualty lists.

159

Fredericksburg in December of 1862. The town would host two major battles. Burnside attempted to attack the Army of Northern Virginia on the heights behind the town on 13 December 1862 only to fail. Months later, Maj. Gen. John Sedgwick would succeed against a much smaller force in a fight that was an adjunct to the Battle of Chancellorsville 2-4 May 1863.

mand, his fate was sealed by the humiliating "Mud March" the following January, when he persevered in an attempt to flank the Army of Northern Virginia despite extraordinarily heavy rains which made it virtually impossible for the army to move. Burnside now demanded that Lincoln relieve seven generals or find a new army commander. The President removed Burnside, replacing him with Hooker.

Shortly afterwards Burnside was given a departmental command in the Ohio Valley. He did well in this post, taking strong measures against Copperhead activity—including the shadowy "Knights of the Golden Circle" and even capturing the elusive Confederate raider John Hunt Morgan. That autumn, Burnside took to the field with considerable success in order to defend Knoxville from Confederate Lt. Gen. James Longstreet. In consequence, he was restored to command of the *IX Corps*.

During the opening stages of Grant's Overland Campaign in the Spring of 1864, Burnside's corps operated in conjunction with, but not under the command of, Maj. Gen. George Meade's *Army of the Potomac*. Burnside performed his duties well, even after the corps was brought under Meade's direct command. It was Burnside who planned the operation which subsequently became known as the "Battle of the Crater" (30 July 1864). The disastrous outcome of the operation was primarily due to interference on the part of Grant and Meade— 24 hours before the action was to begin they replaced a special-

ly-trained black division with an untrained white one—but Burnside was relieved of command. Kept idle for the rest of the war, he resigned from the service on 15 April 1865.

After the war Burnside grew prosperous in railroading, served three terms as governor of Rhode Island and represented his state in the Senate from 1874 to his death.

A big, genial, impressive looking man with enormous "Burnsides"—whence "side burns"—Burnside was by no means an incapable commander. A good administrator and satisfactory organizer, he was fairly successful as a corps commander, at his best with modest forces. Perhaps no one understood his abilities and limitations better than he did.

The bewhiskered Ambrose Burnside.

Albert Sidney Johnston

Kentucky-born Albert Sydney Johnston (1803-1862), one of nine children, was educated at Transylvania College before entering West Point, from which he graduated in 1826. After a period of garrison duty, he served in the Black Hawk War, before resigning in 1834 to care for his ailing wife. When she died, in 1835, he briefly attempted to take up farming. In 1836 he enlisted as a private in the Army of the Republic of Texas, rising to brigadier general and army commander within a year, despite being seriously wounded in a duel with a jealous subordinate, an injury which left him slightly lame and subject to occasional numbness and pain in his right foot. The following year he was named Secretary of War of Texas. Resigning in 1840, Johnston settled down in Brazoria County. Johnston served briefly as colonel of the *1st Texas Volunteer Foot Rifles* and then as a staff officer during the Mexican War, and was shortly afterwards commissioned colonel in the United States cavalry. Serving in various posts, he was given the newly

formed *2nd Cavalry* in 1855. In 1857 Johnston was made a brevet brigadier general and commanded the so-called "Mormon Expedition" and the garrison of Utah.

The outbreak of the Civil War found him commanding United States forces on the Pacific coast. He soon resigned his commission and was named a full general in the Confederate Regular Army on 31 August 1861, to rank from 30 May. He was shortly afterwards assigned to command all Confederate forces west of the Allegheny Mountains.

While Johnston strove to organize and equip his forces, they were involved in a number of small actions through the balance of 1861 most of which were inconclusive or reverses. Nevertheless, the situation in his department at the beginning of 1862 was satisfactory.

The loss of Forts Henry and Donelson in February radically altered this state of affairs. Concentrating forces from all over the West, Johnston prepared a counterstroke which he deliv-

Albert S. Johnston traveling through the wilderness from California to serve in Confederate ranks. His role in the war would be short as he was killed at Shiloh in April of 1862.

ered at Shiloh on 6 April 1862. Johnston's attack completely surprised Ulysses S. Grant's forces, which nevertheless put up a stubborn fight. At about 2:30 p.m., while directing operations on his left flank, Johnston rode too far forward and was hit in the leg by a musket ball which severed the femoral artery. None of his staff officers having the presence of mind to apply a tourniquet, Johnston bled to death within minutes. The next day Grant, somewhat reinforced, went on to win the battle.

Johnston's death "at the moment of victory" rapidly became part of the legend of the "Lost Cause," the claim being advanced that had he lived, the battle would have been won. In fact, there is little in Johnston's career to justify the oft-stated conclusion that he was a brilliant commander. Indeed, the plans for the Confederate attack at Shiloh were extraordinarily poor: Johnston's corps attacked in successive waves, rather than each on an individual front, so that, had Grant's men been ready, the attackers would have suffered a devastating defeat. As it was, the Confederate forces became so intermingled, that command control was largely lost. At best Johnston was a capable organizer and administrator who never was tested in action.

A Confederate warrior who fell before his skill's could be truly tested, Albert Sidney Johnston.

Daniel Butterfield

One of Union Maj. Gen. Daniel Butterfield's most important services to the war effort—and to American military tradition—occurred one beautifully calm night during the Peninsular Campaign, when, as the *Army of the Potomac* lay encamped at Harrison's Landing, he composed "Taps."

RIGHT:
Roanoke Island's Fort Bartow comes under destructive fire from Federal warships during Burnside's campaign against the Carolina coast.

Soldiers engage in games of chance in a covert casino located in a wood outside Memphis, Tennessee. Though cards and dice were coveted by soldiers to ease the boredom between campaigns, most threw such evidence of their sinfulness away before engaging in battle.

Originally from New York, Daniel Butterfield (1831-1901) studied law and travelled extensively in his youth. At the outbreak of the war he was superintendent of the eastern operations for American Express, of which his father was a founder. He enlisted as first sergeant in, and was subsequently elected colonel, of the *12th New York Militia*, in which Dan Sickles and Francis Barlow also served. This was the first Federal outfit to set foot in Virginia.

He was in the Shenandoah Valley during the Bull Run Campaign and was subsequently promoted brigadier general of volunteers. Butterfield led a brigade in the Peninsular Campaign—subsequently being awarded a Medal of Honor for his services at Gaines' Mill, where he was wounded—and in the Second Bull Run Campaign. He later led a division, and subsequently *V Corps* at Fredericksburg, having risen to major general of volunteers.

Appointed chief-of-staff of the *Army of the Potomac* when Hooker assumed command, he continued in this post under Meade and was badly wounded at Gettysburg. After the battle he engaged in an undignified dispute with Meade as to whether the latter intended to abandon the fight on the night of

1 July, and was removed as chief-of-staff.

Butterfield subsequently served in the West, first as Hooker's chief-of-staff and later commanding a division in the *XX Corps* during the Atlanta Campaign until relieved due to ill-health.

At the end of the war he remained in the regular army as colonel of the *5th Infantry*, but resigned in 1869. He subsequently became a highly successful businessman, confidant of President Grant and world traveler. His skills as an organizer were called upon many times, and he directed Sherman's funeral, the Washington Centennial celebrations and Dewey's triumphant return after the Spanish-American War. A good chief-of-staff, Butterfield performed his duties well, but he allowed his friendship with Hooker to color his relationship with Meade and his conduct after Gettysburg was frankly disloyal to his commanding officer.

Butterfield is responsible for two of the most enduring of American military customs. Based on an idea of Philip Kearny, he designed the badges which each corps in the *Army of the Potomac* wore for identification purposes, a system which was eventually extended to all Union armies, and he wrote "Taps".

A fife and drum outfit serving in the Federal army.

Henry Halleck

A native of New York, Henry Halleck (1815-1872) ran away from home rather than take up farming and was eventually adopted by his maternal grandfather, who saw to it that the brilliant and ambitious young fellow received an excellent education (Phi Beta Kappa, Union College). At West Point Halleck was assigned as an assistant professor even before graduating 3rd in the class of 1839. He entered the engineers and helped design the harbor defenses of New York before touring French coast defenses in 1844. He wrote several important works, including *Report on the Means of National Defense* and *Elements of Military Art and Science* and translated Henry Jomini's *Political and Military Life of Napoleon from the French*. Halleck saw administrative service in California during the Mexican War, emerging with a brevet, and later served as inspector and engineer of lighthouses and on the fortification board for the Pacific Coast. He somehow also found time to help frame the Constitution of the State of California and study law. In 1854 he resigned from the army and founded a major law firm in California. Refusing a judgeship and a U.S.

Senate seat, Halleck devoted himself to his profession, to writing, to business and to the state militia, becoming an authority on mining and international law and quite wealthy in the process.

At the outbreak of the war he was appointed a major general in the regular army at the suggestion of Winfield Scott. Great things were expected of Halleck, but he proved an inept field commander. This fact took some time to become apparent as when he commanded in the West in 1862 his subordinates included Ulysses S. Grant and William S. Rosecrans. Appointed general-in-chief of the army in July of 1862, Halleck's great administrative abilities proved immensely valuable. Despite the fact that he acted more as a clerk-in-chief, he did much to promote a more efficient organization of the army and managed to keep the troops supplied and reinforcements forthcoming, but could have done far more to coordinate the activities of the Union armies. In early 1864 he was replaced by Grant and demoted to the status of chief-of-staff, a task which he performed to perfection. After the war he held various admin-

When none of his staff could tell George B. McClellan how deep the Chickahominy River was, Lt. George A. Custer put spurs to horse, plunged in, rode across, turned around, rode back and, as his mount regained the bank, said "That's how deep it is, General."

Confederate Brig. Gen. Nathan "Shanks" Evans, a fine tactical commander, had an orderly who carried his "barrelita," a special wooden container which held a gallon of whiskey, just in case the general had the need for a drop in the midst of battle.

Maj. Gen. Edwin Vose Sumner, the oldest corps commander in the *Army of the Potomac*, was nicknamed "Bull Head" because a musket ball is alleged to have once bounced off his head.

istrative posts until his death.

Had there never been a war, Halleck—whose pre-war army nickname "Old Brains", conferred in recognition of his great intellectual achievements, was eventually replaced by "Old Wooden Head"—might have remained a soldier of great promise, rather than a great disappointment.

Camille J. Polignac

Rebel and Yankee gunboats engage each other in the naval battle outside Fort Pillow on 6 June. The Federal fleet under Captain Charles Henry Davis annihilated the enemy force and captured the garrison for the Union.

Conferred Maj. Gen. Edward "Allegheny" Johnson, was often called "Old Clubby" because he was wont to lead his troops into battle waving a heavy old walking stick rather than the more traditional sword.

Not inclined to give the benefit of the doubt to a foreigner, Confederate troops referred to Prince Camille Armand Jules Marie de Polignac as "Polecat" until their first battle with him, when he led them into the fray crying "Now you will see whether I am a 'Polecat' or a 'Polignac,' Charge!"

Robert Smalls

Robert Smalls (1839-1915) was born into slavery in Beaufort, South Carolina, and, unusual for a slave, received a rudimentary education, learning to read. In 1851 his master removed to Charleston, where young Smalls was permitted to work as a boatman for day wages. On the outbreak of the Civil War Smalls, who by then was married and had two children, was impressed into the Confederate Navy. He was made steersman of the armed transport *Planter*, which carried goods and supplies to the various forts and installations in the vicinity of

Charleston harbor. As about a dozen of the vessel's crew were fellow-slaves, Smalls soon began to plot an escape.

In the small hours of 13 May 1862 *Planter* was lying at her normal berth, near army headquarters on the Charleston waterfront. Although steam was up, the captain and the other white crew members were all ashore. Smuggling his wife and children aboard, Smalls took command of the ship. Quickly casting off, he steered her boldly for the harbor entrance. Since the little ship was a familiar sight, none of the troops on guard

While there was considerable international tension over the "Trent Affair," when a Union warship removed Confederate officials from a British merchant ship, the crisis was resolved so courteously that in February of 1862 several thousand British troops were permitted to cross Maine on route to Canada, where they had been sent to beef up the garrison in the event of war with the United States.

One of the most important battles of 1862 was fought on 5 May, when 1,500 Mexican troops armed with Brown Bess muskets and Baker rifles—British war-surplus which had been used at Waterloo in 1815—soundly thrashed 7,500 Frenchmen at Puebla, thereby keeping Mexico City in *Juarista* hands for another year.

In response to the American seizure of the British vessel H.M.S. Trent, Her Majesty's *troops are sent to Canada as war with United States seemed inevitable. Fortunately, cooler tempers prevailed and tensions between the two countries eased.*

Curtis King, who was 80 when he joined the *37th Iowa* in November of 1862, was probably the oldest enlisted man in the war, and was further distinguished by having several sons, 20 grandsons and four or five great-grandsons all in blue.

Maj. Gen. William Wilkens of the Pennsylvania state militia was undoubtedly the oldest officer in the war, being 83 when commissioned in 1862.

The troops could always tell when Confederate Maj. Gen. Sterling Price was getting ready to fight, because he invariably wore a certain multicolored plaid hunting shirt which they nicknamed his "war coat."

Rebel raiders in Missouri during a bloody raid against a Unionist town. The guerrilla fights during the Civil War were at times exceptionally bitter and bloody with both soldiers and civilians becoming casualties.

Maj. Gen. Earl Van Dorn.

thought anything amiss as she steamed past in a rather leisurely fashion, Confederate flag proudly streaming behind and whistle tooting in her usual salute. As soon as the ship was out of range, Smalls ordered full speed and headed for the blockading Union warships. As one of the blockaders approached, Smalls hauled down the Confederate colors and hoisted a white flag.

Smalls' exploit made him a hero throughout the North, and a prosperous man as well, for as "captain" he received a sizable share of the prize money which was awarded him and his men. Lincoln promptly appointed him a pilot in the Navy. In this capacity he served on a number of vessels, being cited for courage under fire while serving on the ironclad *Keokuk* during the naval assault on Charleston in 14 April 1863. That Decem-

ber, Smalls was given a ship of his own, thus becoming the first black man to command a ship in the United States Navy.

After the war Smalls returned to his native Beaufort. He served as a Republican in both houses of the South Carolina legislature from 1868 through 1875, when he was elected to Congress. With the exception of the 1879-1881 term, Smalls served in the House of Representatives until 1887, making a reputation as an advocate of civil rights legislation. Thereafter he was United States Collector of the Port of Beaufort during Republican administrations from 1889 to 1913, and as delegate to the state constitutional convention of 1895, he fought a losing battle to preserve the remnants of civil rights for blacks in South Carolina.

Earl Van Dorn

Mississippian Earl Van Dorn (1820-1863) graduated from West Point in 1842. His initial service was on the Texas frontier, where he fought in a number of engagements with the Comanches, incurring four serious wounds in one skirmish. During the Mexican War he was wounded once again, earning two brevets in the process. Remaining in the army after the war, he served on the frontier, in garrison, and against the Seminoles. Transferring to the cavalry, by the eve of the Civil War he was a major in the *2nd Cavalry*, serving under Albert Sidney Johnston and Robert E. Lee.

Resigning upon the secession of Mississippi in January of 1861, he was made a brigadier general of the state militia, and shortly promoted to major general of the militia when Jefferson Davis resigned to become President of the Confederacy. Entering Confederate service as a colonel in March of 1861, Van Dorn served briefly as commander of the Mississippi River forts below New Orleans before being assigned to command the Department of Texas, where he performed the unusual feat of capturing the famed Union steamer *Star of the West*, object of the first shot of the war during her relief attempt at Sumter in January of 1861. Promoted brigadier general in July and major general in September, Van Dorn was shortly transferred from Texas to Virginia and given a division to command and, incidently, being entrusted with one of the first three Confederate battle flags. The following January he was assigned to command the Trans-Mississippi Department, which he did with little success, culminating in the Confederate reverse at Pea Ridge (7-8 March).

Once again transferred, Van Dorn was given overall direction of the Army of Mississippi, entrusted with the defense of his home state and particularly Vicksburg, and also of the Army of Western Tennessee, which was supposed to defend

the western portions of that state. Defeated at Corinth (3-4 October 1862), Van Dorn was superseded and assigned to command the cavalry of the Army of Mississippi, under John Pemberton. It was at this point that Van Dorn, hitherto not particularly successful, began to show some promise as a commander.

Van Dorn's cavalry proved extremely adept at interfering with the supply lines of Union Maj. Gen. Ulysses S. Grant, greatly impeding his efforts to capture Vicksburg, most notably by his capture of the Federal supply depot at Holly Springs in December of 1862 and the action at Thompson's Station the following March. As a result, Van Dorn was rapidly emerging as one of the war's better cavalrymen when, on 7 May 1863, an irate husband walked into his headquarters and gunned him down.

A small, handsome, elegant man, Van Dorn, like many Civil War commanders, proved a failure largely because he was promoted beyond his abilities. Starting out as an army commander, a post for which he lacked the administrative skill and strength of character, Van Dorn did not find his niche until the war was nearly two years old. Death overtook him just as he was beginning to develop as a cavalry commander.

One unusual aspect of the Confederate attack on Corinth, Mississippi, on 3 October 1862 was the fact that there was an earthquake as the troops were moving into position.

When asked why he never touched alcoholic beverages, Stonewall Jackson remarked, "Why, sir, because I like the taste of them, and when I discovered that to be the case I made up my mind at once to do without them altogether."

When some of his troops seemed hesitant under fire at the Battle of Winchester (Sunday, 25 May 1862), Confederate Brig. Gen. Richard Taylor shouted "What the hell are you dodging for?" whereupon Stonewall Jackson, who "never condoned cursing, especially on the Sabbath" turned to him and in a mild voice said "I am afraid you are a wicked fellow."

Carl Schurz

A native of Rhenish Prussia, Carl Schurz (1829-1906) was educated at the universities in Cologne and Bonn. In 1848 he abandoned his doctoral studies and served the German Revolution as a junior officer. Upon the defeat of the revolution he fled, first to Switzerland and then to France. Expelled from France, he lived briefly in England and then migrated to the United States in 1852. He began a career as an orator and politician with a strong anti-slavery message, settling in Wisconsin.

At the start of the war he was minister to Spain, but resigned in 1862 to urge immediate emancipation of the slaves. Lincoln demurred, but made Schurz a brigadier general of volunteers, a political move designed to enhance German-American support for the war. Schurz led a division with some ability in the Second Bull Run Campaign. Made a major general in March of 1863, his division performed poorly as part of *XI Corps* at Chancellorsville that spring. At Gettysburg he briefly commanded the corps, but neither it, nor his division performed with brilliance, though he did manage to hold the line on Cemetery Hill on 2 July. Later that year Schurz went West with his division, where it again did poorly at Chattanooga. Relieved, he spent the next year in administrative posts and stumping the country for Lincoln's reelection. Later he served ably as chief-of-staff to Maj. Gen. Henry W. Slocum's *Army of Georgia*.

After the war Schurz became one of the most prominent political leaders in the country, championing a variety of progressive causes, and one of the few steadfast spokesmen for black civil rights in print, on the podium and in the Senate. His political influence was enormous, particularly wherever there

were large numbers of German-Americans, and there are probably more monuments to his memory in more different places than any other Civil War figure of comparable rank.

Sentries maintain a lonely guard over shallow graves of soldiers killed during the Battle of Antietam.

Elizabeth Cooper Vernon of Philadelphia was so proficient in the use of firearms and in the manual of arms that, at the start of the war, she was engaged to drill a company of young men who had volunteered for service.

At least one woman served as a "drummer boy" during the Civil War, a resident of Brooklyn named Emily, who disguised herself as a boy and enlisted in Michigan, serving in the *Army of the Cumberland* until mortally wounded at Lookout Mountain.

When, at Corinth, Mississippi, on 30 May 1862, a Union officer refused to permit some Sanitary Commission workers to provide his brigade with fresh water, an imperious female voice was heard to cry "Halt!" which the troops immediately did, much to the chagrin of their commander, who knew the fate of those who crossed "Mother" Bickerdyke.

When questioned by some Indiana troops as to whether she was "Secesh" or "Union," an old mountain woman replied, "A Baptist, an' always have been."

Allan Pinkerton, head of intelligence for the *Army of the Potomac*, is said to have evaluated the suitability of women to serve as agents by means of phrenology.

The aftermath of battle, a hospital for those wounded and crippled by the tools of modern war.

168

The Women

Clara Barton

For many people the war was a liberating and maturing experience. Under the pressures of the conflict, many men and women who were of little note rose far above the ordinary. One such was Clara Barton (1821-1912), a native of Massachusetts. Nothing in the first forty years of her life suggest anything but the ordinary. Trained as a teacher, Clarissa Harlowe Barton was working as a clerk in the Patent Office when the war broke out. Appalled at the lack of facilities for the troops, she began, voluntarily and unofficially, to minister to the casualties in the field. Often arriving while the fighting was still going on, Barton was frequently under fire—a wounded man was once killed in her arms—and her skirts were several times pierced by bullets. She developed and supervised a network of volunteer nurses and welfare workers. By the end of the war she was Superintendent of Nurses to the *Army of the James* and charged with compiling a master list of missing troops, which helped identify numerous unknown dead. After the war Barton went on to found the American Red Cross, served once more in the field during the war with Spain, wrote and lectured.

Lincoln

"In the Matter of Nathaniel Gordon"

It required the personal intervention of Abraham Lincoln to get Congress to authorize the enlistment of chaplains of the Jewish faith.

One day, finding that the entire Cabinet was opposed to a proposal which he had made, Lincoln smiled and said "The measure passes by a majority of one."

Although the importation of slaves into the United States was banned in 1808, the trade was too lucrative to be halted entirely. As a result, an unknown number of Africans were brought into the United States as slaves right down to the end of the Civil War. To be sure, efforts were made to suppress this illicit trade, and under an act of 1820 engaging in the slave trade was classed as piracy, punishable by death. But, as with the drug trade in contemporary society, parochial interests and corruption made such laws difficult to enforce. Although by treaty, Britain's Royal Navy was charged with enforcing the international ban on the slave trade, British seamen were loath to intercept vessels wearing the American flag due to the often testy relations between the two nations. Thus, all that a slaver had to do was run up the "Stars and Stripes" to be secure against search and seizure. The United States Navy did, of course, have its own anti-slavery patrol, but this was more of a token force than a determined effort. Hampering American efforts to stop the slave trade was the fact that a significant proportion of the nation was devoted to the "peculiar institution." As a result, even when slavers were caught "red handed" they were rarely brought to trial, and never convicted. That is, until 1861, with the Civil War well underway.

The first—and only—person convicted under the 1820 act was Nathaniel Gordon, caught by the naval blockade while trying to run a cargo of slaves into the Confederacy in late 1861. Gordon was given the maximum sentence. Appeals followed, but at each level the sentence was confirmed, even by pro-slavery Chief Justice Roger B. Taney. As a last resort, Gordon's lawyers penned an appeal to Lincoln for executive clemency. The President responded:

> . . . if this man had been guilty of the worst murder that can be conceived of, I might perhaps, have pardoned him. You know the weakness of my nature, always open to appeals of repentance or of grief; and with such a touching letter, and such recommendations, I could not resist. But any man who would go to Africa and snatch from a mother her children, to sell them into interminable bondage, merely for the sake of pecuniary gain, shall never receive pardon from me."

On 21 February 1862 Nathaniel Gordon became the first, and only, person in American history to be hanged as a slave trader. The importation of slaves into the United States did not cease until the Civil War was over.

President and Mrs. Lincoln greet visitors during a New Years Day reception at the White House.

Incident at the Navy Yard Hospital

The suffering caused by the war grieved Lincoln greatly. He often visited the more than forty military hospitals in the vicinity of Washington to speak with the wounded and offer what comfort he could. One such occasion was on 27 September 1862, little more than a week after Antietam.

It was a Saturday, and the president set out early, intending to visit as many hospitals as possible. Beginning with that at Georgetown University, he visited hospital after hospital until, towards evening, he arrived at that at the Navy Yard. As the President passed among the wounded men, he chanced to come upon a badly wounded Confederate, "little more than a child." Lincoln knelt by the boy's bedside, exchanged a few words with him and said a silent prayer. Then Lincoln passed on to sit with other men. After a time the tired President took his leave, and left the hospital.

As Lincoln was entering his carriage one of the nurses came out and said that the dying Confederate boy had asked to see him again. Though tired and drained, the President left his carriage and returned to the boy's side.

"What can I do for you?" asked Lincoln.

In a barely audible voice the boy replied, "I am so lonely and friendless, Mr. Lincoln, and I am hoping that you can tell me what my mother would want me to say and do now."

Kneeling once more at the soldier's bedside, Lincoln said, "Yes, my boy, I know exactly what your mother would want you to say and do. And I am glad that you sent for me to come back to you. Now, as I kneel here, please repeat the words after me."

Then, slowly, the dying soldier repeated the words which his only friend uttered in a soft, weary voice:

Now I lay me down to sleep,
I pray the Lord my soul to keep.
If I should die before I wake,
I pray the Lord my soul to take.
And this I ask for Jesus' sake.

President Lincoln on a visit to the Army of the Potomac *in October of 1862 to impress Gen. McClellan to move on the offensive.*

War and Society

Blacks in the Ranks

Black men were involved in some of the earliest actions of the Civil War. Indeed, Nicholas Biddle, a black freeman from Pottsville, Pennsylvania, was widely regarded as the first casualty by Rebel action. Biddle was injured by a brick-bat on 18 April 1861 when the *27th Pennsylvania*, in which he was serving as an officer's orderly, was attacked by a Baltimore mob, one day before the more-widely publicized attack on the *6th Massachusetts*. And, indeed, when Lincoln issued his call for volunteers, black men immediately offered themselves for service. Black volunteer companies were rapidly organized in New York, Boston and Cleveland; a battalion was offered in Washington. However, public sentiment was by no means favorable. Moreover, such a move might have had an explosive effect on the wavering loyalties of the slaveholding Border States. As a result, all such offers of service were rejected.

Though Frederick Douglass and other black leaders tried to keep the issue alive, little progress was realized for more than a year. Only gradually, as casualties mounted and as the issue of emancipation came to the fore, did the hostility towards blacks in the ranks ease. In July of 1862, Congress authorized the President to raise black troops and formal authority to raise black regiments was granted by the War Department on 25 August 1862. But even before that black men had begun to don the uniform of the Republic.

The first black unit raised for Federal service was the *1st South Carolina Volunteers*, organized by Brig. Gen. David Hunter on the Carolina sea islands beginning on 7 May 1862. Political considerations soon caused the regiment to be disbanded, though *Company A* continued in existence informally until the regiment was reactivated that November, by which time other black regiments had already mustered in. Meanwhile, the Navy had been enlisting blacks for over a year: as early as August of 1861 black men were serving as gunners on Union warships. The first properly authorized black unit in Federal service was the *1st Kansas Colored Volunteers* (later the *79th U.S. Colored Troops*), which began organizing in July of 1862, although it was not officially completed for service until January of 1863 by which time it had already been in action.

The first full black regiment to be mustered in was the *1st*

Louisiana Native Guards, authorized by Maj. Gen. Benjamin Butler, on 27 September 1862, an outfit which had actually been raised for Confederate service in 1861 by the free black men of the state. Additional regiments of this corps were on duty by the end of the year.

The Emancipation Proclamation removed all formal obstacles to black recruitment, though the racism of individual commanders and political leaders often impeded efforts to raise troops in particular areas.

The first black military organization to enter combat was the *1st Kansas Colored Volunteers*, at Island Mounds, Missouri, on 29 October 1862. Black troops participated in an increasing number of actions. Over the next eight months they served with particular distinction at the Siege of Port Hudson (27 May-9 July 1863) and the Battle of Milliken's Bend (6-8 June 1863), where black recruits beat off an assault by superior numbers of Confederate veterans. However, public recognition was long in coming, until the black *54th Massachusetts* lost over 25 percent of its strength in the attempt to storm Fort Wagner, on Morris Island, S.C., on 18 July 1863.

Black troops served well, despite considerable discrimination

Most of the officers in black regiments were white. Nevertheless, about 75 black men—some estimates place the figure as high as 100—held commissions as officers, mostly in company grades in the Louisiana regiments. Nine black men attained the rank of major and one became a brevet lieutenant colonel, Dr. Alexander T. Augusta, a Canadian physician who gave up a lucrative practice in Toronto to fight for the Union. In addition, Lt. Col. William N. Reed of the *1st North Carolina Volunteers* (*35th U.S. Colored Infantry*) was widely considered to have been "bound to both races by the ties of consanguinity."

The 54th Massachusetts makes its gallant but fruitless charge against the ramparts of Fort Wagner guarding Charleston harbor. The gallant deeds of the regiment inspired the 1989 film, Glory.

and mistreatment. Until nearly the end of the war the pay for black enlisted men was $10.00 a month, regardless of rank, from which $3.00 were deducted as a clothing allowance, leaving but $7.00, little more than half what white private soldiers earned—the *54th Massachusetts* refused to accept any pay until the inequity was rectified. Moreover, black troops often found themselves doing more than their fair share of fatigue duties. They were involved in about 5 percent of the combat actions of the war, about 450 engagements, including some of the most sanguinary, such as Olustee (20 February 1864). Indeed, statistically black combat casualties were 35 percent higher than white, partially because of a Confederate penchant for massacring blacks captured in arms. About two dozen black men—both army and navy—were awarded the Medal of Honor. During the last two years of the war black troops served in every theater, and were particularly important in the Mississippi Valley, where they constituted a significant proportion of Federal forces.

Altogether 178,975 black men were recruited for the armies, of whom 2,751 were killed in action, mortally wounded, or murdered by Confederate troops. Black troops amounted to roughly 12 percent of total Union manpower at the end of the war, by which time the "black iron hand" of the Federal armies amounted to 120 infantry regiments, seven cavalry regiments, a dozen heavy artillery regiments and ten batteries of light artillery, for a total of 140 regiments. It was the largest black army that had ever been seen.

Afro-Americans who served with the Federal army during the Civil War. Some are Northern freemen, others are escaped slaves.

Afro-American troops at drill after their participation in the catastrophic battle for the Crater at Petersburg in 1864.

Comparative Strength of the Armies

Attempting to compare the strengths of the armies at various periods in the war is rather difficult. While the total number of men enrolled at any given time is relatively easy to ascertain, the number available for operations is much less so. Both armies suffered a great deal from desertion. By some estimates 300,000 Yankees and 200,000 Rebs went over the hill during the war, and possibly far more. In the Confederate Army it was not unheard of for troops to desert during the winter and return to duty in the spring. In addition, many men were often on detached duty. As a result, the number of men present for duty was always less than the number enrolled. At the end of the war, when Union manpower was officially 1,000,516, fully 202,709 men were listed as "absent"—20.2 percent! The two armies also differed as to the way in which they tabulated

manpower available for duty, with the Confederate figure omitting, for example, about 7 percent of the men when compared with the Union base of calculation. A final complicating factor is that forces on garrison and occupation duty might be relatively far from the fighting, but nevertheless included in the figures of those present for duty. On this table the column "Enrolled" includes everyone who was carried on the rolls of the armies on the date given. The figure "Present" excludes deserters and men in hospitals. However, this figure includes troops assigned to garrisons and occupation duty. Thus, in January of 1863 about 190,000 Union troops were committed to holding Washington and securing lines of communication in Maryland, West Virginia, Virginia, Kentucky, Western Tennessee, Northern Mississippi, and Missouri, so that over 25

The first income tax in American History was instituted by the Union on 1 July 1862, a measure which was copied in the Confederacy nine months later.

The first national conscription law in American history was passed by the Confederate Congress on 16 April 1862.

Compared to the numbers of men in the armies, the manpower of the sea services —navy, marines, revenue service— was relatively insignificant. Officially there were 132,544 enlistments in Union forces afloat. The United States Navy peaked at some 50,100 men at the end of the war, including about 3,500 Marines. Total enlistments in the Confederate sea services were probably between 12,000 and 15,000 men, although the peak strength of the Confederate Navy appears to have been about 5,000, plus about 1,000 Marines, figures attained in early 1864.

percent of the Union troops available for service were rendered non-effective by perhaps 30,000 Confederate guerrillas and partisans. This was one reason why the Confederacy was able to muster 75-80 percent of Union strength in most battles, despite the considerably greater Union manpower.

Rounded figures are estimates based on incomplete data. The figure given for the Confederacy on 1 January 1861 is for the South Carolina militia and volunteers; that for the following 1 April is for troops already mustered into Confederate Service, including some 5,000 at Charleston and about 2,000 at Pensacola, but omits some troops still under state jurisdiction, perhaps another 5,000 in South Carolina alone. Union figures for these two dates are for the Regular Army only, a call for volunteers not yet having been made.

TOP RIGHT:
A Southern portrait of German soldiers that served in the Yankee armies. Many Confederates maintained an intense hatred of the German immigrants who served in Federal ranks calling them "Hessians."

An assortment of camp punishments created to instill discipline in the volunteers who wanted to play at war.

The Units

The 1st Minnesota

Generally regarded as the first regiment to be accepted for Federal service, the *1st Minnesota* was offered by Alexander Ramsay on 14 April 1861, even before Lincoln's first call for volunteers had gone out, and was promptly accepted by Secretary of War Simon Cameron. Two weeks later, on 29 April, the *1st Minnesota* mustered in for three years service under Col. Willis A. Gorman. After a brief period of training, the regiment "took the cars" to Washington, reaching the capital on 26 June, thereby making what would be the longest journey of any regiment to join the Eastern armies. This regiment, which

for a long time wore a distinctive black uniform with red shirt and black hat, was the only Minnesota outfit in the East during the war and fought in every battle of what would become the Army of the Potomac, from First Bull Run to Appomattox.

At First Bull Run, the *1st Minnesota* was a brigade in Col. Samuel P. Heintzelman's *3rd Division*, which formed the Federal right, and sustained the heaviest casualties of any Union regiment in the battle, 180 men. During the battle the regiment refused to leave the field until being ordered to do so three times. The following October, the regiment formed the

In order to provide a landing force to support the Union river flotilla on the Mississippi, the *Mississippi Marine Brigade* was formed from army volunteers in mid-1862, comprising the *1st Battalion Mississippi Marine Brigade Infantry*, the *Mississippi Marine Brigade Light Artillery Battery* and, inevitably, the *1st Battalion Mississippi Marine Brigade Cavalry*: appropriately enough, the "horse marines" were raised in Missouri.

The *131st* and *133rd New York*, which mustered into Federal service in July of 1862, were recruited largely through the efforts of the New York City police, who later also helped raise the *161st*, *173rd* and *174th New York Infantry* and the *14th New York Cavalry*.

Guilty of thievery and cowardice, a soldier is ceremoniously drummed out of the ranks.

175

At Shiloh the 2nd Texas fought in un-dyed uniforms which greatly resembled shrouds, eliciting remarks such as "Who were them hellcats who went into battle dressed in their graveclothes?"

Though the *53rd New York* ["The d'Epineuil Zouaves"] was recruited by Col. Jobert d'Epineuil in August of 1861 for three years service, it proved so full of goldbrickers, drunks, brawlers and rowdies that it was discharged the following March.

Confederate troops pause at a ford to roll up trousers and take off shoes before crossing.

One of the fortifications pro-tecting Richmond along the James.

The Confederate Regular Army

On 6 March 1861 the Confederate Congress enacted legislation providing for the creation of a regular army for the Confederacy and authorizing Jefferson Davis to raise as many as 3,000 men in order to support the South Carolina state troops investing Ft. Sumter at Charleston. Recruitment for this force was never seriously undertaken and it never amounted to much, as most Southerners preferred their state volunteer regiments in the "Provisional Army of the Confederate States," the equivalent of the Union's "Volunteer Army."

Despite this, Davis persisted in maintaining the fiction that there existed a regular establishment, in order to lay the foundation for the post-war period. Davis believed that after the war the Confederacy would require a regular force of about 10,000 men, including a half-dozen infantry regiments, a cavalry regiment, an artillery corps, an engineer corps, and various staff departments. At the start of the war six general officers were commissioned in the regular service, as were many members of the various staff corps, usually before passing into the Provisional Army. In addition, several regiments were actually activated.

Altogether seven infantry regiments, five cavalry regiments and a battery of light artillery were actually raised in the regular army in addition to small bodies of specialized troops plus four provisional regiments and two battalions of engineers. These formations were mostly activated through the conversion of existing state units or the merger of small contingents from several states. There is considerable confusion in tracing the ctivities and history of these organizations. Changes in desig-

nation were common, and some units are sometimes referred to as battalions and at others as regiments. Enumeration was erratic, so that a perusal of the *Official Records* reveals mention of eleven regiments and two battalions of cavalry plus seven regiments and five battalions of infantry, which were in reality all the same five cavalry regiments and seven infantry regiments in various manifestations, guises and redesignation.

In the end, it seems likely that perhaps 750 of the men enrolled in the regular establishment during the war were officers, including the six senior-most men in the Confederate Army, Samuel Cooper, Albert Sidney Johnston, Robert E. Lee, Joseph E. Johnston, Pierre G.T. Beauregard and Braxton Bragg, who ranked as generals, the only grade above colonel. Probably no more than 1,000 men were in organized formations at any one time and only about 5,000 were ever enrolled, of whom fully 1,279 deserted. Only one regular outfit was with the Army of Northern Virginia, the 1st Provisional Engineer Regiment, serving from its organization in the Spring of 1864 to Appomattox. Only two Regular Army formations achieved any distinction. The 5th Confederate Regiment, a sort of "foreign legion" composed of men of many different nationalities, but mostly Irish, fought under Gen. John B. Hood in Tennessee in 1864. The 8th Confederate Battalion, raised from Yankee prisoners of war and colloquially known as the "Galvanized Yankees," performed yeoman service in covering the escape of the Confederate government through North Carolina in the period after the fall of Richmond, holding Salisbury for a day against a Union cavalry division.

Confederates of G.B. Anderson's Brigade attempt to subdue a Yankee sutler in order to pillage his expensive wares.

The Pennsylvania Bucktail Regiments

Three of the bravest and most effective regiments in the Union Army bore the collective nickname "Bucktails." When Lincoln made his first call for volunteers in April of 1861, the response in Pennsylvania was so enthusiastic that the state's quota was rapidly oversubscribed by over 30 per cent. For political reasons, then-Secretary of War Simon Cameron refused to accept the additional men into Federal service. Rather than turn them away, Gov. Andrew G. Curtain had the great foresight to convince the state legislature to foot the bill to enroll, equip, train and maintain them as state troops. Thus was born the *Pennsylvania Reserve Corps*, comprising thirteen fine infantry regiments, which were eventually mustered into Federal service as the *30th* through *42nd Pennsylvania Volunteers*. The entire corps formed a division in *V Corps* which proved one of the toughest formations in the *Army of the Potomac* until mustered

out in early 1864. It was, however, the *13th Pennsylvania Reserves*—the *1st Pennsylvania Rifles* or the *42nd Pennsylvania Volunteers*—which became famous as the *"Pennsylvania Bucktails."*

The *13th Pennsylvania Reserves* was recruited as a rifle regiment from among the hardy lumbermen and backwoodsmen of the wild northern part of the state—one company whitewatered down to the regimental rendezvous. Before a man would even be considered for service he had to produce a bucktail in proof of his marksmanship. The regiment's nickname, "Bucktails," derived from the habit the men had of fastening this trophy to their hats. Initially armed with a variety of rifles, each man providing his own favorite shooting iron, the regiment was equipped with Sharps breechloading rifles in time for Gettysburg, and later carried Spencer repeat-

Confederate troops attempt to escape the trials of war by enjoying amusements in camp.

Enlisted for occupation and security duty, the *37th Iowa* was composed entirely of men over 45 years of age: the average age was 57, and a few men were well up in their 70s and more.

Pennsylvania Bucktails *display their superior brand of marksmanship against Confederate targets.*

Engaged at close quarters the Pennsylvania Bucktail Rifles *take on a Confederate force under Turner Ashby during the Battle of Harrisonburg.*

ing rifles. Although formally attached to the *Pennsylvania Reserve Division*, the *13th* frequently served in a more or less independent role, as skirmishers and sharpshooters. Indeed, for some months in early 1862 it did not even serve intact. During the Peninsular Campaign, four companies served in the Shenandoah Valley under Col. Thomas L. Kane, later a brigadier general, fighting at Harrisonburg and Cross Keys, while the rest of the regiment fought with the *Army of the Potomac* from Mechanicsville to Malvern Hill. The regiment was reunited in time for Second Bull Run, under Col. Hugh W. McNeil, who was killed at Antietam.

Heavily engaged at Fredericksburg, where it suffered 161 casualties, the regiment, along with the *Pennsylvania Reserve Division*, was shortly afterwards transferred to the defenses of Washington. During the opening phases of the Gettysburg Campaign two of the division's three brigades volunteered for field service. The *Pennsylvania Reserves* rendered excellent service at Gettysburg, and the "Bucktails" were rather seriously engaged around Little Round Top, where Col. Charles F. Taylor was killed.

The regiment went on to serve in the Mine Run and Bristoe Station Campaigns, and in Grant's Overland Campaign in the Spring of 1864, until mustered out on 11 June. In not quite three years of Federal service, the *13th Pennsylvania Reserves* suffered 609 casualties, 52.2 percent of the 1,165 men who served, including 162 battle deaths. A number of men who reenlisted and all those who, having joined the regiment after it had mustered in still had time left on their enlistments, were transferred to the *190th Pennsylvania*, and thus many of the "Bucktails" continued to serve to the end of the war. Meanwhile, additional "Bucktail" regiments had taken the field.

Impressed by the fighting qualities of the *13th Pennsylvania Reserves*, in July of 1862 Secretary of War Edwin M. Stanton authorized Maj. Roy Stone, one of the regiment's veterans, to recruit a "Bucktail" brigade. Acting with commendable speed and efficiency, Stone shortly recruited two full regiments. The *149th Pennsylvania* mustered in at Harrisburg at the end of August, with Stone as colonel, and the *150th* mustered in a few days later under Col. Langhorne Wister. For some time the two regiments served as part of the garrison of Washington, where *Company K* of the *150th* was detailed to provide a bodyguard for the President, which service it performed to the end of the war.

In February of 1863 the regiments were grouped with the *143rd Pennsylvania* as a brigade in *I Corps*, with Stone in command. But lightly engaged at Chancellorsville, the regiments were heavily involved in Gettysburg where they helped open the wall on 1 July and so lost their colonels and lieutenant-colonels there. The *149th* suffered 336 casualties of 450 men engaged (74.7 percent), the *150th* had 264 out of 400 (66.0 percent), and the 143rd 253 of 465 (54.4 percent). The two "Bucktail" regiments served in all the subsequent campaigns of the *Army of the Potomac* until Petersburg, by which time they were in two different divisions of *V Corps*.

In February of 1865 they were transferred to prisoner-of-war guard duty, in which capacity they served until mustered out. Although the two new "Bucktail" regiments never equalled the original in fighting skill, they amassed quite creditable records. Of 1,454 men who served in the *149th*, fully 613 (42.2 percent) became casualties, as did 431 of the 1,008 (42.8 percent) in the *150th*. The "Bucktails" proved themselves to be among the finest fighting regiments in the Union Army.

The Ways of War

The Cavalry

In both armies the cavalry began the war looking to play a glorious role in the grand tradition of the eighteenth century and the Napoleonic Age, as the arm of shock, bringing about a decisive decision on the battlefield. But even in Napoleonic times the boot-to-boot charge with lance and saber was beginning to become a risky venture, and notably so against seasoned troops. By the Civil War the rifled musket had made the cavalry charge not merely risky, but frankly obsolete unless the circumstances were particularly favorable, such as against very green troops. As a result, the cavalry spent much of the war looking for a role. And in the end, it found an excellent one.

As it developed during the war, the role of the cavalry came to encompass a considerable variety of activities. The missions of the mounted arm included conducting reconnaissances, establishing and maintaining contact with enemy forces, screening the movements of friendly forces and raiding against enemy lines of communication. Any serious fighting was best done dismounted, using carbines and serving as light infantry, though the saber and the pistol and even the shotgun, were useful in mounted skirmishes.

The cavalryman's favorite role was raiding, for it gave him a chance to run free, causing as much destruction as possible and avoiding the monotonous burdens of patrol duty. Moreover, raids tended to catch the attention of the public, already inclined to be overly fond of the troopers. However, while raids sometimes could have a useful effect on the course of a campaign, they were distinctly less important than reconnoitering and screening before the army. These were missions which never ended, for the need to seek out information on the enemy, and to deny it to him, never ceased. Thus, unlike the infantry and the artillery, which relatively speaking had plenty of time to spare between campaigns, the cavalry worked most of the time. Not in combat, but in patrolling, scouting and serving on picket. These were boring, grueling tasks which placed a heavy burden on the troopers and an even greater strain on their mounts. Casualties among the horses were always higher than those among their riders and a regiment could easily run through two or three issues of horses in a year.

The organization of the cavalry was very similar on both sides. A Union regiment consisted of a headquarters and twelve companies, which could be organized into three battalions of four companies or six squadrons of two companies as the situation dictated. At regimental headquarters the officers included a colonel, a lieutenant colonel, three majors, three lieutenants serving respectively as regimental adjutant, quartermaster and commissary and a surgeon with his assistant. The headquarters staff included a sergeant-major, three sergeants serving respectively as quartermaster, commissary and saddler, a farrier (blacksmith) and two hospital stewards. Each company had a captain, a first and second lieutenant, a first sergeant, a quartermaster sergeant, a commissary sergeant, five other sergeants, eight corporals, two teamsters, a wagoner, two farriers, a saddler, two musicians and about 70 troopers.

The youngest officer in the war was undoubtedly E.G. Baxter (born 10 September 1849), who enlisted in the Confederate 7th Kentucky in June of 1862 and was made a second lieutenant when not quite 14.

Stuart's command crosses the Potomac into Virginia after an October 1862 raid into Pennsylvania. The troopers confiscated horses and other supplies from the Yankees during a jaunt that successfully embarrassed Union commanders.

During 1862 the *Army of the Potomac* had an average of 28 wagons for every 1,000 men.

A photograph of the archetypical Federal cavalryman serving in the Western Theatre.

A Federal scouting party on the move in the placid waters of the Potomac.

A Confederate cavalry regiment normally consisted of a headquarters and ten companies. On paper, at least, the headquarters staff was virtually identical to that of the Federal regiment, though with only two majors. Each company was supposed to have a captain, three lieutenants, five sergeants, four corporals, a farrier and his assistant and about 85 troopers. On paper then, the Union cavalry regiment had about 1200 men, while the Confederate one ran to only about 900. In practice, however, the number was far less, due to casualties and a lack of replacements. At Gettysburg, for example, Union regiments averaged a little more than 360 men and Confederate ones about 280.

In both armies several regiments formed a brigade. Federal brigades had from three to six regiments and Confederate ones normally about five, but occasionally as few as two. In rare instances a battery of horse artillery was attached to a brigade, but this was more normally found at a higher level. In both armies the usual cavalry division was composed of two or three brigades, and a division of, say, 3,600 troopers with two batteries. All of this usually occupied about four miles of road. J.E.B. Stuart's Cavalry Division in the Army of Northern Virginia eventually grew to six brigades plus a large contingent of horse artillery. This proved rather clumsy and soon after Gettysburg the division was reorganized as a corps.

The cavalry of the *Army of the Potomac* had been formed into a corps of three divisions and a sizeable contingent of horse artillery by Maj. Gen. Joseph Hooker in February of 1863, a move marking the beginning of the maturation of the Federal cavalry, which until then had been significantly inferior to that of the Army of Northern Virginia.

Since the Regular Army had six regiments of cavalry at the start of the Civil War (the *1st* and *2nd Dragoons*, the *Regiment of Mounted Rifles* and the *1st*, *2nd* and the newly raised *3rd Cavalry*, which were respectively redesignated the *1st* through *6th Cavalry* in August of 1861, with devastating effects on

morale) it might have been expected that the Union cavalry would have been more effective, at least at the onset of the war, than was that of the Confederacy. However, this was not the case, for the regular regiments had important duties to perform on the frontier. There was also a relative shortage of good riding stock and a relative lack of riding skills in the comparatively urban North. More importantly, the Union was tardy in forming brigades and divisions of cavalry, which left the mounted forces without centralized direction.

It was the Southern cavalry which first developed as an efficient combat arm. And the South benefitted from the fact that some of her sons were among the finest cavalrymen ever known, such as Turner Ashby, who died early, Nathan Bedford Forrest, a gifted amateur in the West who was perhaps the only Confederate cavalryman who really understood that war meant damaging the enemy more than securing personal glory, the youthful Joseph Wheeler, another "westerner" and famed J.E.B. Stuart, who served with the Army of Northern Virginia. With such leadership, the Confederate cavalry developed an

early and significant edge over that of the Union, an advantage which it maintained for much of the war.

Eventually, of course, excellent cavalrymen began to emerge in the Union ranks, men such as John Buford and Elon Farnesworth, who died soon after attaining high rank, Alfred Pleasanton, who started in the East and ended up in the Trans-Mississippi, Benjamin Grierson and James H. Wilson, who distinguished themselves in the West, and Judson Kilpatrick, George A. Custer and Philip Sheridan, who distinguished themselves with the *Army of the Potomac*.

By the time of Vicksburg and Gettysburg the Federal cavalry had matured to the point of being able to stand up and trade blows successfully with that of the Confederacy. This was due partially to the creation of distinct cavalry corps, which put all the troopers in an army under one central direction for operational purposes, and partially due to the introduction of the Sharps carbine, which gave the Union troopers a considerable advantage in firepower.

The first indication of this maturity in the West was Benjamin H. Grierson's raid from La Grange, Tennessee, to Baton Rouge, Louisiana, a seventeen day, 800 mile expedition which wrecked havoc with the Confederate rear-area in April of

BOTTOM:
A detachment of Texas cavalrymen on patrol in northern Virginia.

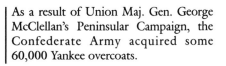

As a result of Union Maj. Gen. George McClellan's Peninsular Campaign, the Confederate Army acquired some 60,000 Yankee overcoats.

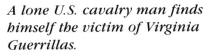

A lone U.S. cavalry man finds himself the victim of Virginia Guerrillas.

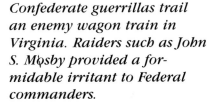

Confederate guerrillas trail an enemy wagon train in Virginia. Raiders such as John S. Mosby provided a formidable irritant to Federal commanders.

1863, during the opening phases of Grant's final drive on Vicksburg. In the East the change was signaled by Brandy Station (9 June 1863), at which the Yankee troopers surprised J.E.B. Stuart's cavaliers and then, in the long, involved action which followed, pretty much gave as good as they got. Then came all the little cavalry skirmishes along the Blue Ridge and South Mountain chains in the early phases of the Gettysburg Campaign, in which the Yankees came off the better more often than not. This newfound skill and determination became particularly evident when, during this same campaign, Stuart, in order to restore the luster to his bruised reputation, took most of his men off on a raid into Maryland and Pennsylvania, disappearing from Lee's sight for over a week. Though Maj. Gen. Alfred Pleasanton, commanding the *Cavalry Corps of the Army of the Potomac*, was neither as brilliant nor as spectacular a trooper as was Stuart, he did his job, keeping his three divisions close in hand, screening before the advance of the army and seeking out the enemy. As a result, Lee was taken totally by surprise when Henry Heth ran into Union cavalrymen on the Chambersburg Pike northwest of Gettysburg on the morning of 1 July. Stuart tried to set things aright with his attack against Union communications along the Hanover road on the afternoon of 3 July, but his troopers were outfought and

outridden in a crazy melee fought on foot and horse. The old edge had gone, and gone forever.

RIGHT:
Federal Cavalry plunges into a sharp contest with Rebel skirmishers outside of Fairfax Courthouse, Virginia.

Anti-slavery guerrillas who fought in Kansas and Missouri, the Jayhawkers. Though fighting for the Union, Jayhawkers were a vicious band of looters who sacked whole towns robbing loyalists and secessionists alike.

Organizations in Service

The regiment was the basic unit of military organization in the Civil War. Because the military policy of the Union differed from that of the Confederacy it is difficult to gain a accurate notion of the number of regiments which were in service during the war.

This exercise is complicated by a number of factors. To begin with, in the first months of the war, many regiments were mustered into Federal service for only three months. Upon discharge, they often re-enlisted for a longer term, usually for three years, but two years, one year and even nine months were not unheard of. Furthermore, from time to time during the war, short-service militia regiments were called into service, often for as little as two weeks. In some cases such regiments had mustered once or twice before. An additional complication is that the Union continuously raised new regiments, rather than maintain existing ones at full strength through infusions of fresh manpower. This practice inflated the number of regiments, and at the same time had a pernicious effect on the

efficiency of the army, for veteran outfits were allowed to waste away to nothingness, to be replaced by often totally green ones. Only three states avoided this practice, preferring to send new troops to flesh out veteran regiments: Minnesota and Iowa activated few new regiments after August of 1862, and Michigan ceased raising new regiments after December of 1862. Further confusing the figures is the fact that from time to time regiments were disbanded or converted to another arm. No finer example may be found than in the case of one West Virginia regiment: the *2nd Virginia* was organized in November of 1861, and became the *2nd West Virginia* the following year, then the *2nd West Virginia Mounted Infantry* in June of 1863, which became the *5th West Virginia Cavalry* in January of 1864!

As if this were not sufficiently confusing, a number of formations appear to have been credited to more than one state, so that, for example, the *11th Wisconsin Battery* later became *Battery L, 1st Illinois Light Artillery*, while *Company D of the*

69th New York, was composed of Irishmen from Chicago. Finally, most of the black regiments originally raised as state volunteers were transferred to Federal service: thus, the *1st Kansas Colored Volunteers* became the *79th United States Colored Infantry*, while the *22nd Regiment, Corps d'Afrique*, became the *94th U.S.C.I.*

The situation in Confederate service was considerably better. Enlistments, initially for one year, were extended for the dura-

tion in the spring of 1862. In addition, there was a fairly constant flow of new manpower into depleted regiments, which kept effectiveness high: as the French had learned in their revolution, amalgamating green men with seasoned ones turns them into good soldiers rather quickly. There was, to be sure, some transfer of regiments between the state volunteers in the Provisional Army and the small Regular Army, and there was some redesignation of units from time to time, which tend to complicate tabulating the number of regiments, but the situation is far less cloudy.

If one equates separate battalions and companies into regiments the Union mustered about 2,070 regiments of all types, while the Confederacy had about 765. However, it is important to note that for both armies, no account has been taken of state troops, militia, or home guards unless mustered into national service: thus two regiments of the Georgia line which rendered outstanding service to the Confederacy during the Atlanta and Carolina Campaigns are omitted, as are many New York and Pennsylvania militia regiments who turned out to help stem Lee's invasion of Pennsylvania in 1863. In addition, marines are not included, though both sides raised the equivalent of several battalions, some of which saw service in the field from time to time.

* * *

The troops in Federal regiments raised by the separate branches of the service were normally credited to the individual

The battle flag of a Confederate infantry regiment measured 48″ by 48″, while that of a Union regiment was 72″ by 78″.

Early in the war the Union armies were using 600 different types of artillery ammunition.

LEFT:
Citizens of the Empire State who answered Lincoln's call for troops, men of the 71st New York at Camp Douglas.

BOTTOM LEFT:
Continuously humiliated by Stonewall Jackson during his 1862 campaign in the Shenandoah Valley, ragged and dejected members of Freemont's Army proceed to their next defeat.

Federals take time off from the war to enjoy what pleasures they can on Christmas of 1862.

RIGHT:
Southerners of Company A of the 5th Georgia Infantry.

Hardfighting Westerners of the 21st Michigan. While their counterparts in the East faced defeat or uncertain and costly victories, the Western armies racked up impressive wins at places like Pea Ridge, Forts Henry and Donelson, and Shiloh.

states or territories, although raised entirely by the Federal government. The Regular Army was, of course, the permanent standing military force of the Federal government, which expanded considerably during the war: indeed, several regular infantry regiments—and all heavy artillery regiments—ought to be counted as more than one regiment since they contained 24 companies rather than the normal ten.

The United States Volunteers included two categories of troops, sharpshooters and so-called "Galvanized Yankees," Confederate prisoners-of-war who volunteered for service against the Indians rather than endure the pleasures of POW camps, who more correctly should be called "Galvanized Confederates." The Corps d'Afrique was a term used for black regiments raised in Louisiana and vicinity before they were incorporated into the United States Colored Troops, many of whom had originated as state regiments. The Veteran Volunteers was supposed to be a special corps recruited from among physically fit discharged veterans, who were relieved of some onerous duties: designed to entice seasoned men back into the ranks, the experiment was not a success. The Veteran Reserve Corps was composed of veteran soldiers unfit for serious combat, but able to perform various less onerous military duties.

Confederate Indian Regiments:
Aside from Indians who served in state regiments, each side

recruited in the Indian Territory, known today as Oklahoma. Union Indian troops, mostly Cherokees and Creeks, were organized for self-defense purposes. The Confederacy recruited from a number of different tribes, all of which had Southern roots, and most of which were at least technically slaveholding. The Indian troops recruited for Confederate service were:

Cherokee: 1 Bn infantry, 2 Rgts mounted rifles
Chickasaw: 1 Rgt and 2 Bns cavalry
Choctaw: 3 Rgts infantry, 2 Rgts cavalry
Creek: 2 Rgts infantry
Mixed: 1 Rgt mounted rifles
Osage: 1 Rgt infantry
Seminole: 1 Rgt cavalry

These were organized into three brigades:
1st: the Cherokee, Chickasaw and Osage units.
2nd: the Choctaw units, about 1,000 men.
3rd: the Creek, Seminole and mixed units.

The 1st Indian Brigade was commanded by Stand Watie, a Cherokee who was the first American Indian to achieve general's rank. Note that, as with many Confederate cavalry and mounted infantry outfits, the Indian troops occasionally found difficulties in securing horses. As a result, by the end of the war some of the mounted outfits were serving as infantry.

Ballooning

The ancient dream of flight was not achieved until 5 June 1783, when the Montgolfier brothers launched a hot air balloon, with the first manned ascent taking place on 21 November. The military potential of the balloon was recognized quite early. In 1793 the armies of Revolutionary France began to make use of balloons for observation and reconnaissance. Military use of balloons grew as the years went by. In 1849 the city of Venice became the first to be subject to what is generally considered a twentieth century horror, aerial bombardment. By mid-century, ballooning had become relatively commonplace, with commercial and sporting applications as well as military. As a result, on the outbreak of the Civil War a number of people came forward to offer their services as "aeronauts."

Maj. Hartman Bache, a grandson of Benjamin Franklin, was among the first to talk the War Department into considering the use of balloons. Availing himself of the services of John Wise, a balloon "manufacturer" from Lancaster, Pennsylvania, Bache procured a varnished raw silk balloon for $850. This reached Washington in July of 1861, shortly before First Bull Run. Entrusted to the care of Maj. Albert J. Myer, the Chief Signal Officer, the balloon proved less than useful—Myer tried to tow it fully inflated into a position from which he could observe Confederate movements during the battle. As a result, he missed the battle entirely, and the thing tore in the bargain. Sent back to Washington, the balloon was repaired, but broke its tether one day and had to be brought down by rifle fire, thus technically becoming the first victim of anti-aircraft fire. Although he was hardly to blame for Myer's lack of experience, Wise received no further orders from the War Department.

Not that there was a shortage of prospective suppliers.

Even before Bull Run, Brig. Gen. Benjamin Butler, commanding at Fortress Monroe on the Virginia coast, had been approached by John LaMountain with a proposal to use balloons for reconnaissance. A native of Troy, New York, LaMountain, was a former seaman who had gained some fame as a prewar aeronaut. Among his achievements was a flight of 1,100 miles eastwards from St. Louis in only 24 hours. On 31 July LaMountain went aloft from the fortress and provided valuable information on Confederate dispositions in the vicinity. This was only the beginning, and he made several more ascents over the next few months, even using the armed transport *Fanny* to tow his balloon into position, technically making her the first aircraft carrier in history. Among his other achievements were the first nighttime reconnaissance flights, during which he estimated Confederate numbers by counting campfires, a trick which the wily Rebels quickly caught on to and promptly imposed history's first "black out." However, there were those who questioned the value of LaMountain's work, charging that much of the information which he supplied was unreliable, a matter which is difficult to determine more than a century after the fact. In any event the army parted ways with him in early '62.

The most important Civil War aeronaut was "Professor" Thaddeus Lowe. Only 29 at the start of the war, Lowe had already established a reputation as an inventive and daring balloonist, with a number of long-range voyages to his credit and several transatlantic attempts as well. On June 1861 he lofted his *Enterprise* 500 feet above the Capitol building to

Holding the map is Professor T.S.C. Lowe with his father. Lowe was a pioneer in the field of aerial reconnaissance during the Civil War.

Professor Lowe, an aeronaut in the service of the Army of the Potomac, *inflates his balloon* Intrepid *for a reconnaissance mission during the Battle of Fair Oaks.*

the largest being the 32,000 cubic feet *Intrepid*, which had an envelop of 1,200 yards of silk and cost $1,500.00. Hundreds of ascents were made, including several by McClellan himself. In addition to using wagon-mobile balloon equipages, Lowe made extensive use of the barge tender *George Washington Parke Custis*—named after Robert E. Lee's father-in-law—which was fully equipped to service and launch balloons, thus also technically being even more qualified to be termed the first aircraft carrier. As always, experience proved the best teacher. It was quickly found that free balloons were too unreliable and dangerous. Nor was great altitude of particular value. Although a tethered balloon could easily reach 1,500 feet, with a view in excess of 50 miles, 300 feet was militarily far more useful, at which the view was 15 miles. Dawn was the best time for reconnaissance, as the observer could locate enemy positions and estimate manpower on the basis of breakfast campfires. Balloons proved useful for engineers interested in mapping terrain, observing fixed defenses, locating bridging sites in anticipation of advances, and similar work. In addition, balloons were of some use in helping to spot artillery fire, a feat which Lowe accomplished for the first time on 24 September 1861, when he directed mortar fire against some Confederate patrols in the environs of Washington, communicating with the gunners by telegraph. The presence of balloons with the *Army of the Potomac* caused the Confederates to somewhat modify their activity in camp, so they also had a nuisance value. Although the Confederates often fired on balloons, they never managed to bring one down. Indeed, there was greater danger in being part of the ground crew, since fire directed at the balloon often landed among them. Amazingly, although Lowe's balloons used hydrogen, none ever seem to have accidentally gone up in flames.

demonstrate the capabilities of balloons, telegraphing a message to Lincoln in which he described the view. This convinced the president of the potential usefulness of balloons. As a result, the United States Balloon Corps was set up, with Lowe at its head despite some bureaucratic opposition. The bureaucrats were right in a number of ways. The balloons had limited mobility. When deflated they could be moved with relative ease, but could not be lofted at need, as the larger ones required several hours to inflate, while inflated balloons could be towed behind wagons, but only at very low speed. A further disadvantage was that generating sufficient hot air to inflate a balloon was a long and difficult process. This latter problem was resolved when Lowe invented a portable gas generator which permitted the use of more efficient, if more dangerous, hydrogen.

Despite the drawbacks, balloons had their uses, as was soon demonstrated in the Peninsular Campaign. The U.S.B.C. used seven balloons during the campaign with considerable success,

The Confederacy also developed an interest in ballooning, though their efforts were hampered by a lack of resources. Despite romantic tales, the few Confederate balloons which did see service were not made from silk dresses. There would have been far too many small panels and an excessive number of seams which even the best varnishing would have proven difficult to make leak proof. The Southern aeronautical effort was under the command of Capt. Edward Porter Alexander, the Chief of Ordnance of the Army of Northern Virginia, and former associate of Union Maj. Albert J. Myer in the creation of the Signal Corps. The balloons were first built by Dr. Edward Cheves of Savannah, an old experimentor.

The first Southern aeronaut, however, was Lt. John R. Bryan, who's enthusiasm for the service appears to have declined in direct proportion to the number of ascents he made. During the Peninsular Campaign two balloons were used at Richmond, which had a municipal gas works. They were in-

Alas for romance, it is not true that the last silk dresses in the Confederacy were captured by the Federals on 4 June 1862, during the Peninsular Campaign, in the form of a stray balloon which had been made through the generosity of the ladies of Richmond.

George B. McClellan's movement of the bulk of *The Army of the Potomac* by water from Washington to the Virginia Peninsula in late March of 1862 was the largest seaborne movement of troops in history until World War I.

The Intrepid *makes an ascent as Professor Lowe undertakes a mission to investigate Confederate positions. Lowe could communicate information to the ground through the use of a special telegraph.*

flated at the gas works and towed to their observation position by locomotive, a far more effective mode of transport than wagons. An attempt was also made to use river boats to tow balloons around. This was abandoned when the armed tug *C.S.S. Teaser* ran aground and its precious cargo fell into Yankee hands on 4 July 1862. The crew of one of the Rebel balloons had an exciting afternoon once when they became the object of the attentions of three rounds from a 3″ Rifle which Union Capt. Thomas W. Osborn of *D Battery, 1st New York Light Artillery* had rigged for high angle fire. The Rebel aerostatists were, however, able to avoid gaining the dubious distinction of becoming the first fliers to be shot down in flames.

During the Seven Days, the Confederate captured three of Lowe's inflating mechanisms, but made no use of them. In addition to operations at Richmond, at least one balloon was employed at Charleston in the Spring of 1863, under the direction of Charles Crevor, but it caught an unfortunate wind one day and drifted off never to be see again.

The use of balloons was most extensive in early and mid-1862. Many Union commanders were very enthusiastic about them. McClellan, Fitz John Porter, Irvin McDowell and Benjamin Butler all made ascents. But the numerous problems attendant upon the use of balloons limited their effectiveness. In addition, there was considerable bureaucratic in-fighting over administrative control of the U.S.B.C. At various times it was under the authority of the Corps of Topographical Engineers, the Quartermaster Corps and the Corps of Engineers, while it battled with the Military-Telegraph Corps over control of telegraph apparatus and with the Signal Corps over control of signals. This squabbling did much to impair the efficiency of the balloon corps. Nevertheless, by the spring of 1863 over 3,000 ascents had been made, mostly in the Eastern Theater, although one balloon did see service in the West. Then in May of 1863, Maj. Gen. Joseph Hooker cut Lowe's salary, reduced his staff, interfered with his operations and subordinated him to the Corps of Engineers. Frustrated, Lowe, who, it must be said, was not easy to get along with and careless about his bookkeeping, resigned on 8 May. Without him the U.S.B.C. rapidly declined and it was disbanded in June of 1863, by which time the Confederates had long since abandoned the use of balloons for lack of resources.

FAR RIGHT:

A frigid reveille in a Federal camp. The winters in both the West and East could be exceptionally bitter with some troops freezing to death on numerous battlefields. (Courtesy of the West Point Museum Collections, United States Military Academy, West Point, New York)

A sluggish army on the move. Baggage trains and gun carriages attempt to negotiate the mire of a muddy road during an advance.

Machine Guns

By the mid-nineteenth century technology had progressed to the point where the dream of a self-loading, continuous firing gun was finally within reach. By the time of the Civil War several inventors were working on machine guns and they made serious efforts to get the armies to adopt their devilish devices, with little success. Five of these weapons are of particular interest.

Ager Union Repeating Gun: The Ager was a crew served, crank operated, hopper fed piece firing pre-capped .58 caliber metallic cartridges at about 120 rounds per minute. Lincoln witnessed a test firing in June of 1861 and immediately dubbed it the "coffee mill" gun, a nickname which stuck. He also bought 10 of them that October at $1,300 each and McClellan acquired another 50 in December at about $735 apiece. Altogether 63 were made, including the demonstration models. There is some rather unreliable evidence that the Ager gun was first used in action by the *28th Pennsylvania* while on picket along the Potomac in January or February of 1862. This same regiment definitely used one in action on 28 March 1862 in a skirmish at Middleburg, Virginia, when, according to observers, some Confederate cavalry was cut to pieces at 800 yards. Despite this, the regiment's commander, Col. John W. Geary—who later proved a capable division commander—soon returned the pieces in his charge with the comment that they were "inefficient and unsafe to their operators." Some use was made of the Ager gun during the Peninsular Campaign. The *56th New York* employed a battery of the wheeled guns at Yorktown in April of '62 and several—possibly the same battery—were used at Gaines' Mill (27 June). While there was some satisfaction over the resultant destructive effects on the enemy, this was not sufficient to justify wider use of the weapon. Nevertheless, since the pieces were on hand, they were occasionally used through to the end of the war, notably by the navy on the Mississippi and during the protracted investment of Petersburg. The Confederacy acquired several Ager guns, two being taken by Brig. Gen. Isaac R. Trimble's North Caro-

lina Brigade at Gaines' Mill after a hard fight, and about a dozen by Stonewall Jackson when he seized Harper's Ferry in September of 1862, but there is no record of their being put to any use. Although the Ager gun had some value, it was a clumsy device, and dangerous to use, being prone to misfires. In addition, the breech seal was not very good and fragments of cartridge casing were often scattered about. William Tecumseh Sherman was slightly wounded in this fashion in early 1863.

Bellinghurst-Requia Battery Gun: This piece was invented by

Requia, a man but vaguely known, and promoted by Bellinghurst, who came from New York, but is equally ill-known. Their device was essentially a somewhat modernized version of the late medieval *ribauld*. It had 25 breech loading barrels laid alongside each other at a slightly divergent angle to provide some "spread" to the bullets. The bullets, standard musket rounds, were fixed so as to project from a rod-like clip which had a powder train running along its length which could be set off by a single percussion cap. Upon firing, the spent clip was discarded and another put in its place. With practice, a crew of

Federals go into battle.

The Confederate defenses at Ft. Henry on the Tennessee River were so badly designed that, when some Federal naval officers rowed over to accept the surrender of the place on 6 February 1862, their boat floated right through the sally port, the Tennessee River being then in flood.

When the Orleans Guards, a Louisiana volunteer battalion, went into action at Shiloh, they discovered that their stylish blue uniforms had the unfortunate effect of causing their Rebel comrades to mistake them for Yankees, so they reversed their coats and fought all day with the white linings showing.

The 21st Massachusetts *and* Hawkin's Zouaves *rush Confederate fortifications on Roanoke Island.*

three could get off seven volleys in a minute—175 rounds. The principal flaws were that the powder train was exposed to the weather, burned irregularly in the best of circumstances and could misfire. As a result, the piece, which was mounted on a light artillery-like carriage, saw only limited use by Union forces in the defense of covered positions, such as bridges, hence its name "covered bridge gun".

Gatling Machine Gun: The first version of Dr. Richard Gatling's machine gun was used by Union forces on an experimental basis. A crew served weapon, it had good rate fire, initially about 250 rounds per minute using paper wrapped caliber .58 caliber musket cartridges, which were gravity fed from a hopper, while a crank operated the firing mechanism, rotating the six barrels to avoid overheating. With the introduction of metallic cartridges the rate of fire could be increased to 600 rounds per minute. However, the device had a number of flaws, not least of which was that Gatling found his Southern

origins an obstacle to securing a proper hearing. In addition, the piece was heavy, being mounted on a light artillery-type carriage. There were also some technical flaws, the most notable being a difficulty in aligning the barrels to the chamber. The early model resolved this by making the diameter of the base of the barrels greater than that of the .58 caliber chambers, and tapering the bore towards the muzzle, which meant that the rounds had poor velocity and accuracy. These bugs might have been worked out, but Gatling's factory burned down after only a few pieces had been produced. By the time Gatling got back into production it was 1864 and interest in machine guns, never very great, had declined. Nevertheless, he was able to demonstrate a somewhat more advanced model to Maj. Gen. Benjamin Butler. Impressed, Butler prodded Massachusetts into buying a dozen at $1000 apiece and these were used with limited success during his operations against Petersburg. In early 1865 Gatling demonstrated a much improved tentially bottle up David G. Farragut's ocean-going vessels in the river. In addition, she was a powerful reinforcement to the defenses of Vicksburg.

Realizing the danger which *Arkansas* posed, Farragut acted swiftly, knowing that she would need time to effect repairs. That very night he ran the fleet past Vicksburg once again, concentrating part of his fire on *Arkansas* as she lay alongside the river bank. Although the damage inflicted by the fleet was relatively light, repairs took rather a long time. Not until 3 August was *Arkansas* again ready for "sea." By that time she was desperately needed to support an attempt to retake Baton Rouge from the Yankees.

Arkansas sortied on 4 August, without the Yankees learning of it. Things went well at first and, unpursued, she steamed steadily down river. But the next day her engines began to give trouble and she had to anchor in order to effect repairs. On the morning of 6 August she raised steam again and was making good progress when her engines once more gave out, virtually within sight of Baton Rouge. As nothing could be done to get her going again, and with a Federal squadron led by the powerful ironclad *Essex* approaching, *Arkansas* was abandoned and burned. Union domination of the "Father of the Waters" was never thereafter threatened by Confederate warships.

Stephen H. Mallory, Secretary of the Navy for the Confederacy. Mallory was instrumental in the creation of the C.S.S Virginia which wreaked havoc upon a Federal fleet in the Hampton Roads.

U.S.S. Monitor and C.S.S. Virginia

Ironclad warships began to come into vogue shortly before the outbreak of the Civil War, with France and Britain having several in service and other powers striving to catch up. As a result, both the Union and Confederate navies very early began to consider acquiring such for their own use.

It was Confederate Secretary of the Navy Stephen R. Mallory who made the first move. Since the Union retained virtually the entire prewar navy, the South would always be hopelessly behind in conventional warships. By quickly beginning to build ironclads, the Confederacy might gain an immediate advantage over the Union, permitting it to break the blockade. Under Mallory's prodding, the Confederate Congress appropriated $2,000,000 for ironclads. Mallory immediately authorized the reconstruction as an ironclad of the hulk of the frigate U.S.S. *Merrimack*.

Merrimack, one of the most powerful conventional warships in the world when completed in 1855, had been burned and sunk at the Gosport Navy Yard when Union forces evacuated the place on 20-21 April. There were many technical problems to overcome in order to realize the completion of this project. Although the precious drydock had survived intact, most of the facilities at the Gosport yard had been severely damaged or destroyed. In addition, the South had slender iron working facilities—only the Tredegar Iron Works in Richmond were capable of producing armor plate—and little in the way of a steam engine industry. Nevertheless, Mallory acted with commendable speed. Within a short time he had collected an effective team to oversee the work, consisting of John Porter, an experienced naval architect, William Williamson, a naval

engineer and John Brooke, a former officer in the United States Navy and an inventive ordnance specialist.

The sunken hulk of the frigate was raised on 30 May and work began at once. The vessel was cut down almost to the waterline, while her engine—which had been none too good before the ship was torched and had now been subject to five weeks immersion— was refitted and lowered deeper into the hull. Eschewing traditional superstructure and rigging, a sloping casemate structure was built just above the waterline, and a broad flat deck extended outwards from this, overhanging the hull. There were may delays in converting the vessel. Not only did Tredegar take until February of 1862 to produce the 723 tons of armor required, but a shortage of suitable flatcars hampered its delivery plate. The ship was finally ready for service in March of 1862.

As completed, the newly rechristened *C.S.S. Virginia* was 275 feet long and had a 38.5 feet beam. She drew 22 feet, was top-heavy, not very maneuverable and slow: as a 4,600-ton frigate her engines were barely sufficient to propel her along at nearly nine knots, as an ironclad the vessels displaced over a thousand tons more and she could barely make 7.5 knots. *Virginia*'s casemate was built up with 30″ of pine, covered by 4″ of oak, over which were laid two layers of 2″ iron plates, all at a 35 degree angle to help deflect shells. In addition, there were 1″ iron plates extending below the waterline under the overhang to protect the hull: this was supposed to extend nearly two feet, but as completed was barely 6″ deep. The ship had ten guns: a 7″ muzzle loading rifle on a pivot at the fore and the after end of the casemate, plus three 9″ Dalghren smoothbores and one 6″ rifled muzzle loader along either side. She also had a 1,500 pound cast iron ram fixed to her bow.

Finding a crew for *Virginia* was difficult. No officer was appointed to command her, so that Lt. Catesby ap Rogers Jones, was technically in command. The other officers were all mostly Old Navy men as well. But there was a shortage of common seamen in the South. About 80 old salts were released from regiments in the Norfolk-Suffolk area, but most of the ship's crew of about 300 were landsmen. On 8 March *Virginia* was ready for her trials, which would also be her first operational sortie, with Cdr. Franklin Buchanan, commanding the James River defenses, aboard and acting as captain. Buchanan was an Old Navy veteran who had resigned in anticipation of the secession of his native Maryland, only to try to withdraw it when Maryland remained loyal!

Accompanied by a couple of small gunboats, *Virginia* steamed slowly into Hampton Roads at about 1:00 p.m on that Saturday, making slowly for the nearest of the blockading Union warships, two old sailing vessels, the 50-gun frigate *Congress* and the 24-gun sloop-of-war *Cumberland*. Fire was opened at about 2:00. In the ensuing engagement, *Cumberland* was rammed, *Virginia's* iron beak wrenching loose in the process, while *Congress* was run aground and set on fire. *Cumberland* went down at about 3:30, with her guns still firing and flags still flying. Meanwhile, *Virginia* continued to pound *Congress*, killing McKean Buchanan, brother to Franklin, who was himself wounded in the exchange. At about 4:30 *Congress* struck, but some infantry regiments on the shore nearby kept up such a heavy fire on *Virginia*, that Lt. Catesby ap Rogers Jones, who had assumed command from Buchanan, resumed firing on the helpless vessel. By this time three powerful steam frigates attempted to intervene but ran aground. *Virginia* tried to approach *U.S.S. Minnesota*, a sister of the old *Merrimack*, but the tide was ebbing and she could not get close. It being about 5:00 p.m., Jones decided to retire. In some three hours of combat, *Virginia* had suffered superficial damage, including a leak when her ram had been wrenched off, which reduced her already low speed still further. About a score of her crew had been injured in the engagement, in which hundreds of Union seamen had become casualties. *Virginia* steamed slowly back up the Elizabeth River.

At dawn the next morning the little Confederate flotilla sortied once again, making for Old Point Comfort, where *Minnesota* was still firmly aground. Lying near the grounded warship was an odd looking raft-like object with a boxy projection. It was the Union's first ironclad, *U.S.S. Monitor*.

With recent developments in Europe in mind, and some information about Confederate intentions, Union Secretary of the Navy Gideon Welles proposed the construction of iron-clads in May of 1861. In August the Navy advertised for proposals and 17 were received. A board appointed to examine the proposals deemed two likely prospects and construction of these was authorized. One was an ironclad steam frigate, which became *U.S.S. New Ironsides*, one of the most successful ships of the war, and the other was an ironclad gunboat, *U.S.S. Galena*, which was to prove unsuccessful.

The designer of *Galena*, Cornelius Bushnell, asked John Ericsson, the distinguished naval architect and inventor—among other things, he had perfected the screw propeller—to review his proposal and perhaps give him some advice. Ericsson approved Bushnell's plan, and then showed him a dusty model of a peculiar looking ironclad vessel, which he claimed to have once offered to French Emperor Napoleon III: no record of such an offer has ever been found in French archives. This vessel was to be built entirely of iron, with a very low freeboard and virtually no superstructure, save for a large revolving turret with two 11″ guns.

Ericsson, who had a long-standing feud with the Navy Department, had not bothered to submit his design for consideration, but Bushnell immediately recognized its revolutionary nature. He pulled some strings and got Ericsson some introductions which led, after much acrimony, to a $275,000 money-back guaranty contract to build the vessel. Ericsson did it in 124 days: the ship was laid down at a slip on what is now Monitor Street in Greenpoint, Brooklyn, on 25 October 1861, was launched on 30 January 1862, and commissioned on 26 February. *U.S.S. Monitor* was completed on time and under budget, though not to specifications, Ericsson ignoring a clause which required that she be rigged as a sailing vessel.

The new ship was unique. Displacing a little less than a thousand tons, she looked like a 172′ long, 41′6″ wide raft on which was perched a 20′ wide and 9′ high turret. The only other features were two 6′ tall smokestacks, two 4′6″ air intakes and a pilot house which jutted about the same height above the deck forward. The ship was heavily armored, with nine 1″ layers of plate on the gun port covers and eight on the turret sides. The hull was plated with 2″ to 4.5″ and the decks had 1″. Although designed for eight knots, she could make only about six, and had barely 14 inches of freeboard, so that she was awash in anything but a flat calm. *Monitor* had only two guns, huge 11″ smoothbores. She had a crew of 58 officers and men under Lt. John L. Worden, U.S.N.

After a few trials in New York harbor, *Monitor* steamed for Hampton Roads on 6 March 1862. She arrived there on the night of the 8th, just in time to see *Congress* blow up spectacularly. Taking station to protect *Minnesota* she awaited the morrow.

There is little to say about the celebrated *"Monitor-Merri-*

Lincoln's Secretary of the Navy, Gideon Welles.

Among the many technical innovations on the famed U.S.S. Monitor, is the often overlooked fact that she was the first warship to have flush toilets.

Although the famous clash between *U.S.S. Monitor* and *C.S.S. Virginia* on 9 March 1862 ushered in the age of ironclad warships, neither vessel suffered a single man killed or permanently injured.

RIGHT:
The U.S.S. Cumberland *is devastated by a galling fire from the C.S.S. Virginia. The naval battle at Hampton Roads demonstrated the inability of wooden vessels to take on ironclads. (Courtesy Civil War Library and Museum)*

Dueling Ironclads. The awkward U.S.S Monitor *fights the equally strange C.S.S. Virginia to a stalemate in the first fight between ironclads in military history.*

mack" duel. It began at about 9:00 a.m. and for two hours the two ships, neither of which was very speedy nor very maneuverable, fired on each other and circled around, with little effect. Each attempted to ram, and *Monitor* once managed to deliver a glancing blow to her adversary, with little effect. At about 11:00 *Monitor* broke off the action for a time in order to bring more ammunition up from her magazine into the turret. About half an hour later she returned to the fray. Soon afterwards a lucky shot struck *Monitor* in the pilot house, temporarily blinding Worden. His second-in-command, Lt. Samuel D. Greene, was in the turret at the time, and the ship drifted off into the shallows, temporarily out of action, before he could assume command.

Seeing the foe drifting away, *Virginia* turned her attention on the nearby *Minnesota*, opening a devastating fire which set her ablaze and sank one of the tugs trying to get her off the shoals. With his ship burning about him, Capt. G.J. Van Brunt let loose a full broadside at the Confederate vessel, 23 guns of 8″, 9″ and 10″ caliber. Every round struck *Virginia* square, and every one bounced off. Just as it seemed *Virginia* was about to make an end to the wounded frigate, *Monitor* returned to the fray. They again circled each other, firing away with little effect. Finally, riding high as her coal was depleted, *Virginia* broke off the action, shortly after noon and steamed away. The battle was over.

In about three hours of pounding each other, both ships had taken some damage. *Monitor's* pilot house had been badly battered, while some of *Virginia's* armor had been severely

strained by her opponent's 11″ balls. Casualties had been few, even Worden recovered within a few weeks. Tactically it had been a draw. But it need not have been so, for *Monitor* was using reduced charges in her 11″ guns. Later experimentation would demonstrate that charges twice the size of those used were possible, and it is probable that had such been used at Hampton Roads that morning *Virginia* would have suffered grievously. As it was, both sides came away claiming the honors of the day.

There was never a rematch, and, indeed, neither vessel ever fought again, both coming to sad ends: *Virginia* was blown up on 9 May, after an operational life of but two months, when the Confederates evacuated the Norfolk area, and *Monitor* foundered in a gale off Cape Hatteras on 31 December 1862,

where her hull was recently rediscovered and is now the object of intense study.

Although tactically a draw, the first battle between ironclads had important strategic consequences. *Virginia* was, after all, unable to break the Yankee hold on Hampton Roads, which permitted the Peninsular Campaign to go on and furthered the blockade of the South. And, of course, the engagement was decisive for the introduction of the iron warship.

The turret of *U.S.S. Monitor* was made by the Novelty Iron Works.

So radical was John Ericson's proposed warship *Monitor*, that his contract with the Navy included a clause requiring repayment of all monies advanced if she was unable to steam at 8 knots for 12 miles.

LEFT:
Within the hull of the Virginia, *cannoneers train their sights on the turret of the Federal ironclad* Monitor.

BOTTOM LEFT:
U.S.S. Monitor *and C.S.S.* Virginia *exchange blows during the fight in Hampton Roads. The contest would be the last for both ships as the former would be lost in a gale and the latter destroyed when the Confederates lost the naval yard at Norfolk. (Courtesy Civil War Library and Museum)*

Gunners in the turret of the Monitor *unleash a blast at the* Virginia *during the epic confrontation between the two ironclads.*

Leading a charge against the outnumbered 23rd and 47th Virginia Regiments at Kernstown, Col. Erasmus B. Taylor audaciously rides into the ranks of the enemy at the head of his troops.

Although the Medal of Honor was the only decoration officially authorized by Congress for general distribution, a number of other decorations were granted during the war. These were mostly awarded by cities or towns or on the authority of particular commanders. The "Fort Sumter and Fort Pickens Medal" was awarded by the New York Chamber of Commerce to the 168 men who had held these two posts in 1861. The "Kearny Medal" was created by the officers of Maj. Gen. Philip Kearny's division in his memory and Maj. Gen. D.B. Birney, who had succeeded Kearny, created the "Kearny Cross," some hundreds of which were awarded for valor, including two to battlefield nurses, Ann Ethridge and Marie Tebe. Brig. Gen. Quincy Gillmore awarded several hundred of his "Gillmore Medal" to enlisted men involved in operations around Charleston, South Carolina, in mid-1863. Maj. Gen. Benjamin Butler awarded 200 medals—known as the "Butler Medal"—to black troops of the *XXV Corps* for distinguished conduct at New Market Heights and Chaffin's Farm in September of 1864. The "*XVIII Corps* Medal" was created by Maj. Gen. James B. McPherson in late 1863 for troops of his command. A number of other localities granted decorations, as did several regiments, but none were awarded in great numbers.

202

also for "distinguished soldierly conduct." And in the Navy it could be awarded for heroism not connected with combat, such as rescues at sea. As a result, the Medal of Honor was granted for deeds which would today merit a considerably lesser decoration.

Nearly 2,400 Medals of Honor were awarded during the Civil War, many on the most dubious pretexts—the entire *27th Maine* received it on one occasion—and often as a result of political pull. In 1916 a review board was convened which disallowed hundreds of such questionable awards, including that to Dr. Mary Walker, which was restored in 1977. As a result, the official awards of the Medal of Honor for the Civil War are:

Personnel Awards	Awards Ratio per 1000	
	Enlisted	Battle Deaths
Army 1,199	0.59	12.6
Navy 310	3.67	146.0
USMC 17	2.53	114.9
Dr. Walker 1		

TOTAL 1,527

Some idea of the manner in which the Medal of Honor was awarded during the Civil War can be gained by considering the Gettysburg Campaign. From the time the armies left the Rappahannock lines on 9 June, through 26 July 1863, when they returned, there were some 65 awards of the Medal of Honor. Nearly 60 of these were for deeds performed during the battle itself, the highest number of awards for a single engagement in history. The reasons for some of the awards are frankly enigmatic. Thus, 2nd Lt James K. Durhen, of Company E, *17th West Virginia*, received one for his conduct at the Battle of Winchester (14 June) during which he "led his command over the stone wall, where he was wounded." Many awards went to men who captured Confederate battle flags, fifteen for this reason to men who were on Cemetery Ridge on 3 July, the record being held by the *19th Massachusetts*, which received four, followed by the *14th Connecticut*, with three. Several went to men who saved the colors from the enemy, and many to soldiers who rescued wounded comrades from imminent capture. A great many were awarded for the defense of the artillery, particularly on 2 July. Thus, 2nd Lt. Edward M. Knox, who held his *15th New York Battery* in position until he was down to one gun, which he helped drag to safety despite being severely wounded, and Bugler Charles W. Reed, of the *9th Massachusetts Battery*, who prevented the capture of the wounded battery commander, and Capt. John B. Frasset of *Company F, 23rd Pennsylvania*, who led his regiment to the relief of a beleaguered battery, retaking it from the Rebels all received one. A number of officers received the Medal of Honor for refusing to leave the field despite severe wounds, most notably Lt. Col. H.S. Huidekoper of the *150th Pennsylvania*, on 1 July. Six men received the Medal of Honor for one incident, when, on 2 July, Sgt. John W. Hart and five other volunteers of the *6th Pennsylvania Reserves* braved intense fire to storm a log cabin which was sheltering five Rebel snipers near the Devil's Den, capturing them all.

Some of the awards are poignant, such as that to Pvt. Jefferson Coates of *Company H, 7th Wisconsin*, who, on 1 July, displayed "unsurpassed courage in battle, during which he had both eyes shot out." Several awards were for consistent distinguished conduct under fire, most notably that to Sgt. Harvey M. Munsell of *Company A, 99th Pennsylvania*, who received his for "gallant and courageous conduct as color bearer," a feat which he performed through 13 separate engagements during the war, and those to Col. Joshua Chamberlain of the *20th Maine* who helped defend Little Round Top and to Brig. Gen. Alexander Webb, who held "the Angle."

The people who did not receive a Medal of Honor are almost as interesting as those who did. Lt. Alonzo H. Cushing of *Battery A, 4th Artillery*, who, on 3 July, died defending Cemetery Ridge literally to the last round, did not receive one, though his sergeant, Frederick Fuger, who survived, did. Neither Brig. Gen. Strong Vincent nor Col. Patrick H. O'Rorke of the *140th New York*, who both fell at the head of their troops during the defense of Little Round Top, received one. This was because very few of the awards were made posthumously. Indeed, remarkably few of the awards were made at the time. Most were granted many years later—the last Civil War awards were made during World War I—and were frequently the result of considerable politicking on the part of the awardee and his regimental veterans organization. This was one reason why Maj. Gen. Daniel Sickles received a Medal of Honor for his less than sterling performance commanding *III Corps* on 2 July, while neither Maj. Gen. John F. Reynolds nor Maj. Gen. Winfield Scott Hancock did for their unusually heroic and valuable services. Reynolds died during the battle, and Hancock in 1886, before Medal of Honor collecting became a fad.

On 13 October 1862 the Confederate Congress authorized the award of a decoration to men "conspicuous for courage and good conduct on the field of battle." Such men were to be elected by the troops of their company after each engagement in which the company had been particularly distinguished. No awards were ever made under this provision. However, another measure provided for the publication of a "Roll of Honor" after each engagement, which was to be read to the troops at a formal parade, a practice which continued almost to the end of the war. In addition, about 200 men in both the army and navy received special promotions for "Valor and Skill" under the terms of an act adopted in April of 1862, and a number of officers were voted the "Thanks of Congress."

Irritated by the Federal presence on the Mississippi River, Confederate snipers take shots at an enemy steamer.

War and the Muses

The Battle Hymn of the Republic

Tunesmith who forged the stirring lyrics to the Battle Hymn of the Republic, *Julia Ward Howe.*

Julia Ward Howe (1819-1910), the daughter of a wealthy New York banker and mother of six, was noted as an abolitionist, women's rights advocate, writer, poetess and reformer. Editor, with her husband, Samuel G. Howe, of the abolitionist journal *Commonwealth*, she had several books to her credit before the Civil War. After the war she wrote several more books, became prominent in the international peace movement, and was the first woman elected to the American Academy of Arts and Letters. Despite all of this noteworthy activity, Mrs. Howe is today best remembered for "The Battle Hymn of the Republic."

In December of 1861 Mrs. Howe paid a visit to the *Army of the Potomac* in the company of Governor John A. Andrew of Massachusetts and several other friends. One evening, as their carriage passed among the camp fires of the army, a regiment marched by singing "The John Brown Song." It was an inspiring scene, but the nonsensical words of the song seemed wrong. That night, as Mrs. Howe lay asleep in her bed at the Willard Hotel, some words came to her which somehow seemed more fitting. She got up and jotted them down in the dark. The next day she revised them and thus was born "The Battle Hymn of the Republic."

The song first appeared in print in the February 1862 issue of *The Atlantic Monthly*, for which Mrs. Howe was paid $4.00, a goodly sum at the time. It rapidly became one of the most popular, and certainly the most enduring, of all Civil War songs.

One chilly day late in 1862, a group of Yankees chanced to come upon some Rebels engaged in baptizing a comrade in the Rapidan River, whereupon they joined in the hymn singing.

By mid-1862 Union Army bakeries at Fortress Monroe in Virginia were turning out 30,000 loaves of bread a day.

The Battle Hymn of the Republic

Mine eyes have seen the glory of the coming of the Lord:
He is trampling out the vintage where the grapes of wrath are stored;
He hath loosed the fateful lightning of His terrible swift sword:
    His truth is marching on.

I have seen Him in the watch-fires of a hundred circling camps;
They have builded him an alter in the evening dews and damps;
I have read His righteous sentence by the dim and flaring lamps:
    His day is marching on.

I have read a fiery gospel writ in burnished rows of steel:
"As ye deal with my contemners, so with you my grace shall deal;
Let the Hero, born of woman, crush the serpent with his heel,
    Since God is marching on."

He has sounded forth the trumpet that shall never call retreat;
He is sifting out the hearts of men before His judgement-seat:
Oh! be swift, my soul, to answer him! be jubilant my feet!
    Our God is marching on!

In the beauty of the lilies Christ was born across the sea,
With a glory in his bosom that transfigures you and me;
As he died to make men holy, let us die to make men free,
    While God goes marching on.

1 8 6 2

The Battle-Cry of Freedom

George F. Root wrote a number of important songs during the Civil War, including "Tramp, Tramp, Tramp" and "Just before the Battle, Mother," both of which became quite popular. But his most lasting effort was certainly "The Battle-Cry of Freedom." Written in 1861, the song did not catch on until the following year, by which time it had been popularized by two of the most notable singing groups in the nation, the Lombard Brothers and the Hutchinson Family. The song soon became a favorite among the troops, who often sang on the march and in camp. It is said that Confederate troops during the Seven Days and after Fredericksburg despaired of victory when they heard it being sung by the Yankees despite their recent defeats.

Between those working the streets and those in the approximately 450 "sporting houses," there were an estimated 7,500 "ladies of the evening" in Washington in early 1862.

Among the many activities in which they indulged when they had nothing better to do while in camp, the troops of both armies were wont to pass the time by staging lice races.

The Battle Cry of Freedom

Yes, We'll rally round the flag,
Boys, we'll rally once again,
Shouting the battle cry of Freedom,
We will rally from the the hillside, we'll gather from the plain,
Shouting the battle-cry of Freedom.

Chorus: The Union forever,
　　　Hurray! boys, Hurrah!
　　　Down with the traitor, up with the star;
　　　While we rally round the flag boys, rally once again,
　　　Shouting the battle-cry of Freedom.

We are springing to the call of our brothers gone before,
Shouting the battle-cry of Freedom;

And we'll fill the vacant ranks with a million freemen more,
Shouting the battle cry of Freedom.—Chorus

We will welcome to our numbers the loyal, true and brave,
Shouting the battle-cry of Freedom;
And altho' they may be poor, not a man shall be a slave,
Shouting the battle-cry of Freedom.—Chorus

So we're springing to the call from the East and the West,
Shouting the battle cry of Freedom;
And we'll hurl the rebel crew from the land we love the best,
Shouting the battle cry of Freedom.—Chorus

The imperious "Little Mac,"
George Brinton McClellan.

205

Barbara Fritchie

In July of 1862 the War Department discovered that the Union armies had one musician for every 41 soldiers, a ratio which was soon sharply reduced when regimental bands were abolished.

Since the troops usually preferred something with a little alcohol in it, they often resorted to various time-honored soldier's concoctions, such as "champagne," a fermented beverage made with three parts of water and one of corn and molasses.

One of the most famous Civil War poems, "Barbara Fritchie" is based on an incident which occurred during the Antietam Campaign in September of 1862. The poem itself recounts the tale as legend has it. For it is indeed a legend. However the truth, as recounted by several eye-witnesses, is in its way, even more interesting. As Stonewall Jackson's men were passing through Frederick, Maryland, on 6 September, Mrs. Mary A. Quantrill, the loyalist in-law of the notorious Confederate border-ruffian William C. Quantrill, was standing by her gate with her little daughter, both boldly waving Union flags. At first the troops were annoyed at this, but as Mrs. Quantrill and her daughter persisted, irritation turned to admiration, and a Confederate officer—not Jackson, who passed down another street—saluted, saying "To you, madam, not your flag." Barbara Fritchie, already a fixture of town folklore for having once met George Washington, got attached to the story: her daughter even supplied her with a flag which was pointed out as "the" flag. The tale spread, eventually reaching John Greenleaf Whittier, who wrote the poem in good faith.

Barbara Fritchie

Charge of the 9th New York against the Confederate right at Antietam or Sharpsburg. Despite almost shattering Lee's line, the timely arrival of Southern reinforcements wiped out the gains of the New Yorkers.

Up from the meadows rich with corn,
Clear in the cool September morn,

The clustered spires Frederick stand
Green-walled by the hills of Maryland.

Round about them orchards sweep,
Apple and peach trees fruited deep,

Fair as the garden of the Lord
To the eyes of the famished rebel Horde,

On that pleasant morn of early that fall
When Lee marched over the mountain-wall;

Over the mountains winding down,
Horse and foot, into Frederick town.

Forty flags with their silver stars,
Forty flags with their crimson bars,

Flapped in the morning wind: the sun
Of noon looked down, and saw not one.

Up rose old Barbara Fritchie then,
Bowed with her fourscore years and ten;

In her attic window the staff she set,
To show that one heart was loyal yet.

Up the street came the rebel tread,
Stonewall Jackson riding ahead.

Under his slouched hat left and right
He glanced; the old flag met his sight.

"Halt!"—the dust brown ranks stood fast.
"Fire!"—out blazed the rifle blast.

It shivered the window, pane and sash;
It rent the banner with seam and gash.

Quick, as it fell, from the broken staff
Dame Barbara snatched the silken scarf.

She leaned out the window-sill
And shook it forth with a royal will.

"Shoot if you must, this old gray head,
But spare your country's flag," she said.

A shade of sadness, a blush of shame,
Over the face of the leader came;

The nobler nature within him stirred
To life at that woman's deed and word:

"Who touches a hair of yon gray head
Dies like a dog! March on!" he said.

All day long through Frederick street
Sounded the tread of marching feet:

All day long that flag tree tost
Over the heads of the rebel host.

Ever its torn folds rose and fell
On the loyal winds that loved it well;

And through the hill-gaps sunset light
Shone over it with a warm good-night.

Barbara Fritchie's work is o'er,
And the Rebel rides on his raids no more.

Honor to her! and let a tear
Fall, for her sake, on Stonewall's bier.

Over Barbara Fritchie's grave,
Flag of Freedom and Union, wave!

Peace and order and beauty draw
Round thy symbol of light and law;

And ever the stars look down
On thy stars below Frederick town!

Stonewall Jackson's Way

No other commander in the war inspired as much song and poetry as did the "Gallant Stonewall." Indeed, so numerous are the pieces dedicated to him that Bruce Catton once remarked "A volume could be compiled of poetic tributes to the great Stonewall." One of the best, and certainly the liveliest, was written by Dr. John W. Palmer, wandering adventurer, journalist, and, at the last, Confederate officer.

Stonewall Jackson's Way

Come, stack arms, men! Pile on the rails,
Stir up the camp-fire bright;
No matter if the canteen fails,
   We'll make a roaring night.
Here the Shenandoah brawls along,
There burly Blue Ridge echoes strong,
To swell the brigade's rousing song
   Of "Stonewall Jackson's way."

We see him now—the old slouched hat
   Cocked o'er his eyes askew,
The shrewd, dry smile, the speech so pat,
   So calm, so blunt, so true.
The "Blue-Light Elder" knows 'em well;
Says he, "That's Banks—he's fond of shell;
Lord save his soul! we'll give him—well,
   That's Stonewall Jackson's way."

Silence! ground arms! kneel all! caps off!
   Old Blue-Light's going to pray.
Strangle the fool that dares to scoff!
   Attention! it's his way.
Appealing from his native sod,
In *forma pauperis* to God—
"Lay bare thine arm, stretch forth thy rod!
   Amen!" That's Stonewall's way.

He's in the saddle now. Fall in!
   Steady! the whole brigade!
Hill's at the ford, cut off—we'll win
   His way out, ball and blade!
What matter if our shoes are worn?
What matter if our feet our torn?
"Quick -step! we're with him before dawn!"
   That's "Stonewall Jackson's way."

The sun's bright lances rout the mists
   Of morning and by George!
Here's Longstreet struggling in the lists,
   Hemmed in an ugly gorge.
Pope and his Yankees, whipped before,

"Bayonets and grape!" near Stonewall roar;

Ah! maiden, wait and watch and yearn
   For news of Stonewall's band!
Ah! widow, read with eyes that burn
   That ring upon thy hand.
Ah! wife, sew on, pray on, hope on!
Thy life shall be forlorn.
The foe had better ne'er been born
   That gets in "Stonewall Jackson's way."

Throughout all of his campaigns Thomas "Stonewall" Jackson was wont to suck on lemons, though no one could ever figure out how he obtained them.

So infrequently did Thomas "Stonewall" Jackson draw his sword that it eventually rusted in the scabbard.

In order to warm himself one cold day in January of 1862 the usually abstemious Stonewall Jackson took a glass of whiskey in the mistaken belief that it was wine, with the result that he very soon opened his coat, complaining that it was too warm, and talked more freely than at any other time in the war.

A Federal artillery battle suffers a close call while going into position during the Battle of South Mountain (14 September 1862).

Tenting Tonight

One winter's night near Fredericksburg, a Federal band struck up a number of patriotic tunes, and, when one of the Rebels listening from across the Rappahannock shouted "Now give us some of ours," ran through some Southern airs as well, ending the program with "Home, Sweet Home," amid cheers from both armies.

Over 75 percent of the 15,000 Union graves in the Fredericksburg National Cemetery are marked "unknown."

Although written early in the war by Walter Kittredge, of New Hampshire, a popular singer of the day, "Tenting Tonight" was too overtly defeatist and pessimistic to find a publisher. But Kittredge sang it when he joined the army, and it soon became immensely popular with the troops on both sides.

Tenting Tonight

We're tenting tonight on the old camp ground,
Give us a song to cheer our weary hearts,
A song of home, and the friends we love so dear.

Chorus: Many are the hearts that are weary tonight,
　　　　Wishing for the war to cease;
　　　　Many are the hearts looking for the right
　　　　To see the dawn of peace.
　　　　Tenting tonight, tenting tonight,
　　　　Tenting on the old camp ground.

We've been tenting tonight on the old camp ground,
Thinking of days gone by, of the loved ones at home
That gave us the hand, and the tear that said "good-bye!"—Chorus

We are tired of war on the old camp ground,
Many are dead and gone, of the brave and true
Who've left their homes, others have been wounded long.—Chorus

We've been fighting today on the old camp ground,
Many are lying near; some are dead
And some are dying, many are in tears.

Last Chorus: Many are the hearts that are weary tonight,
　　　　　　Wishing for the war to cease;
　　　　　　Many are the hearts looking for the right,
　　　　　　To see the dawn of peace.
　　　　　　Dying tonight, dying tonight,
　　　　　　Dying on the old camp ground.

The bodies of men who gave their lives for the cause of the Union are given a hasty burial in a shallow grave. Only about a third of the soldiers who died in the Civil War fell in combat. Most were killed by disease and other causes.